This Book Belongs To

Royal Mothers

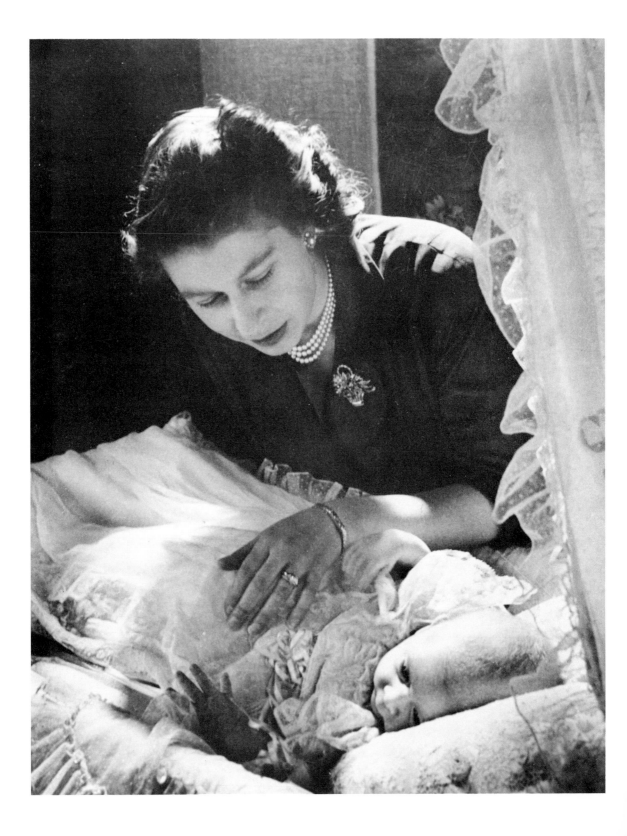

Royal Mothers

From ELEANOR OF AQUITAINE
to PRINCESS DIANA

by Ann Wallace *and* Gabrielle Taylor

Piatkus

To Robin, Michael and Hannah
and to Noel
with our love

© 1986 Ann Wallace and Gabrielle Taylor

First published 1987 by
Judy Piatkus (Publishers) Limited of
5 Windmill Street, London W1P 1HF

British Library Cataloguing in Publication Data

Wallace, Ann
  Royal mothers: from Eleanor of Aquitaine
  to Princess Diana.
  1. Royal houses—Europe—History
  2. Mothers—Europe—History
  I. Title   II. Taylor, Gabrielle
  929.7'092'2   D107

ISBN 0-86188-505-8

Designed by Sue Ryall

Front jacket illustrations depict
Queen Victoria and child (top right)
Anne Hyde and child (bottom right)
Elizabeth Bowes-Lyon and child (bottom left)

Phototypeset in 10/12 pt Linotron Palatino
Printed and bound in Great Britain at
The Bath Press, Avon

Contents

Picture Credits

Introduction

The early medieval kings, descended from Norman stock, ruled not only England but their lands across the Channel. They and their wives were cosmopolitans who travelled frequently around Europe, led crusades to the Holy Land, built massive castles and amassed great wealth. From their extravagant, expansive lifestyle sprang the romantic image of the age of chivalry, of knights in shining armour, of troubadours and courtly love. But it was also a time of harsh brutality and terrible poverty for the rest of the population. There were few towns and most people lived in dank, dark hovels in the countryside. Even their language was foreign to their rulers from across the sea.

Although we touch on events and the queens of the House of Normandy, our story really starts with the exciting Eleanor of Aquitaine, who married Henry II and epitomised the true spirit of motherhood as we know it today. She fought fiercely for her eight children—the last of whom was born when she was 44 years old. She supported them, loved them and would have died for them.

The royal mothers of medieval England were perhaps the hardiest of them all; giving birth in tents, fighting battles, becoming involved in political skirmishes and enjoying an instinctive emotional attachment to their children. The period ends with Anne Neville, who died of a broken heart after the death of her only son.

Through the centuries, there are stories of great cruelty—Sophia, wife of George I, was imprisoned by her husband for the last 31 years of her life. She kissed her children of 12 and 7 goodbye and never saw them again. There are stories of intrigue—was the son of James II and Mary of Modena really a changeling smuggled into the lying-in chamber in a warming-pan? There are stories of great tragedy—the beautiful Charlotte, the fairytale princess of the Georgian era who died in childbirth at the age of 20.

But above all, there are the stories of sadness, of babies miscarried and stillborn, of children rarely surviving beyond infancy. Queen Anne, who succeeded William III, had 17 pregnancies in 16 years and only one baby survived beyond infancy. Perhaps it's not surprising that royal children were kept apart from their parents, handed to wet nurses and brought up in their own residences away from court. Perhaps their mothers could not face the thought of becoming too close to children that might so easily die.

The one common denominator in all the royal births was the obsessive, overwhelming desire for an heir—a healthy baby, preferably male—who would secure the line and keep the family in power. While this natural desire still remains today, the risk of failure has been greatly reduced by modern medicine in childbirth.

It was Elizabeth Bowes-Lyon, the Queen Mother and someone never originally destined for the throne, who brought a breath of change to the scene. Her daughters were raised away from the limelight, allowed to be treated as ordinary upper-class children until the Abdication focused attention on them.

The Princess of Wales is, of course, the most modern of royal mothers, raising her children to be normal, happy little boys who go to the local nursery and are allowed a freedom from protocol that has rarely been seen in royal circles, even at their young age. But for all that, William and Harry are princes. The monarchy today is now clearly enlightened and free from so much of the trappings and ceremonial that surrounded it for so long. The road to that freedom has been a long one—but, it makes fascinating reading.

A typical childbirth scene of the fifteenth century,
showing how little home births, at least,
have changed through the ages.

The Plantagenets

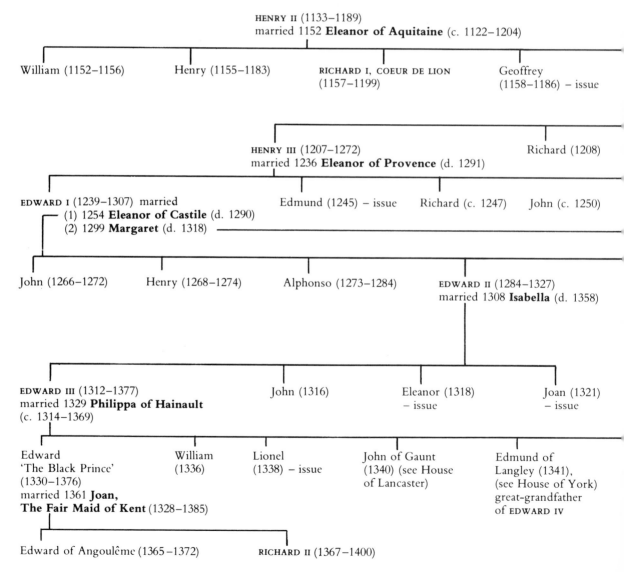

HENRY II (1133–1189)
married 1152 **Eleanor of Aquitaine** (c. 1122–1204)

William (1152–1156)   Henry (1155–1183)   **RICHARD I, COEUR DE LION** (1157–1199)   Geoffrey (1158–1186) – issue

HENRY III (1207–1272)
married 1236 **Eleanor of Provence** (d. 1291)   Richard (1208)

EDWARD I (1239–1307) married
(1) 1254 **Eleanor of Castile** (d. 1290)
(2) 1299 **Margaret** (d. 1318)   Edmund (1245) – issue   Richard (c. 1247)   John (c. 1250)

John (1266–1272)   Henry (1268–1274)   Alphonso (1273–1284)   **EDWARD II** (1284–1327)
married 1308 **Isabella** (d. 1358)

EDWARD III (1312–1377)
married 1329 **Philippa of Hainault**
(c. 1314–1369)   John (1316)   Eleanor (1318) – issue   Joan (1321) – issue

Edward
'The Black Prince'
(1330–1376)
married 1361 **Joan,
The Fair Maid of Kent** (1328–1385)   William (1336)   Lionel (1338) – issue   John of Gaunt (1340) (see House of Lancaster)   Edmund of Langley (1341), (see House of York) great-grandfather of **EDWARD IV**

Edward of Angoulême (1365–1372)   **RICHARD II** (1367–1400)

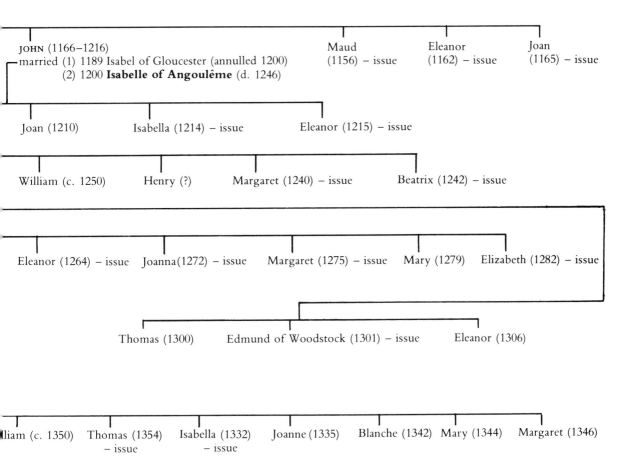

JOHN (1166–1216)
married (1) 1189 Isabel of Gloucester (annulled 1200)
(2) 1200 **Isabelle of Angoulême** (d. 1246)

Maud
(1156) – issue

Eleanor
(1162) – issue

Joan
(1165) – issue

Joan (1210)   Isabella (1214) – issue   Eleanor (1215) – issue

William (c. 1250)   Henry (?)   Margaret (1240) – issue   Beatrix (1242) – issue

Eleanor (1264) – issue   Joanna (1272) – issue   Margaret (1275) – issue   Mary (1279)   Elizabeth (1282) – issue

Thomas (1300)   Edmund of Woodstock (1301) – issue   Eleanor (1306)

lliam (c. 1350)   Thomas (1354)   Isabella (1332)   Joanne (1335)   Blanche (1342)   Mary (1344)   Margaret (1346)
– issue   – issue

HOUSE OF LANCASTER

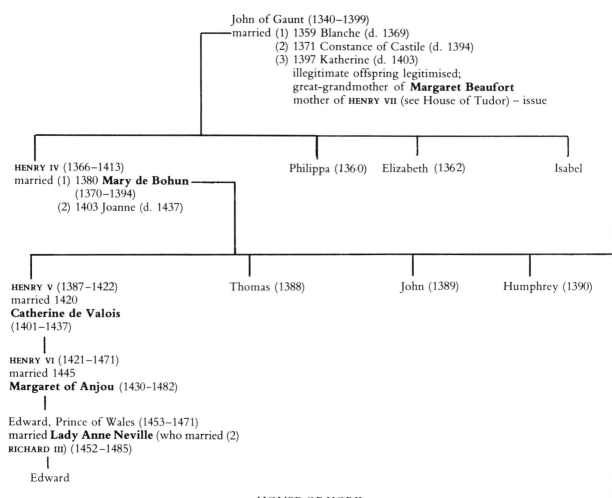

John of Gaunt (1340–1399)
married (1) 1359 Blanche (d. 1369)
(2) 1371 Constance of Castile (d. 1394)
(3) 1397 Katherine (d. 1403)
illegitimate offspring legitimised;
great-grandmother of **Margaret Beaufort**
mother of HENRY VII (see House of Tudor) – issue

HENRY IV (1366–1413)
married (1) 1380 **Mary de Bohun**
(1370–1394)
(2) 1403 Joanne (d. 1437)

Philippa (1360)   Elizabeth (1362)   Isabel

HENRY V (1387–1422)
married 1420
Catherine de Valois
(1401–1437)

Thomas (1388)   John (1389)   Humphrey (1390)

HENRY VI (1421–1471)
married 1445
Margaret of Anjou (1430-1482)

Edward, Prince of Wales (1453–1471)
married **Lady Anne Neville** (who married (2)
RICHARD III) (1452–1485)

Edward

HOUSE OF YORK

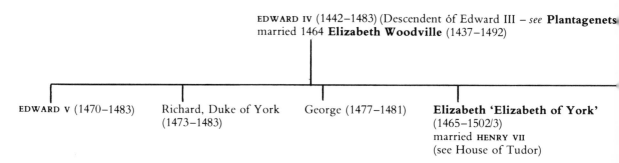

EDWARD IV (1442–1483) (Descendent óf Edward III – *see* **Plantagenets**
married 1464 **Elizabeth Woodville** (1437–1492)

EDWARD V (1470–1483)   Richard, Duke of York   George (1477–1481)   **Elizabeth 'Elizabeth of York'**
(1473–1483)   (1465–1502/3)
married HENRY VII
(see House of Tudor)

Blanche (1392) – issue   Philippa (1393)

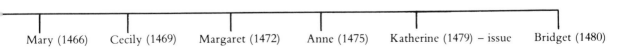

Mary (1466)   Cecily (1469)   Margaret (1472)   Anne (1475)   Katherine (1479) – issue   Bridget (1480)

In an era that has been marked down in history for its romance, royal wives were far from meek and dutiful. Beneath their flowing mantles, their jewelled gowns and their feminine coifs and kirtles, they were very tough women indeed. Politically astute, they could be fiercely supportive and loyal to their husbands and sons as they followed their men on campaigns and often fought alongside them on the battlefield. They could also be grasping, scheming and aggressive, capable of leading their own armies in support of their own cause. They were such an indefatigable bunch, these queens and princesses of the Dark Ages, it's not so surprising that not one of them actually died in childbirth—in spite of bad sanitation and the great risk of sickness and disease. But the infant mortality rate was appallingly high; the causes of death were many, including the ever-present threat of such scourges as bubonic plague, known as the Black Death.

Whatever the cost in precious lives the ultimate aim was to provide a supply of healthy sons to continue the royal line: medieval princesses may have been independent of spirit and capable but they were not thought fit to rule. Through their marriage settlements they were used simply as pawns in games of international politics. By marrying a suitably-endowed princess a king could add considerably to his kingdom—as in the case of Henry V who, through his marriage to Catherine of Valois, also made himself heir to the crown of France.

Matilda of Flanders, wife of William the Conqueror, arranged her family rather well. Her first four children were sons, followed by six daughters, and two of the sons succeeded to the throne, becoming William II and Henry I.

When Henry I died in 1135, his daughter Matilda fought for the throne against her cousin Stephen of Blois. The result was 20 years of civil war. Sometimes Matilda reigned, but mostly Stephen was King. Their quarrelling only came to a halt towards the end of Stephen's life, when he agreed to pass over his son's claim to the throne in favour of Matilda's eldest son, Henry,

from her marriage to Geoffrey, Count of Anjou. It was Geoffrey, so the story goes, who, through his habit of decorating his hat with a sprig of golden broom (*Planta Genista*), came to be nicknamed Plantagenet by his friends—and thus, unwittingly, named the royal house that was to rule for the next 300 years.

What was life really like for royal mothers in those days? Kings and queens, princes and princesses and their huge households moved around frequently for political reasons and in times of war. They also moved to get away from the stench of their crowded castles and to allow time for them to be cleaned.

When Edward I and his family travelled, as they did constantly between their royal houses, onlookers might have noticed in the retinue two men on horseback carrying between them a small litter. It was covered in green cloth and lined with crimson silk and contained the baby Princess Eleanor, daughter of Eleanor of Castile. They were looking at what was probably the country's first baby carriage.

Eleanor of Castile, Edward's first wife must, like most other royal mothers, have been a trendsetter of her time. Another was Philippa of Hainault, wife of Edward III and mother of the Black Prince. Philippa was revered, almost like a saint, in her own lifetime and became a model mother—statues and paintings of the Madonna and Child were based on figures of Philippa and her fine, healthy son.

When it came to domestic detail, few historians troubled to record any of the day-to-day life of the queens and their households in early medieval England. They devoted most of their efforts to the political activities, power struggles and social intrigues of these powerful queens. Nevertheless, we do know that a lot of ceremonial surrounded a royal birth, both before and afterwards. There was the lying-in period, for which the mother was provided with a specially decorated chamber, and afterwards came the child's christening and the mother's purification or 'churching', both of them surrounded by almost as much splendour as at a wedding.

A noble birth of around 1485.
The baby is already swaddled
in the arms of an attendant.

Bearing in mind the very public way of life in the royal castles, it is easy to see why the custom of having a lying-in chamber was thought so important. When the whole of life revolved within and around the castle walls—when there was an ever-present stream of visiting nobles and foreign dignitaries seeking audience with the king, not to mention officials of the household, ladies-in-waiting, messengers and scores of servants—a castle offered very little privacy. A lying-in chamber, where the mother-to-be could withdraw from view and be alone for a while, was a necessity. She usually planned the decoration herself—the bed covers, drapes and wallhangings, and she even had special dishes and drinking vessels. The room had an altar where Mass would be said, and there, with her meals brought to her, she stayed until her baby was born, visited only by her husband, ladies-in-waiting and the priest. This became the accepted custom for generations of royal births.

Meanwhile, it was left to others to raise the children, who were even housed in separate apartments so that the parents would not be disturbed by crying babies. Once any noble mother gave birth, she seldom, in fact, saw her baby. She was not expected to care for the child in any way—not even to feed him. Born without any of the comforts or medical care that we take for granted today, it was customary for the new-born baby to be handed over to a carefully chosen wet nurse.

It was considered a very important job, an honour even, to be a royal wet nurse. She was picked—sometimes from scores of eager applicants—for her glowing good health, so that there was no risk of disease being passed on through her milk.

Dressed in specially-designed gowns, which opened at the bodice so the dress did not have to be pulled off the shoulder to feed the baby, the wet nurse did her duty by suckling the child with her own milk, even chewing his food for him until he grew his own teeth. Usually it was a poor peasant woman whose own child had died at birth, but occasionally a new mother would be willing to hand over her own baby to someone else to have the honour of raising a royal infant. And it was a job that went on for some time. Milk from cows or goats was not considered fit for human consumption in the Middle Ages and did not figure in the daily diet, so breastfeeding continued until the child was two or even three years old.

Clothes for baby Plantagenets were simple—no frills and flounces or tiny sizes—just yards of plain linen or wool swaddling cloth. It was thought that swaddling would prevent deformity; there was even a fear that the infant's arms and legs could drop off if they were not given adequate support. So, for the first 18 months of a child's life, the body was soothed with ointments and tightly bandaged from the neck down. The little arms and legs were encased in splints and layer upon layer of cloth, the head covered with a biggin or bonnet. It was both uncomfortable and unhygienic, yet this was a practice that persisted until early in the eighteenth century.

Christenings, however, were important occasions when infant princes and princesses were dressed like adults. They wore rich velvet mantles trimmed with fur, and a long silk stole hung down from the baby's head to the feet of the godparent who held the baby.

This was the pattern of life for royal mothers and their babies in the Middle Ages. The same traditions endured, handed down from generation to generation, long after the Plantagenet line ended with the Wars of the Roses and the rule of the House of Tudor began.

A royal christening procession: the godmother with her train bearer and posy carrier.

ELEANOR OF AQUITAINE
1122 ~ 1204

Queen of Hearts

Henry II, great-grandson of William the Conqueror, married a lady of great determination and drive—the beautiful and highly cultivated Eleanor, daughter of the Duke of Aquitaine. She was eleven years his senior and for her it was a second marriage. She was well-educated, and could read Latin and write poetry at a time when most girls were illiterate; she was well-travelled, and in her teens had inherited the lands of Aquitaine from her father.

As a spirited 15-year-old, she had married the future King Louis VII of France. She was adored at court and at first Louis was eager to please his fun-loving young wife, but gradually he grew tired of superficial court life and turned instead to religion. He cut his hair short and spent long hours in prayer. Whilst Louis' people welcomed the change in their king, Eleanor longed for excitement. To spice up her life she even dressed in armour and led a crusade to the Holy Land.

Eventually, Louis decided he must marry again, not because of Eleanor's conduct but because, after eleven years of marriage, she had given him only two daughters and he desperately needed heirs. Eleanor controlled a large part of France, but even this counted for little with Louis who was determined to have sons to secure his kingdom—daughters, after all, could lose their lands through marriage.

So Eleanor and Louis were divorced and she became a desirable match—perfect for Henry II, despite the age difference. They married at

Whitsuntide in 1152, and where Eleanor's fertility by Louis had been in question, with Henry there were no problems. Their first child, William, died at the age of three, but he was followed by Henry, Matilda, Richard, Geoffrey, Eleanor, Joanna and, finally, John who was born on Christmas Eve 1166, when Eleanor was 44. Altogether, she gave birth to three kings and two queens—a remarkable record when infant mortality was so high.

Despite her frequent pregnancies Eleanor had immense energy and a love of life that she never lost. She was an indefatigable traveller not only in England and France, but across Europe to the Mediterranean and the Holy Land. Journeys were made on horseback or, when she was pregnant, in rickety wagons protected from the weather by awnings of skins.

Because the court was constantly on the move, Eleanor could have no favourite home in which to give birth to her children. Wherever the court happened to be at the final stages of pregnancy was where she had her baby—be it by the Thames at Bermondsey, where her first daughter by Henry II, Matilda, was born, in the great castle at Angers in France, birthplace of Joanna, or at Beaumont Palace, Oxford, where she gave birth to both Richard and her youngest son, John. But Eleanor did make sure she had certain home comforts. From the cheerless surroundings of the misty Thames-side palace at Bermondsey, she arranged for shipments of her favourite wines from home, herbs and spices, gold and silver plate and bales of silk.

Eleanor, ever a leader of style and fashion, had

An engraving of Eleanor taken from the effigy on her tomb at Fontevrault.

a big influence on the lighter, and artistic side of her children's upbringing. She introduced to the court the newly-fashionable entertainment of the troubadours, the knightly poets whose songs—of love and the crusades—accompanied by lute, harp, and viol became the pop music of the time. One such poet who received more royal patronage than most was Bernard de Ventadour. He fell hopelessly in love with Eleanor and dedicated his best known songs to her.

Such light-hearted diversions helped raise Eleanor's spirits when life at court was anything but fun. For Eleanor had problems, not only in the shape of the fair Rosamund, the King's favourite, who lived at his hunting estate at Woodstock, but her husband's reign was also darkened by his involvement in the murder of Thomas à Becket. The horrifying act shocked the whole of Christendom and caused Henry to do penance for the rest of his life. The family was finally torn apart by a long-running quarrel which was fought on both sides of the Channel. The quarrel was, in fact, brought about by the King's generosity and triggered off the very events he had hoped to prevent. To avoid a bitter feud between his sons after his death, he decided to make settlements on them in his lifetime and actually had his eldest son, 15-year-old Henry, crowned in Westminster Abbey while he was still alive. So England actually had two kings for a time, Henry the Old and Henry the Young.

Only John, born after the shareout, was left without his own territory. At first his father regarded it as a family joke and nicknamed the child 'Lackland', but once John was old enough to be betrothed and, therefore, needed a marriage settlement, the King suggested that his elder brother Henry should hand over three castles from his French possessions. The idea was dynamite. Prince Henry at once turned to the King of France for support and Eleanor, ever the supportive mother, fiercely protective of the claims of her power-hungry, quarrelsome sons, rushed to their defence in the rebellion against their father. Only John, aged six, stayed on his father's side.

Eleanor is reputed to have disguised herself as a man to follow her sons into battle, but nevertheless she was captured and taken to Salisbury Castle, where she was imprisoned for 13 years and afterwards at Winchester. While held captive she comforted herself with beautiful clothes and ordered scarlet capes, grey furs and embroidered coverlets for herself and her servant girl.

She was still there when her eldest son, Henry, died of dysentery and her husband, tired, old and still fighting, died at Chinon in France in 1189. Now he was succeeded by his son Richard, who had acquired his mother's territory in Aquitaine.

The new King sent a messenger from France ordering that Eleanor should be released from her imprisonment and be made Regent until his return. She was now in her mid-sixties but this resilient, energetic woman was ready once again to get into her political stride. She celebrated her freedom by ordering the release of prisoners around the country and then went on a tour, exacting oaths of allegiance to the new King.

As Eleanor had grown even more alienated from her husband, so she had turned increasingly to her sons for company and support. Indeed, she had personally encouraged them to rebel against their father. Richard had always been her favourite. He was, in fact, everybody's favourite; like his mother, he had become the golden boy of his time, the very embodiment of the age of chivalry. Tall, fair, handsome—and brave. Not for nothing was he called *Coeur de Lion*.

But Richard had one fault which Eleanor tried to overlook until he inherited the crown, and it became vital that he should marry and have an heir. The worrying fact was that Richard preferred the company of men to women. Could he have suffered from an overdose of mother-domination? Could he have sought, but looked in vain, for a bride in the mould of the formidable Eleanor he so much adored? At the age of eleven he had been betrothed to nine-year-old Alais, a princess of France, but it came to nothing. Now in her new role, the still forceful Eleanor took the matter into her own hands. She had heard that Richard had been attracted by a high-minded Spanish princess and she resolved to arrange the marriage.

Eleanor was nearing her seventies when she set out in the dead of winter, 1190, and headed south across the Pyrenees to Pamplona. Her mission accomplished, she then made the equally perilous return journey back through southern France, across the Alps and through Italy to Sicily. With her travelled Berengaria, daughter of King Sancho of Navarre. A bride for Richard. The Princess's feelings were not recorded. Doubtless she had heard only heroic tales of her handsome groom. The marriage took place in May 1191 in the Orthodox Cathedral at Limassol in Cyprus; King Richard magnificently attired in scarlet and silver and cloth of gold. After three days of celebration, he left on a crusade and from then on the couple seldom met. Berengaria was still childless when Richard died eight years later. He had been wounded by an arrow during a siege at Chaluz in France and he sent for his aged mother. She rushed to his side from Fontevrault, where she was living in retirement and he died in her arms. Of all her sons, only one now survived —Lackland John, the youngest of her family.

Even at the age of 80, Eleanor still had work to do. She still took an active part in the power struggle between John and her grandson Arthur of Brittany, the son of Geoffrey. And so, towards the end of her life, she crossed the Pyrenees to Spain, a tremendous feat in those days, once more to negotiate a marriage. This time it was to arrange the betrothal of her granddaughter, Blanche of Castile, to Louis VIII, and to accompany her back to France.

Eleanor spent her last days at Fontevrault, where she died at the age of 82—an unusually long life in those days. She was undoubtedly a complex character, capable of inspiring love and hate. One contemporary writer, Gervase of Canterbury, described her as 'a very clever woman, most noble of blood, but fickle'. Others, Shakespeare among them, saw her as domineering and ruthless in her ambition for power. She was even accused of being possessed by the devil, others were bewitched by her aura of glamour; few could ignore her. Hers was a remarkable life for any age.

Fontevrault—Eleanor's home in her final years.

ISABELLE OF ANGOULÊME
c.1187 ~ 1246

John had been betrothed at the age of 10 to a young heiress, Hawise of Gloucester, and the couple were later married at his castle at Marlborough. It was, of course, an arranged marriage and it turned out to be even less successful than most. It was sad, loveless and childless, and after ten years they parted.

John chose his next bride for himself—not only for the French lands he would acquire, but also because he was attracted by her personality. She was only 12 or 13 years old at the time, and already betrothed to Hugh le Brun, Count of la Marche. Even then, John recognised in her a spark of the strength of his own mother, for she, too, grew up to be a woman of great spirit and independence. Her name was Isabelle of

The Stolen Bride

Angoulême and only weeks after John stole her from Hugh, without any of the formality of an engagement, he married her in August 1200 and they set off for England. On the way they called at Fontevrault, where John presented his child bride to his elderly mother, Eleanor.

It was a traumatic experience for Isabelle to leave her home in the heart of the French countryside. With a husband she barely knew, she set out on the first long journey of her lifetime, and made her first ever sea-crossing, on her way to Westminster Abbey to be crowned Queen of England. Around £30 was spent on her child-size robes which had to be specially made for the coronation, after which the couple set out on a tour of the realm.

*An illuminated manuscript showing
the royal travelling coach.*

When royalty travelled in the Middle Ages the entire court—the government and royal household—went too. The chancellor, treasurer, chamberlain, clerks and other high officials progressed round the country together, delivering justice, settling local disputes and holding court. They took everything with them, travelling on horseback and carrying furnishings, utensils and equipment, clothes and bedding in wagons and carts. Only the food for the whole household did not have to be carried—that was provided by the estates where the party stayed; in fact a royal progress was a useful way of ensuring that all the provisions—the meat and crops—produced at all their various residences were used up.

For young Isabelle, this was just a taste of what was to come, for in her future years as John's consort she was to spend much of the time on the move. They spent their first Christmas together at Guildford where 'the king distributed many raiments of a festive nature to the knights'. Then, in the dead of winter, they made the long cold journey north across the Humber to Scarborough, Durham, Newcastle and Carlisle. They were back in the south in time to be in Canterbury for the Easter ceremonies.

Isabelle was 20, and her husband in his 40s when their first child, Henry, was born at Winchester in 1207. He was followed two years later by a second son, named Richard after his warrior uncle, then came three daughters, Joan, Isabelle and Eleanor. Five pregnancies did not prevent Isabelle from being with her husband on his campaigns. Indeed, children in the Middle Ages were generally given little consideration and certainly not regarded as an obstacle by a royal mother wishing to travel with her husband. Childhood as we know it today did not exist. Once out of infancy, children were expected to behave like adults. Toys were simple and few, schooling severe. Although there were some notable exceptions, mothers were distant from their children, who were often sent away to grow up in other households. The high mortality rate was a sad, everyday fact—but a baby who died was usually quickly replaced by another.

The marriage between King John and Isabelle appears to have been a true love match. Isabelle accompanied the King on nearly all his campaigns, even though at times she was in grave danger. Once, when he was under siege, cut off

A lifelike portrait of Isabelle
of Angoulême based on her effigy at Fontevrault.

21

from his family while barricaded in a fortress at Roche-aux-Moins, King John ordered that Isabelle and two of his children, Joan and Richard, should be brought to him. Another time Isabelle herself was besieged by rebels while she was isolated at Chinon in the valley of the Loire and John had to send mercenaries to rescue her.

In spite of all John's troubles—the unrest across the Channel and the rebellious barons at home, who forced him to sign the Magna Carta—he and Isabelle somehow managed to enjoy for a time a wonderfully relaxed family life. A favourite home was the hilltop fortress of Corfe Castle, high above the Dorset coast, which also served as a prison for John's prisoners of war. It was in the safety of Corfe that the family gathered for feasts and celebrations, when they entertained generously with huge banquets with music, dancing and entertainments. The atmosphere was lighthearted when the young Queen and her children danced to the music of lutes and guitars, oboes, kettledrums and bassoons. And the King, now nearly fifty, lavished on his family all the comforts, the beautiful clothes, jewels and ornaments he could offer. But such time was running out.

In the face of impending invasion by the French, Isabelle waited with her children in the safety of Corfe Castle while her ailing husband led his army up the coast of East Anglia. And there disaster struck. Overtaken by the treacherous tides on the edge of the Wash, part of the King's party—the men and horses carrying the baggage train bearing, among many other valuables, the crown jewels and the King's own priceless collection of gold and silver—were swept away by the rushing tidal waters.

The King, meanwhile, had been taken ill with dysentery. Weak and in great pain he was carried on a litter to the Bishop of Lincoln's castle at Newark where, in spite of great efforts to save him, he died on October 18, 1216.

*An illustration of King John
hunting a stag, taken from
a medieval manuscript.*

Faced now with the prospect of direct rule from France or a boy King, the barons chose what they considered the lesser of two evils and supported the new young King. Henry III, just nine years old, was hurriedly crowned in Gloucester Cathedral ten days after his father's death—not with the royal crown, which had been lost in the muddy waters of the Wash, but with Isabelle's own golden circlet. The barons decided that the Bishop of Winchester should become the boy's guardian and 70-year-old William Marshal, Earl of Pembroke, always a loyalist leader, was appointed Regent.

Isabelle, widowed and alone, returned to France—and to the man to whom she was once betrothed, Hugh, Count of la Marche. For she had discovered that his father had died on a crusade and the young Hugh was 'alone and without heir' and being persuaded by his friends to find a wife. Ironically, Isabelle's own daughter, Joan, had once been betrothed to him as well. But she was obviously too young, and anyway it had to be a French wife, someone nearer his age. 'Dearest son' wrote Isabelle, to nine-year-old Henry III. 'If that [marriage to Joan] were to happen all your lands in Poitou and Gascony and ours too would be lost . . . we have therefore taken the said Hugh, Count of la Marche, as our Lord and husband.'

Isabelle, home once more in Angoulême, started family life all over again. She gave her husband five sons, one of whom became Bishop of Winchester. And, like Eleanor before her, Isabelle then retired to the abbey at Fontevrault, where she lived until her death.

ELEANOR OF PROVENCE
C. 1222 ~ 1291

A Loving Mother

One medieval mother who paid more attention to her children than most was Eleanor of Provence. She was 14 when she married Henry III, who although he ascended the throne at nine, did not marry until he was 30, and it seems to have been an idyllic marriage. After their wedding in 1236, Henry took his young bride to his favourite home, the magnificent palace at Westminster.

He spent a fortune on luxurious decorations and paintings, most of them dedicated to the saintly King Edward the Confessor who founded the adjoining Abbey, and he ordered 1,000 men a day to work on the place until it was considered one of the finest in Europe. It was an impressive sight to the young Eleanor—at least until a month later when the Thames overflowed its banks and flooded the palace to such an extent that people were rowing in boats in the Great Hall. But floors, even in palaces, were designed to withstand the occasional flood. They were simply covered in sawdust and strewn with rushes, which could be renewed periodically and the floor swept.

Sweet-smelling herbs— lavender, mint, camomile and basil—were used to purify and sweeten the often putrid air. Carpets as floor coverings were unheard of— but rich tapestries covered cold stone walls and tables and added a little warmth and comfort to hard oak benches. Eleanor's apartments at Westminster were decorated in luxurious style. She even had the comfort of a bath-house, complete with hot and cold running water drawn from tanks filled from cauldrons heated in a furnace, and the kitchens were considered the most extensive and modern in Europe. The palace also contained three chapels, and the windows of the building were expensively glazed— yet another rare luxury in the days when glazing was often transported from one royal house to another whenever the court was on the move. As the finishing touch, the King personally organised the building of latrines, well away from the living quarters.

*Westminster Hall was already almost 200 years old
when it became the favourite home of Henry and Eleanor.*

This was the comfortable world into which Eleanor's children were born and, unlike most high-born mothers of her time, she actually enjoyed their company and was determined to keep them around her. Her dedication to her children sounds almost too good to be true in an age when children were largely overlooked. Instead of arranging for the new-born Prince Edward to be housed and cared for in a household away from the palace, it was decided that a new nursery wing should be built in the fresh country air at Windsor. When Edward was two months old Henry ordered 'the chamber of our son, Edward, to be wainscoted, and iron bars to be made to each of the windows of the same chamber'. When he was 18 months old, and no doubt toddling around, his father asked for the nursery to be extended. And when Lady Margaret (the future Queen of Scotland) was born, she required even more space. It is recorded that an order went out for 'another lodging for the use of the children of two storeys with two chimneys.'

And so the castle grew with the family—in fact, the nine children born to Eleanor and Henry were the reason for the construction of a whole new courtyard known as the Queen's herb garden, adjoining Eleanor's chamber. Gradually Windsor, which until this time had been regarded mainly as a stronghold, became the family's main home.

Tragically—though not uncommon for the times—four of Eleanor's sons died in infancy and a daughter, Catherine, was born deaf and dumb. She was sent to Swallowfield in Berkshire to be cared for by her nurse and was given a pet goat from the royal forest for company. When she died, aged three, in 1257, £51 2s 4d was spent on her funeral and a monk, known as the Hermit of Charing, was paid to pray perpetually for the little girl's soul.

The peace of family life at Windsor was shattered violently one day in May 1251 when a terrifying thunderstorm broke over the castle. 'It fell', we are told, 'with that stroke upon the bedchamber of the Queen where she was then abiding with the children and her household, crumbled the chimney to powder, cast it to the ground, and shook the whole house.' The storm also destroyed 35 oak trees in Windsor forest and several farm buildings. It was about ten years before rebuilding began on a new stone chamber with marble pillars and 'wainscoting to be painted of a green colour with gold stars'.

Eleanor and her children were reluctant to return to Windsor after their terrifying experience and apart from hunting expeditions, they spent more time in the safety of the royal apartments at the Tower and Westminster. Apart from its role of stronghold, prison and grim place of execution, the Tower was, in fact, a royal home for centuries. Certainly the family felt secure and protected there, especially in times of unrest. At one time, the king even kept his treasure there, in the safest place of all—a chest under his bed. The royal apartments were at the top of the White Tower, the great fortress built by William the Conqueror. Reached by a steep spiral staircase, with walls at least eleven feet thick and with only narrow slits for windows, the apartments were above the royal chapel of St John. For Eleanor, though, it was a noisy, dirty, depressing place, set close to the teeming streets of the city and the river traffic. Life at the Tower must have been very different after the tranquillity of Windsor. By the time Margaret, the Queen Mother, took over the residence in 1307 air pollution was so bad that Londoners were banned from lighting bonfires or beacons which could foul the atmosphere round the Tower.

Characteristically, Henry and Eleanor made the Tower as comfortable as possible. The whitewashed walls were hung with tapestries, the King had a painting of winter over the fireplace in his bedchamber, and the walls in Eleanor's room were decorated with roses. For the children, though, life at the Tower was fun, because there they had their own menagerie. It was begun when the King of France, Eleanor's brother-in-law, sent the gift of an elephant—probably the first ever to be seen in England, and a house was especially built for it at the Tower.

The Tower of London in this period was a prison,
a stronghold and, in troubled times, a safe royal refuge.

Later they were given a lion, white leopards and a bear to add to the royal zoo.

Eleanor and her children were indulged and obviously adored by Henry, who spoilt his family with gifts and comforts. A glimpse at their household accounts gives an idea of their standard of living. One record says that Eleanor spent £145 42s 4d on jewels for her own use, 'eleven rich garlands with emeralds, pearls, sapphires and garnets' and £1,691 12s 1d for 'horses purchased and robes for the Queen's family, in mending robes, in shoes, saddles, reins, almonds, wax, and other necessaries for the wardrobe'. But although Eleanor spent freely on herself, she also gave generously to others. One account lists 'secret gifts and private alms' amounting to £4,017 10s 3d and 'oblations for holidays, and alms distributed daily, and by the wayside, £151 18s'.

No doubt mindful of his personal motto 'He who does not give what he holds does not receive what he wishes', Henry was especially generous to the poor. Several times a year beggars were invited to eat in the hall at Westminster and afterwards sent home with bread. And if the family were not in residence at Christmas, 6,000 beggars took over the palace for four days and were given a royal feast. The old and handicapped occupied the Great Hall while the rest ate in the White Hall, children were given their meal in the painted chamber and the Queen's own apartments, and afterwards entertained by court jesters.

Christmas was a splendid time of feasting and merry-making. The Great Hall of Windsor castle, heated by enormous wood fires and lit by hundreds of flares and candles, was the setting for Eleanor and her family as they presided over an enormous feast for their huge number of live-in court officials, ministers and ladies-in-waiting. Food came from suppliers all over the country and quantities were enormous. In 1241, the royal order included 60 boars with heads, 100 bucks, 60 does, 50 swans, 50 peacocks, 2,000 fowls, 600 lambs and 10,000 eels.

Eleanor was not fifty when Henry died in November 1272, but she retired from court life to become a nun beside the Avon at Amesbury, where she remained until her death in 1291, a woman fulfilled after an extraordinarily happy marriage and idyllic family life.

Eleanor arriving by sea from Gascony with her new husband.

ELEANOR OF CASTILE
C.1240 ～ 1290

Lady from Spain

Eleanor's son, who succeeded to the throne as Edward I, married another Eleanor, the Spanish Eleanor of Castile. She too was a devoted wife, a constant companion who was almost always at his side whenever he travelled—on crusades, campaigns and diplomatic missions in Britain and across the Channel. She had at least thirteen children, but only half survived—six died before the age of seven and one at eleven.

Although the King was based at Northampton, Eleanor preferred the comforts of Westminster for her children's quarters. Her Spanish influence soon made its mark on the interior of the palace, and she created an even more sumptuous home than it had been when her mother-in-law was in residence.

Matthew Paris, a gossip writer of the time, described the reaction of Londoners in 1255 when they heard about Eleanor's newly-decorated apartment, dazzled by her extravagant Spanish style. The walls were 'hung with palls of silk and tapestry, like a temple, and even the floor was covered with tapestry. This was done by the Spaniards, it being in accordance with the custom of their country; but this excessive pride excited the laughter and derision of the people.'

To house her large family Eleanor had another nursery annex added to the palace at Westminster—a building which became known as the 'maidenhall' because so many little princesses lived there.

Not only was she a devoted wife, Eleanor also had amazing physical stamina. Two of her daughters were born in a tent while she and the King were on a crusade in Palestine—ignoring the dangers of war and the rigours of the extreme climate, Eleanor still insisted that, pregnant or not, her place was with the King. One daughter died but the other, Joanna, amazingly survived.

In the chill spring of 1284, Eleanor was staying in the half-built castle at Caernarvon when her fourth son, Edward, was born. It was during the King's Welsh campaign and, having conquered their country, it seemed sensible to appease the Welsh with the promise of a prince—a prince given the title Prince of Wales, the first born to an English King. Edward's first wet nurse, Mary Mawnsel, was Welsh, but she later became ill and was replaced by Alice Leygrave, an English nurse, who became a loyal and trusted royal retainer.

Meanwhile, only months after the prince's birth, Eleanor, who was so often faced with bereavement among her children, was dealt another blow. Her two eldest sons had already died in infancy, now 11-year-old Alfonso, the

A reconstruction of the Queen's bathroom at Leeds Castle.

heir to the throne, was also dead. Edward, her prince of Caernarvon, was now the future king.

As a mother, Eleanor enjoyed the time she had with her children and from old records it's possible to get brief glimpses of their happy family life: how—for example—the King provided a model boat and castle for his son Alfonso, as well as a toy cart and a painted crossbow (an important weapon at the time). The first games of hopscotch and marbles are thought to have been played on the flagstones of castle floors, and hoops and balls and shuttlecocks were favourite toys. And the royal children had their own entertainers, too—the mummers, minstrels, fools and court jesters were all employed to bring laughter in an often harsh, medieval world. The children frequently travelled with their parents when they progressed round the country from one royal residence to another, so Eleanor's early innovation, the processional travelling cot, must have been used often.

Eleanor's household accounts also give glimpses into life in the royal nursery. Young boys and girls dressed alike and Eleanor's son, Henry, age about six, daughter Eleanor, ten, and their cousin, John, eight, wore matching shifts, kirtles, overgarments and mantles. They were given gloves trimmed with squirrel fur, little caps of peacock feathers, and black stockings.

When Edward, Prince of Wales, was only two, Eleanor was off on her travels again, this time to France. The King wanted to pay homage to Philip IV, the new French King, as well as settle matters in his own province of Gascony. They were away from home for three years—a long time in the life of a young child. When Eleanor saw her son again he was no longer a baby but a little boy of five years, and he was taken from the royal manor at Langley (later King's Langley) in Hertfordshire to meet his mother when she came ashore at Dover.

The Queen's bedchamber at Leeds Castle
shows the luxury of furnishings
that surrounded royalty.

Eleanor had little time left to enjoy her children's company. Fifteen months later, in 1290, while staying at Harby in Nottinghamshire, she was suddenly taken ill and died in the King's arms. He was devastated. 'My harp is turned to mourning', he wrote. 'In life I loved her dearly, nor can I cease to love her in death.' Grief-stricken, he accompanied her body back to Westminster for burial and, to commemorate the last sad journey home, he later had richly ornamental stone crosses erected to mark the resting places of the bier along the way—at places such as Lincoln, Grantham, Dunstable, St Albans and, lastly, at a tiny village close to Westminster called Charing—a spot known as Charing Cross.

The head and shoulders of Eleanor on her tomb in Westminster Abbey.

MARGARET
c. 1282 ~ 1318

A Second Wife

Ten years later, when he was white-haired and 60, King Edward married again, this time to Margaret, the 17-year-old sister of the King of France. Their wedding in Canterbury Cathedral should have been a double affair, for when he made his marriage contract, Edward also arranged the betrothal of his son, Edward of Caernarvon, with the French King's daughter, Isabella. But as she was only eight, plans for the Prince's marriage had to wait. In fact, it seems that Margaret, just two years older than her stepson, would have made a far more suitable bride for him.

The Prince, however, did not have women or marriage on his mind. He was more preoccupied with his love for Piers Gaveston, a young squire of the royal household—the beginning of a royal scandal that was to cost them both their lives.

Meanwhile the old King and his new young bride continued the family line; Margaret gave Edward three more children. The year after they married, the King set out to invade Scotland for the fourth time and Margaret travelled north with him as far as Brotherton in Yorkshire, on the banks of the Wharfe. There, while Edward continued his journey to meet his army at Carlisle, Margaret gave birth to a son named Thomas. Despite the harsh northern climate, she later followed her husband into Scotland where, at Linlithgow Palace, they spent the winter. The palace was kept warm by blazing log fires and lit by flares and candles throughout the long dark days of winter, and fur-lined covers and warm woollen robes kept Margaret and her infant warm. But the draughty, smoke-filled atmosphere of the ancient building and the monotonous winter diet was a testing experience for the young Queen.

When spring came the campaign continued and Margaret followed the King. With her ladies she was actually allowed to watch from a window the dramatic ending of the seige of Stirling Castle, as

Queen Margaret, from a statue in Lincoln Cathedral.

the old walls were rammed by the English army.

Margaret could never settle anywhere for long—in her first year of married life her husband moved court 76 times. She had two more babies—Thomas was followed by another son, Edmund, then a daughter, Eleanor. And because of their closeness in age, Margaret also proved to be a sympathetic stepmother to Edward's grown-up family.

When the 19-year-old Prince of Wales was banished from court after a quarrel with his father, isolated from his friends and short of money, he wrote to Margaret, asking her to persuade his father to let him see Gaveston. Although we do not know the outcome, records show that Margaret was a supportive and good friend to her stepson all his life.

ISABELLA
1292 ~ 1358

Edward I died, aged 68, on July 7, 1307 at Burgh-upon-Sands, Solway, at the beginning of yet another Scottish campaign. Edward, Prince of Wales, aged 23, was now King and he had to do his duty and marry Margaret's niece, the young Isabella. Marriage plans were rushed through, to be followed by the coronation.

Edward and Isabella made an attractive pair

The She-Wolf of France

when they married in the church of Notre Dame, Boulogne, on January 25, 1308— the French were impressed by the fine figure of the good-looking, fair-haired bridegroom and his pretty 16-year-old bride. It was a popular match. But from the start, Edward made it very clear that Gaveston still held first place in his affections although by now he, too, was

*The betrothal of Isabella
to Edward II in a tent between
Ardres and Calais.*

married—to the King's niece Margaret, daughter of Joan, Countess of Gloucester.

At the coronation in Westminster Abbey only a month after the wedding it was Gaveston, resplendent in rich purple decorated with pearls, who outshone Isabella. He was 'so decked out that he more resembled the god Mars than an ordinary mortal'. And well he might, for he was doubtless wearing the very best of the bride's own jewellery—wedding presents which Edward had presented to him.

Little wonder that Isabella, embittered by her husband's outrageous behaviour, turned against Edward to the extent that, in later years she was given the name of 'She-Wolf of France'. Early in

her husband's disastrous reign she loyally followed him on his campaigns as he tried to regain some of the lands lost after his father's death. But he was an inexperienced warrior who preferred water sports and horse racing—he was something of a Plantagenet playboy—to going into battle.

Eventually, when the Scottish hero Robert the Bruce won victories north of the Border, Edward was forced to plan for battle and, with Gaveston by his side, headed north. Seventeen-year-old Isabella, three months pregnant with her first child, was actually left stranded at Newcastle, abandoned together with the baggage train, to be captured by the Earl of Lancaster. Before long

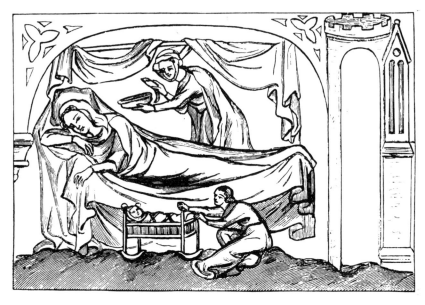

A depiction of a birth in the fourteenth century:
while the midwife attends the mother
a nurse takes charge of the baby.

the country was in a state of civil war. A sort of truce came later that year when Isabella's hated Gaveston was murdered and her son, the future King Edward III, was born. There was public rejoicing at Windsor.

Isabella was frequently enraged by her husband's immaturity in ignoring the responsibilities of kingship, for he preferred to amuse himself with simple country crafts such as thatching, gardening and fishing, and even had a pet lion which he took around with him in a cart. But he did carry out his duty to perpetuate the Plantagenet line. Soon little Prince Edward was followed in the royal nursery by John of Eltham, born in 1316, Eleanor of Woodstock (1318) and Joan of the Tower (1321). But shortly after Joan's birth the King took another court favourite into his circle, Hugh Despenser. And Isabella, no longer the young, helpless childwife, was determined to take revenge. With her young family safely in the care of a team of royal wet nurses and attendants, she was free to make her own political moves. She simply had to wait until the time was right.

Her opportunity came when Edward sent her home to France to plead for the return of lands that had been confiscated. Trouble with the French had been brewing for some time. The King had already banished French traders and Isabella's own French servants had been dismissed. She also suffered the humiliation of having her personal allowance reduced and Eleanor de Clare, wife of the dreaded Hugh Despenser, appointed her housekeeper, with the right to read all her correspondence. Isabella was more than ready to leave for France, and stay there.

When her mission was completed and it was time for the King himself to go to France to pay homage, he pleaded a diplomatic illness and sent the young Prince Edward instead. Isabella could not have hoped for more. Conditions were exactly right to put her plan into operation. With her thirteen-year-old son safely in France she raised an army for the invasion of England.

Meanwhile in Paris there was a reunion with an English exile, Roger Mortimer, who had escaped from prison in the Tower and was now ready to support Isabella's cause. The two became lovers, and together hatched their plot to invade and remove Despenser. When news reached the King and he demanded Isabella's return, she replied 'I protest that I will not return until the intruder is removed, but, discarding my marriage garment, shall assume the robes of widowhead and mourning until I am avenged.'

Isabella's adultery with Mortimer led to her being banished from France but, still refusing to return to the King, she left Paris and travelled with her son Edward to Hainault where she had more business to accomplish. There, at the court of William II, Count of Hainault, Holland and Zeeland, she clinched the marriage between her son and the Count's daughter, Philippa. For Isabella it was an important achievement—not because she had found a bride for her son, but she had acquired a bride's dowry, which was to finance her next move.

Still wearing her widow's weeds, she sailed from Dordrecht. She had the support of Mortimer and John of Hainault, brother of the Count, who were both in command of an army raised with money from Philippa's dowry. They landed on the coast of Suffolk and spent the first night at Walton-on-the-Naze. It was the beginning of the end of the reign of Edward II.

Surrounded by an ever-growing army of supporters, Isabella advanced on London as the King and his supporters headed for the West Country, then continued to Oxford and Bristol. Edward was captured at Neath Abbey, Glamorgan, where he was hiding after trying to sail to Lundy, and eventually imprisoned in Kenilworth Castle. There, faced with the threat that Despenser would be proclaimed King if he did not abdicate, Edward agreed to give up his throne. His son, Edward, was proclaimed King on January 25, 1327.

It is not known whether Isabella's hatred was the cause of her husband's terrible death when he was murdered a year later in a dungeon at Berkeley Castle, but she turned up at the state funeral in Gloucester hypocritically dressed in widow's black. The public were appalled as news of the murder leaked out and the King's tomb in Gloucester Cathedral became a place of pilgrimage.

Isabella's lover, Roger Mortimer, had taken control of the government—but time was running out for him, too. The new King Edward III, just 15 years old, headed another conspiracy to seize power and the couple were arrested one night as they slept at Nottingham Castle. Mortimer was taken to the Tower for trial, and executed on the gallows at Smithfield. Isabella retired to Castle Rising in Norfolk, and in old age became a nun devoting her life to good works.

As a wife and Queen she is marked down in history for her terrible vengeance but little is known about her feelings as a mother, except that she used her son as a powerful pawn in her campaign against her husband and used her daughter-in-law's dowry to pay for her army. Her children had a sad and lonely childhood, torn tragically between warring parents, but their father held them in great affection. Pleading with Edward to return from France he called him 'Our dear and well-beloved son' and great care was taken in the boy's education. In an age when Norman-French was the language at the court and English was spoken only by common people, Edward also studied Latin, Flemish and German as well as the courtly accomplishments of music and dancing, hawking and archery. Books then were becoming more available and in her retirement at Castle Rising, Isabella's library contained many devotional books as well as eight volumes of romantic verse, including one, bound in white leather, about the Arthurian legend.

One thing Isabella did not pass on to her son was her taste for revenge, for although at Castle Rising her freedom was limited, Edward made his mother a very generous annual allowance, which must have made her life very comfortable. Isabella's household book gives a fascinating glimpse of royal life in the fourteenth century. Spices and medicines purchased for the Queen by Peter de Montpellier, her apothecary,

*Castle Rising in Norfolk where
Isabella spent her retirement.*

included 2 pounds of grain fennel, 6 pounds of cloves and $7\frac{1}{2}$ pounds of sweetmeats in tablets. There are payments for the repair of her cutlery, silver goblets and silver washbasins; for a chest of boiled leather bound with iron for holding her salt cellar, and for her bathtubs. There's a receipt for 30 pounds of cotton candles so that workmen under her tailor could carry on with such jobs as fastening 50 gold knots onto her robe after dark, and there is bill after bill for messengers and the cost of horses and carts to move her household around the country.

On a personal note, the records show that Queen Isabella had a fool, Michael, who was reimbursed the sum of 4s 4d for buying shoes and other small necessities for himself, at York on March 20, 1312. She also had a number of hawks and eight greyhounds which she left in the care of a boy during November and December 1311.

Isabella also adopted a Scottish orphan, little Thomelinus, whom she clothed and sent to London to be cared for by Agnes, wife of John the French organist.

Stark walls and bare floors of royal castles were by now being hung more and more with colourful tapestries; hard oak chairs and benches were softened with richly embroidered cushions. Books were beautifully illustrated in brilliant reds, blues and greens and burnished gold, not only by monks but by professional illuminators. Even furniture was often carved by the rising generation of craftsmen. Dogs, stags, and swans were favourite motifs and at Castle Rising, Isabella had the cushions in her private chapel embroidered with butterflies and monkeys. Work such as this was often done by nuns in their convents. Perhaps Isabella herself, reflecting on the misdeeds of the past, turned her hand to needlework in the last years of her life.

PHILIPPA OF HAINAULT
c. 1314 ~ 1369

A Breath of Fresh Air

Philippa of Hainault was a girl who knew her own mind and brought with her a breath of fresh air into the conservative ways of court. Although her dowry had helped to pay for his father's downfall, her marriage to Edward III was a love match, which was rare in those days. Queen Isabella had set out to find a bride for her son at the court of the Count of Hainault at Valenciennes and the Count had not just one but four daughters. Edward, who was with his mother during her stay, had an opportunity to get to know all four sisters. It was tall, dark-haired Philippa who caught his eye, and the feeling, it seems, was mutual. They were married first by proxy, then Philippa arrived in London to be greeted by a scene of typical medieval splendour. It was an era when terrible brutality and punishment was commonplace, but by contrast, people enjoyed themselves with great gusto—with all the jousting, carolling, feasting and dancing essential to medieval merrymaking.

There were more celebrations when Philippa arrived in York for the wedding and where the seventeen-year-old King was waiting. There they kissed and embraced and rode side by side through the crowded streets.

Philippa, just 14, was not the youngest of brides in an age when it was not uncommon for two children aged 12 to marry. They had their first child when Philippa was not quite 16 but, despite their youth, they turned out to be model parents. Philippa chose to turn against tradition and breastfeed her baby, although it was then considered improper for noble mothers to do so. The child, christened Edward—one day to be known as the Black Prince—was born at Woodstock at 10 o'clock in the morning on June 16, 1330. Philippa had made careful preparations for her confinement. Among her requirements for her lying-in chamber were three silver basins and a magnificent bed covered with green velvet embroidered with gold. To care for the baby, Philippa appointed a nurse, Joan of Oxford, who was paid £10 per annum, and she was assisted by Matilda Plumpton, no doubt an under-nursery nurse, who was hired to rock the cradle.

To celebrate Edward's birth there was a grand tournament at Cheapside in London and a viewing tower was built for Philippa and her ladies to watch the spectacle. It was an event which could have turned to disaster. As the 26 knights engaged in the tournament assembled, the scaffolding supporting the tower gave way. The Queen, though shocked, was uninjured but the King, nevertheless, ordered the workmen responsible to be arrested and tried. The result would almost certainly have been execution, but Philippa pleaded and saved the men's lives—just as, years later, she made a historic plea for the brave burghers of Calais. It was typical of the acts of kindness that were to make her one of the best-loved Queens of the age, a saintly figure after the vengeful Isabella. Somehow she was

Phillippa of Hainault with one of her babies,
depicted as the Madonna.

pressures of court, she had time to play with her little son. She also stayed closely in touch with her mother and often had the chance to visit her when she was travelling abroad with her husband. In fact, two of her sons were born while the King was fighting a naval battle off Blankenberge—Lionel, born in Antwerp and John (of Gaunt) in Ghent.

Philippa had 12 children—seven sons and five daughters—and as the family grew, the children had their own household at Woodstock. There, one by one, they were handed over to the care of their governess, Lady Elizabeth St Omer. Prince Edward was followed by Isabella, also born at Woodstock, two years later; Joanne was born at the Tower; and William in Yorkshire, but he died in infancy and is buried in York Minster. Then came Lionel and John and a little girl, Blanche, born at the Tower, who died soon afterwards. She was followed by Edmund, Mary, Margaret, and another son called William who also died. Philippa was forty when she had her last child, Thomas. Eight of her children lived to marry; but Joanne died tragically of the Black Death when she was 15, on her way to be married in Bordeaux.

*A fourteenth century illustration of a
christening showing the baby about to be totally immersed.*

symbolic of a new era of hope and optimism and, with her baby son, Edward, inspired sculptors and artists who used them as models for stained glass windows and statues of the Madonna and Child.

As a teenage mother, Philippa took the young Edward with her when she travelled between the royal houses—from Westminster to Nottingham, Lincoln to Northampton. In the first months of his life he travelled as much as any twentieth-century prince. Woodstock was Philippa's favourite home; she revelled in the freedom of the great park where, away from the

Philippa deeply mourned the three babies she lost. When the first William died in 1336, around 393 pounds of wax candles were burnt by his coffin whenever the cortège stopped on its way to York. His tiny body was wrapped in three cloths of gold which cost £42 11s 1½d, and a further sum of £99 3s 5½d was spent having masses said at churches along the route, and to pay the widows who watched over the body on the journey. But, in fact, Philippa was fortunate that so many of her children survived. In 1348 the dreadful plague, the Black Death, spread to England from the Continent killing one in three of the population and, in some areas, wiping out whole villages.

Both Edward and Philippa indulged their children although the fourteenth century was a tough period for most young people. Once out of their baby clothes and dressed like miniature grown-ups, from the age of around six, they were expected to behave as such, and childish behaviour was severely punished, often with the cane. Many children were sent away at the age of about eight to be apprentices or to study in the homes of tutors.

Philippa's children, though, seem to have been spoiled, even by royal standards. The nursery household at Woodstock was a happy place and the children even had their own minstrel by the name of Gerard de Gay, to entertain them. And they showed appreciation of his efforts when they presented him with a coat they made themselves.

Their father virtuously set out to restore his family's name, to take his powers of kingship seriously and excel on the battlefield. Philippa enjoyed the lighter side of life and the celebrations which followed her husband's victories. She loved brightly-coloured clothes and became a leader of fashion. The style of dress changed in Philippa's time from being loose and flowing to slimline figure-clinging styles, belted and trimmed with huge, richly ornamental buckles. She spent money on fine velvets, cloth of gold and furs trimmed with jewels; there were elaborate gowns to be worn at masques and feasts and tournaments. After John, their fourth son, was born, the King gave her a splendid blue velvet gown embroidered with gold birds and trimmed with four hundred large pearls and thirty-eight ounces of small pearls. She also had her chamber richly redecorated with gold leaf and pearls, and was given a new bed as well as a state cradle for the baby and a less elaborate cradle for everyday use. There were new cups, saucers and spoons, all in silver, and twelve carpets worth £60.

Philippa also took an interest in herbal medicine, a subject she learnt from her mother who gave her rosemary, which, it is thought, was first planted in England for use at the Westminster infirmary and in the royal kitchens.

Away from the court, Philippa's special interest was the development of the cloth manufacturing industry at Norwich. Back in 1331 the King himself wrote to John Kempe of Flanders, inviting him to establish a cloth weaving industry in East Anglia. From then on Philippa made it her duty to visit the newly settled immigrant workers from her homeland and protect their interests. She also actively encouraged the coal mining industry.

As Philippa's large family grew up they caused her some heartache. Edward the Black Prince went to France when he was 16 to fight with his father in the battle of Crècy. Her second daughter, Joanne, was sent to Spain when she was only 15 to marry Pedro, son of Alphonso, King of Castile. There was to be a spectacular ceremony of welcome in the frontier city of Bayonne when the young Princess arrived in a triumphal procession. But tragedy struck. She was suddenly taken ill at Bordeaux and died within hours, an early victim of the plague that was to bring death to thousands in Europe. Philippa and her husband were devastated. They comforted themselves with the thought that 'She, in her innocent and immaculate years, has been transferred to the virgin choir in heaven where, for us below, she will perpetually intercede.'

As a consort, Philippa was not always on the sidelines. She was an indomitable woman, a woman of great courage who was not afraid to command an army herself if the need arose. When the King and Prince Edward were fighting at Crècy she proved her courage by leading the English army against the Scots as they marched south, and took King David prisoner.

Philippa died at Windsor of a dropsical disease, at the age of 55, her husband at her side. She lived to see most of her children married and to know her grandchildren. She died as one of the country's greatest Queens.

Philippa's tomb
in Westminster Abbey.

JOAN
1328 ~ 1385

Fair Maid of Kent

Royal children were often joined in their nurseries by cousins and children of court officials. The children growing up in Queen Philippa's nursery establishment at Woodstock had, as their playmate, a pretty golden-haired little girl whose father had been executed under the Isabella-Mortimer regime. She was Joan, daughter of Edmund Earl of Kent, a granddaughter of Edward I through his second marriage to Margaret. Joan was destined to become the country's most beautiful, wealthy and altogether desirable woman—the 'Fair Maid of Kent', and the first Princess of Wales.

Her outstanding beauty showed itself at an early age, for when she was ten she caught the eye of Thomas Holland, a steward serving in the household. Thomas was 18 and the son of a knight, quite the most unsuitable match for the granddaughter of a king. When Joan was 12, the coupled married without permission and in secret, probably when the King and Queen were away on a campaign overseas.

Meanwhile the Hundred Years War was being fought in Europe, and Thomas, determined to win battle honours and make a name for himself, left to fight in Germany and France, and joined a crusade against the Moors in Granada. Joan kept her marriage a secret and was unable to protest when her mother arranged her marriage with William Montague, the future Earl of Salisbury.

For a time, as Countess of Salisbury, Joan became a sophisticated lady of court society; she loved the round of fashionable gatherings, banquets and tournaments. It was during this episode in her life that the Order of the Garter is said to have been created. Joan dropped her garter at a court ball and Edward III himself picked it up uttering those immortal words *Honi*

A portrait of Joan of Kent from a manuscript in the Abbey of Saint Albans.

soit qui mal y pense ('Evil to him who evil thinks') to quieten sniggering bystanders. Later the King founded the highest order of English knighthood—with a garter as its symbol.

Joan lived with William although she had no children by him, until Thomas Holland returned to England in 1347 and claimed his wife. The Earl had her taken into custody to prevent the couple meeting, while Thomas appealed to the Pope for a divorce between Joan and William. However, all three were together for the royal Christmas gathering in 1348 and the Black Prince, showing his sympathy, presented Joan or 'Jeanette' as he called her, with a silver beaker.

The story had a happy ending for Thomas. The Pope declared in his favour, while William, seeming to show no resentment, found himself a new wife. Joan settled down to married life with Thomas Holland in much reduced circumstances. Much of the booty from his crusades had been spent on the expensive divorce proceedings, and the King gave him a pension of 100 marks a year 'for the better support of his wife'. Four years later their financial problems were resolved. Joan's brother died and she inherited the earldom of Kent, becoming Countess of Kent in her own right, and with the title came lands and income. Thomas was given the courtesy title of Earl of Kent.

Joan was in her early twenties when she became a mother for the first time. There was a son, Thomas, born in 1350, then John, two years later, followed by another son, Edmund, who died in childhood, and two daughters, Joan and Maud. Her husband was governor of an English-held fortress in France when he died shortly after Christmas in 1360, making Joan, still in her early thirties, a widow.

The golden-haired toddler who had shared her nursery days at Woodstock with Edward, the Prince of Wales, was now regarded as one of the most beautiful and desirable women in the world. Her shining glory was her mass of auburn hair which reached to her waist, and it was thought she may have used red dye to enhance the colour (a popular craze among fashion-conscious men and women). Her daringly low cut dresses and her extravagant love of silk and fur turned heads wherever she went.

Edward, the Prince of Wales, was thirty and, in spite of attempts by his father to pair him off with foreign princesses, was still unmarried. He had had discreet love affairs, sometimes conducted while on overseas campaigns, but his adult life had been devoted to gathering battle honours and he had become a national hero. Yet he had always had an affection for Joan and the couple became engaged, despite the King's initial objections to the match. The problem was solved when he applied, on the couple's behalf for a papal dispensation. This was required not only because they were cousins, but because the Black Prince was godfather to two of Joan's sons.

Permission was granted and the wedding took place just nine months after the death of Thomas Holland. The superstar of the age of chivalry and the greatest beauty of the day were married at Westminster on October 11, 1361, in the presence of Queen Philippa. The King did not attend, but two years later he created the Prince Duke of Aquitaine and the couple settled in Bordeaux where they presided over their own glittering court.

Their first child, Edward of Angoulême, was born in 1365 to be followed by another son, Richard, a year later. But their time in France brought sadness to the family. The Black Prince became ill and was bedridden with dropsy, then their eldest child, their favourite son and heir, Edward, suddenly died at the age of six.

The heartbroken family returned to England, but it was a dismal home-coming for Joan. Her husband was now an invalid and her remaining son, the future tragic King Richard II. The family settled at their country home at Berkhamsted, away from the pomp and ceremony of their big official palaces. It was a long and painful death for the Black Prince, who finally died at Westminster in 1376, aged 46. As his father, the King, was senile, and his son Richard, not yet ten, it was left to Joan to protect the interests of the future King. From being the devoted wife, who

had expected to be queen one day, she now turned all her attention to her little boy.

Joan took Richard from her manor house at Kennington to Westminster where the Black Prince lay in state for four months before being taken to Canterbury for the funeral. Together they prayed beside the Prince, then Joan led her son into the Great Hall to be presented to the assembled members of Parliament. And when old King Edward died just a year later, ten-year-old Richard was proclaimed King.

Although a Council of State was set up to rule in his name, he was crowned with traditional pomp and circumstance. The ceremony was followed by a state banquet, which Princess Joan watched from a gallery. The little boy, weighed down by the heavy robes and jewels, found the crown too much for him and it had to be held

Joan of Kent and her son Richard who was crowned King of England at the age of ten.

above his head while he ate. That in itself was a bad omen, but superstitious onlookers shook their heads in horror when the child kicked off one of his precious slippers of St Edward, which he had worn as part of his regalia, and lost it in the crowd.

The coronation over, Princess Joan took her son back to Kennington to grow up in peace and prepare for the rigours of kingship. He was educated by his tutor, Simon Burley, a knight and trusted servant of his father. Although Joan appears to have kept her son out of the public eye, Londoners were invited to the palace to entertain him with mumming and music. There were sporting contests, too, and games of dice, so that he was not isolated from the ordinary people he would be called upon to rule.

Princess Joan was in Canterbury, visiting her husband's tomb and the holy shrine of Saint Thomas à Becket, when Richard unexpectedly made his first public appearance. He was only fourteen but, courageously, just as his father would have done, he rode out to quell an angry mob of peasants, supporters of the rebellious Wat Tyler, who were gathering from all over the country to storm the capital. The Princess hurried back to London to support her son and had to take refuge in the Tower to escape the mobs. She found her son triumphant. Although so young, he already had the skill and diplomacy to disperse the mob who were armed with bows and arrows.

For the rest of her life Princess Joan became increasingly involved in court politics. Although her good looks were fading, her body swollen with dropsy, she was held in great affection by the people. She died, aged 58 on August 7, 1385 at Wallingford, one of the Black Prince's favourite residences. She could have been buried next to the Black Prince, in royal splendour in Canterbury Cathedral. Instead, according to her will, her body was placed next to her first husband, Thomas Holland, in the little church of Friars Minor at Stamford, Lincolnshire.

* * *

Richard II was, like his grandfather, doomed to die tragically, a prisoner. He married twice, but both marriages were childless. His first wife, Anne of Bohemia, died aged 27, possibly of the plague, at the royal palace at Sheen. It had been an idyllic marriage and Richard was so grief-stricken that he refused ever again to return to Sheen, and ordered his Clerk of the Works to raise all the palace buildings to the ground. His second marriage was to a child-wife, eight-year-old Isabelle of Valois—a political match arranged to secure peace with France.

Richard was deposed by his cousin Henry Bolingbroke and died a prisoner in Pontefract Castle after being either suffocated or starved to death. He was 33 years old.

MARY OF BOHUN
c. 1372 ~ 1394

First Lancastrian Queen

The new King, Henry Bolingbroke, Duke of Lancaster, was the son of John of Gaunt, and a grandson of Edward III and Philippa. He took the crown as Henry IV, the first Lancastrian king. Henry was also twice married, first to Mary de Bohun, by whom he had four sons and two daughters, then to Joanne of Navarre, who was childless. Mary de Bohun was an heiress whose estates included lands around the Wye Valley and Monmouth. She was 12 when she married Henry Bolingbroke. Her first child, a son called Henry after his father, was born in the gatehouse tower of Monmouth Castle on September 16, 1387. At the time of his son's birth,

Bolingbroke was making his way home from Windsor and he was crossing the Wye at Walford when the news was brought to him. The proud father was so delighted that he awarded the ferryman with the monopoly of the ford.

Bringing up baby was not high on the list of priorities in Mary de Bohun's household. The young Henry, a weak, sickly infant, was gravely ill for a time. Soon after his birth he was taken from the castle to a village some miles away to be nursed by Joan Waring. In fact Mary de Bohun seldom saw her child for she died when she was 22 and her son, the future King Henry V of England and hero of Agincourt, was about seven. Henry barely remembered his mother, but he always held Joan Waring in affection and thought of her with gratitude. Years later, when he became king, he settled on her an annuity of £20.

After his uncertain start, Henry grew up to be tough and athletic. He learnt to fight the hard way, in the rough, tough hill country of the Welsh Borders. It was the ideal training ground for the future warrior king. He knew Welsh and English, the languages of his people, as well as French and Latin, he was educated in literature and music and he was deeply religious. It was all in preparation for the new breed of monarch to whom Archbishop Arundel referred in his father's coronation address. 'This honourable realm of England ...' he intoned 'had been reduced to destruction by the counsel of children and widows' (a cruel reference to Princess Joan and her son Richard II). 'Now God has sent a man, knowing and discreet, for governance ...'

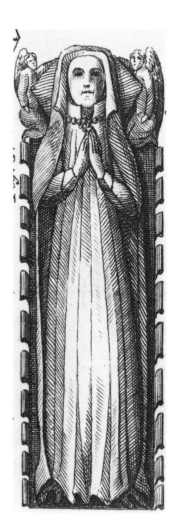

A memorial reputed to be of Mary de Bohun, which was in the chapel of Trinity Hospital Leicester.

CATHERINE OF VALOIS
1401 ～ 1437

Wife of a Hero

Catherine of Valois, who married Henry V shortly after Agincourt in 1415, never really knew her son. The infant Henry succeeded to his father as King of England when he was nine months old and, in accordance with his father's will, was placed in the care of uncles and friends, including the Earl of Warwick and the Duke of Bedford. Catherine found that her son's upbringing was not to be her responsibility.

Catherine herself had a sad and lonely childhood. The child of the mad King Charles VI of France and the scheming Queen Isabel, she was born in the palace of St Pol in Paris, a residence used by the King during his periods of madness. As a child, she was cruelly treated, shut up in a small room and left unwashed and hungry. When Charles, in a time of sanity,

Catherine's mother's apartments were lavish compared with her daughter's

realised his daughter's plight, he sent her away to be cared for in a convent and had his wife imprisoned at Tours.

In spite of the ill-treatment in her childhood, Catherine remained close to her mother, and it was Isabel who was at the centre of King Henry's long-running marriage negotiations which went on for about ten years. There was a lot of hard bargaining on both sides but Henry had a rich prize indeed when, finally, aged 33, he married Catherine in the cathedral at Troyes. The dowry of a million gold crowns, plus sovereignty over all the French lands he had conquered during the long years the two countries had been at war, was a staggering political prize. He had, in fact, made himself heir to the crown of France.

Although it was a marriage which showed the French submission to the English, it is thought that Catherine herself was not unhappy with the match—and when the King kissed her in greeting, at the conference arranged to draw up the marriage contract, Catherine blushed. There were 12 days of festivities—feasts and receptions and presentations of gifts before the wedding and the ceremonial blessing of the marriage bed on June 2, 1420.

Catherine, who had suffered so much deprivation and found so little affection in her young life, revelled in the reception that awaited her when Henry brought her home to England in February the following year. Not even the tumult of war in France at the time of her marriage could spoil her delight. They landed at Dover and travelled to Canterbury, where Catherine stayed a while before joining her husband in London. She drove through decorated streets, watched by crowds of curious Londoners, to her coronation in Westminster Abbey and afterwards she was officially enthroned in Westminster Hall. After the ceremony came a banquet attended by all the nobles and high-ranking officials. It was not only a celebration for Catherine, it was a reception of welcome for the King who had been absent for three and a half years. He was needed by his own Parliament and people.

The coronation over, Catherine accompanied Henry on a royal tour of her husband's kingdom, a country which was deeply in debt. So much had been spent on endless campaigns in France and yet more money was needed. The King and Parliament had to work quickly to raise loans. By May that year Catherine was pregnant, and although the King had intended to stay with her until the birth, he was forced to return to France.

Henry left his wife in the guardianship of his brother, the Duke of Bedford—and with one strange request: that their child should not be born at Windsor. Exactly why is not clear. But Henry was able to cast horoscopes and it could be that Fate demanded the child be born elsewhere. Nor is it known why Catherine ignored, or disobeyed, the request, but she had her baby—a son named Henry—at Windsor on December 6, 1421.

When the King heard where his son had been born he apparently sighed philosophically and prophesied:

I, Henry, born at Monmouth
Shall small time reign, and much get;
But Henry of Windsor shall long reign
   and lose all
But as God will, so be it.

When Catherine joined her husband in France in the spring, leaving her child at Windsor in the guardianship of his uncle the Duke of Gloucester, she found all was not well with the King. He had been fighting dysentery for some time and even had a doctor sent from England to treat him, but there was little to be done. For a while Henry and Catherine, living in great state at the Louvre, held court. Henry even attempted to go into battle once more. But he was too weak to ride and had to be carried on a litter back to his favourite home at Vincennes, where he died at the end of August 1422—never having set eyes on his son.

The marriage of Henry V to Catherine in the cathedral at Troyes.

Catherine accompanied her husband's body on the long, sad journey back to London for the funeral in Westminster Abbey. In his will, Henry appointed his brother the Duke of Gloucester, Regent of England, while another brother, the Duke of Bedford, was to be Regent of France and Governor of Normandy. Bedford, together with the King's friend Richard Beauchamp, Earl of Warwick, were to be responsible for his son's upbringing. There were no official duties for the young Queen Catherine.

She returned to her nine-month-old son at Windsor and, on the first day of Parliament, they rode together to Westminster, seated on a moving throne drawn by white horses. The infant, it was reported, behaved very well. Seated on his mother's knee he was quiet, almost grave, during the proceedings in Parliament.

*The infant Henry VI in
the arms of his tutor and guardian.*

The Earl of Warwick, guardian of the infant king, is seen in a drawing holding the child in full regalia. Then about 18 months old, he wears a velvet gown and cap with a miniature crown; his tiny hands clutch an orb and sceptre.

A month after Henry V's death, Catherine's father, the mad King Charles VI, died, making her son King of France as well. Henry was almost eight when he was crowned King of England in Westminster Abbey, and ten when he was taken to France for a second coronation in the Cathedral of St Denis—the only king to have been crowned in both countries.

After the London coronation there was a special banquet—the menu reads like the fifteenth-century equivalent of a royal nursery tea. Young Henry's eyes feasted upon such delicacies as a boar's head decorated with gold castles; ornamental jelly and custards; a pie flavoured with cheese and sugar sculptures which included figures of the little king.

One wonders what Catherine's feelings must have been as she watched Henry grow towards manhood. Cared for by his nurse, Joan Astley, and with Dame Alice Boteler as his governess, he was tutored for the kingship ahead. Watching from the sidelines, Catherine had little part to play. She was seen at some state occasions, such as the opening of Parliament for the first few years of her son's life, then she disappeared from public view. The only mention of her is when seven-year-old Henry was advised by his governess to give his mother a ruby ring as a New Year's gift. Parliament granted her Baynards Castle as her permanent home, but she eventually retired from court life and married (or lived with) a Welshman named Owen Tudor, who was an officer in her household—and whose family line would give its name to the royal house of Tudor. Their son Edmund Tudor, Earl of Richmond, became the father of the first Tudor King, Henry VII. Owen Tudor ended up in Newgate Prison, Catherine retired to Bermondsey Abbey. She was buried in Westminster Abbey where her son erected a memorial to her.

MARGARET OF ANJOU
1430 ~ 1482

The Warrior Mother

The beautiful but forceful Margaret of Anjou, daughter of Rene of Anjou, King of Sicily, was 15, good-looking and well-grown when she was betrothed to Henry VI in France. When she sailed into Portsmouth for her wedding two years later, in May 1445, she was escorted by 56 ships carrying her vast household which included barons and baronesses and 82 yeomen. The marriage was solemnised in the Benedictine Abbey at Titchfield in Hampshire with a gold and ruby ring, and among the new queen's gifts was a pet lion which she kept at the Tower.

Wine flowed in the streets the day Margaret met the people of London. She wore white damask powdered with gold, and pearls and precious stones in her hair which hung loose to her shoulders. She rode sitting on white cushions in a carriage drawn by two horses

The courtship of Margaret and Henry (centre),
from a fifteenth century tapestry.

47

which were also covered in white damask. The triumphant procession through sunlit city streets from the Tower to St Paul's was the first big event for the people of London in the three days of celebration surrounding her coronation.

Henry VI, once the infant king, was now 23 and a young man who had no taste for war and little desire to lead. But he was scholarly, deeply religious, a man of cultivated artistic taste. He lost the French crown his father had won and, by the time the Hundred Years War ended, only Calais remained as English territory. His mind was on other things. Five years before his marriage he founded Eton College and had started plans for King's College Chapel in Cambridge. Margaret, too, was well educated. She enjoyed reading in French and English, rode well and enjoyed hunting.

But a troubled reign lay ahead for Henry and his French bride. Henry V's prophecy concerning his son was coming true. In 1455 a quarrel broke out which was to change the family's fortunes yet again. Henry's right to the throne was challenged by his cousin Richard, Duke of York. The Wars of the Roses—between the royal houses of Lancaster and York—marked one of the most turbulent periods of British history.

Henry VI and Margaret of Anjou had been married nine years, with the couple getting increasingly anxious to produce an heir, when it was announced the Queen was pregnant. The King was so overjoyed that he settled an annuity of 40 marks on Richard Tunstal, the squire whose job it was to give the news publicly to the King, in front of his court. But the couple's happiness was short-lived. A few months later Margaret was given news that her mother, whom she adored, had died. Then, shortly before her baby was due, Henry fell gravely ill. The mounting pressures of state had proved too much for the young King who became ill both physically and mentally and suffered what has been described as an heredity 'inflammation of the brain'. He recognised no one and it was feared he might die.

Margaret, still suffering the sadness of her bereavement, and awaiting the birth of her first child, had to summon all her strength to take up the affairs of state rather than let them fall into the hands of her husband's all-too-eager rival, Richard the Duke of York (Henry's cousin and heir-presumptive). She felt lonely, isolated from close family contact; suspicious, too, of the motives of so many around her. But she had strength and determination to act alone. The baby was born on October 15, 1453 at Westminster and, as it was the feast of St Edward, she called him Edward. Margaret, for the time being, was happy that the Lancastrian line was secure. She was given her 'churching' ceremony, the traditional rites of purification, at Westminster a month later and her son was baptised in royal splendour wearing a heavily embroidered christening gown.

The King was moved to Windsor in the hope that the country air would help him recover and the Queen took her baby to join him there. With them went the Duke of Buckingham who carried the child in his arms to show him to his father 'beseeching the King to bless him; and the King gave no manner answer.' The King, tragically, still insane, was unseeing.

It had been the custom, on the birth of the eldest son, for the King to recognise the child's rights to succession by taking him in his arms, blessing him and presenting him to his nobles. Henry was still unaware that he even had a son, and Margaret could not make him perform this simple but essential ritual. More than a family tragedy, it was a dangerous political situation of which Margaret was only too well aware. The King's enemies were ready to spread rumours that the child was not Henry's at all. It was even suggested that the Queen's own baby had died at birth and been substituted with a peasant's child.

Parliament appointed the Duke of York 'protector and defender' of the King until either he recovered or Edward became old enough to rule. The baby was given an allowance the same as his father and created Prince of Wales. There were grants and payments to the Queen as well, probably to persuade her to accept the Duke of York.

*The type of scene that would have surrounded
the birth of Margaret's only son.*

At last the King began to recover and by the New Year of 1455 he was well enough to meet his 15-month-old son for the first time. He asked his name and when Margaret told him 'he held up his hands and thanked God'. Henry then told her that throughout his long illness he was unaware of events going on around him.

Henry returned to London and attempted to regain power, to no avail. Margaret was ready to act as Regent herself. A liberated woman of her time, capable, energetic, able to manage her own affairs, she was the strength behind the throne, but public feeling was against her. The Duke of York raised an army and the King was deposed for five months in 1461 and again in 1471.

Margaret, fiercely protective, had one aim—to guard her son at all costs. She loved him passionately and kept him close to her all the time, so he seldom experienced the companionship of other children. It was she who reared her only child, Edward, Prince of Wales, in the mould of a blood-thirsty warrior. He almost grew up on horseback and his early training was on the battlefield. Margaret grew to despise her husband for his weakness and devoted herself to training the boy to be a fighting king. Margaret's stamina and courage attracted the admiration of her supporters; she endured hardship and poverty. When she was penniless on a campaign in Northumberland, she and her husband and son lived for five days on a diet of herrings. And when King Henry was taken captive in London, Margaret was forced to flee with her son, who was barely seven, to Wales. They got as far as Malpas in Cheshire when their bodyguards set about robbing them of their valuables. Margaret and her son escaped with the help of a 14-year-old boy, John Combe of Amesbury. They rode together, three on one horse, all the way over moorland and mountain to the safety of Harlech Castle where they were made welcome by the Welsh.

The little prince was with her, too, at the battle of St Albans. His mother made him president of the court which condemned Bonville and Sir Thomas Kyriel to execution. 'Fair Son, What death shall these two knights die?' she asked. And the child replied that their heads be cut off. At the tender age of seven he had power over life and death. He was thirteen when the Milanese ambassador wrote, 'This boy, though only 13, already talks of nothing else but of cutting off heads or making war, as if he had everything in his hands, or was the god of battle, or was seated on the throne.'

Margaret herself led armies in battles against the Yorkists. She was promised help by the Welsh and she took Edward to Scotland to beg for help in raising an army there. Eventually she fled to France where she spent seven years in exile awaiting her chance to renew the fight.

The chance came, but her hopes died at Tewkesbury in May 1471 when, to her horror, her son Edward, the 18-year-old Prince of Wales, was killed. Shortly after, King Henry was put to death in the Tower.

Margaret was found taking shelter in a convent near Coventry and captured. She spent the rest of her days in France, thanks to a ransom paid by the King of France. All her married life she had been the strength behind the throne, warlike and ambitious, tirelessly energetic. She had suffered long and hard for her husband and, most of all, for her son. Until her death she tried to get their bodies given to her for burial. Even in this she sadly failed.

Harlech Castle, where Margaret and her son
found refuge after their escape.

ELIZABETH WOODVILLE
1437 ~ 1492

Mother of Two Lost Boys

At the time of the agonising struggle for survival of the proud Queen Margaret, another striking figure rose into ascendency at court. She was Elizabeth Woodville, the blonde, beautiful and rapacious wife of Henry's rival—the new King Edward IV. Elizabeth was the eldest daughter of Lord Rivers, the Treasurer of England, and the widow of Lord Ferrers of Groby who had been killed while fighting for Margaret of Anjou— and by whom she had two sons, Thomas and Richard. Edward married her rather impulsively in 1464. It was a quiet wedding near Stony Stratford; only Elizabeth's mother and essential witnesses, and 'a young man to help the priest sing' were present because Edward wanted the marriage kept secret until he was sure his bride would be accepted by his people.

Elizabeth was a woman of refined taste. Even before she married the King she was accustomed to a lifestyle of luxury. They had been married a year when Edward finally made his marriage public and they moved from their first home in the Tower to new apartments at Westminster. Their daughter, Elizabeth, the future wife of Henry VII, was born there five months later, surrounded, no doubt, by a certain amount of disappointment. The royal physicians had studied the stars and assured Edward that the child would be a son. One of them, Master Dominick, was so determined to be the one to pass the good news to the King, that he waited outside the Queen's bedchamber, his ear to the keyhole, during her labour and delivery. At last, he heard the baby cry, knocked on the door and asked the sex of the child. The ladies-in-waiting, not wanting to reveal that the longed-for son was, in fact, a daughter, sent him on his way. Edward, the proud father, declared anyway that he was perfectly happy with his daughter—the stars had prophesied royalty for his first-born, whatever the sex.

Elizabeth Woodville was an ambitious woman, a seeker of fame and fortune, always keen to advance herself and her family up the social ladder. And in her ultimate position as Queen of England she was able to arrange the best possible marriages for members of her family. The Woodvilles were increasingly on the way up. Edward was happy to indulge her wishes, but her ambition was to make her many enemies.

One example of her love of pomp and prestige was seen in the elaborate ceremony of purification after the birth of baby Elizabeth. It was not then the custom for a mother to attend her child's baptism, so instead Elizabeth's churching ceremony was a grand occasion. She arrived, a canopy held over her head, walking between two dukes, followed by her mother and a retinue of 60 ladies. Choir boys carrying candles walked in a procession of the Blessed Sacrament with clergy, musicians, heralds and trumpeters resplendent in brilliant livery. After sung Mass there was a royal banquet which was served in four beautifully-decorated halls and lasted three hours. Protocol was strict, and the food was first ceremoniously tasted for the King while he distributed gifts to the heralds and musicians. Elizabeth sat alone and in silence in a golden armchair while she ate her way through the menu of rich delicacies. Her mother and the King's sister, seated lower down the table, were served after the Queen, all the other ladies knelt.

Daily life at court was more relaxed. When visitors from Holland were entertained at Windsor a few years later, the Queen was seen happily surrounded by her family and ladies of the court, playing bowls and ninepins, while Edward danced with his little fair-haired daughter. Two more daughters, Mary and Cecily, were born after Elizabeth, and Windsor Castle became a very comfortable home for the growing family. The walls of the reception rooms were hung with white silk, there were carpets on the floors and guests were given rooms with soft state beds. There was a bathroom which held two baths covered with tents of cloth. At bedtime guests were served with spiced wine, green ginger and sweet syrups.

Such luxurious hospitality obviously sprang from the sophisticated Woodville influence. One big occasion in the royal year was the Garter Ceremony, an event spread over three days. When the King announced plans for a new Garter Chapel, the Queen and her eleven-year-old daughter, wearing their blue robes, rode to the service on horseback instead of going on foot. The women, always barred from the ceremonial banquet which followed, watched from an upper gallery of St George's Hall as the dishes were passed, one by one in procession, to the King sitting alone on his dais.

But Elizabeth's happy life was coming to an end. The fortunes which brought her so much power, wealth and success changed suddenly and dramatically in the autumn of 1469 when her husband was arrested by the Earl of Warwick and by his own brother, George, Duke of Clarence, who had defected to the Lancastrian side. Edward was taken captive, first to Middleham Castle, the Warwick stronghold, then to the home of the Archbishop of York, from which he escaped and hurried to join Elizabeth in London. Warwick, meanwhile, had been gathering support for the deposed King Henry VI and troops were marching towards London. Edward hurriedly arranged for Elizabeth, who was shortly to have their fourth child, and their three daughters to move to the safety of their apartments at the Tower. Then, his family securely installed, he fled to King's Lynn on the Wash and from there sailed for France at the end of September 1470.

Days later, on October 6, King Henry VI was restored to the throne. He was given accommodation in the palace of the Bishop of London and taken in procession through crowded city streets to St Paul's. But he was no more than a puppet king. Warwick, who was his train-bearer, had taken over the responsibility of government.

Elizabeth, hiding in the Tower, was aware of the ever-increasing activity. Surrounded by supporters of the new regime, she could hear the marching feet of soldiers, the roars of the city mobs, and she was terrified. Stricken with fear she fled to the royal barge and, with her daughters and lady-in-waiting, the faithful Lady Scrope, she escaped up river to Westminster and found shelter in the Sanctuary, a stronghold beneath Saint Margaret's church. Without money or valuables, Elizabeth, now penniless, was befriended by the Abbot of Westminster who gave her food from the Abbey. Meat was provided by a butcher, John Gould, who supplied 'half a beef and two muttons every week'.

Two months later, on the Feast of All Saints, as a cool November mist shrouded the river, a local

Elizabeth's beauty recorded in a manuscript of the period.

midwife, Margaret Cobbe, delivered Elizabeth's fourth child, a son. Her own physician, Master Sergio, was called to attend her and the little prince was baptised and given the name Edward.

The following spring, 1471, Elizabeth felt confident enough to leave the Sanctuary and move with her family back to the Tower. But she did not have to stay there for long. The battle of Tewkesbury in May was decisive. Edward, Prince of Wales, only son of Henry VI was killed, and with him died the Lancastrian cause. Edward IV, after six month's exile in France, was safely on the throne once more.

Life for Elizabeth Woodville, after terrifying months of uncertainty with the whole of her family in danger, could never be the same again. The long ordeal had changed her; she had displayed great courage and strength of character. It was her time in the Sanctuary and her bravery in the Tower that finally endeared her to her people. She was even praised by the Speaker in the House of Commons for her 'womanly behaviour and great constancy'.

Elizabeth had more children during the next few years—Richard, Duke of York, who was betrothed at the age of four to Lady Anne Mowbray, and four more girls—Margaret, who died young, Anne, Catherine and Bridget, and a third son, George, who died in infancy.

Prince Edward was living at Ludlow with his uncle Lord Rivers, hunting, fishing and studying, when news of his father's death reached him in April 1483. Having been proclaimed King, he set out for London and his coronation.

Elizabeth intuitively sensed that her son was in danger. At a meeting of the Council after her husband's funeral, she asked for a military escort to accompany him back to London, but her pleas were ignored. The 12-year-old prince was intercepted by his uncle, Gloucester, who had been appointed Regent, and Buckingham. Elizabeth's worst fears were justified. Gathering her young family together, with food and possessions, she once again moved into the Westminster Sanctuary.

When Gloucester arrived in London with Edward he persuaded Elizabeth that she should let her younger son, the ten-year-old Richard, Duke of York, join his brother in the Tower in preparation for the coronation. There were guards everywhere. Even the river was dotted with boats from which men were keeping watch. There was no way of escape. The Archbishop knew that force would be used if necessary to take away the boy, and Elizabeth knew she must agree. 'I here deliver him, and his brother's life with him, into your hands, and of you I shall require them before God and man,' she said. Turning to little Richard she exclaimed: 'Fairwell, mine own sweet son. God send you good keeping. Let me kiss you once ere you go, for God knoweth when we shall kiss together

*Elizabeth hugs her sons
for the last time.*

again.' And she kissed him and blessed him, then turned her back, tears streaming down her face. She probably knew she would never see either of her sons again.

It was Elizabeth's worst agony, for soon came the dreadful news that her sons were dead. 'When the news was first brought to the unfortunate mother that her sons were murdered, it struck to her heart like the sharp dart of death', wrote Sir Thomas More. 'She was so suddenly amazed that she swooned and fell to a dead corpse. And after she was revived and came to her memory again, she wept and sobbed, and with pitiful screeches filled the whole mansion. Her breast she beat, her fair hair she tore and pulled in pieces, and calling by name her sweet babes, accounted herself mad when she delivered her younger son out of sanctuary for his uncle to put him to death.'

Elizabeth was inconsolable. When it was suggested that a marriage between her daughter Elizabeth and Henry Tudor in exile in Brittany, together with her recognition of Henry as King if he were able to overthrow Richard of Gloucester, would put an end to those who brought her such misery, she readily agreed. But, when Buckingham, one of Henry's most likely supporters, was defeated, the idea seemed hopeless.

Elizabeth stayed in Sanctuary for ten months until March 1484, when she surrendered herself and her daughters. She was then officially recognised as Dame Elizabeth Grey and she gained solemn promises that her children would be safe. In January the following year King Richard III was killed by the forces of Henry Tudor at Bosworth. Henry, the grandson of Catherine of Valois (widow of Henry V) and Owen Tudor claimed the throne through his Plantagenet mother, Margaret Beaufort.

The dark days were over. She saw her daughter Elizabeth marry the new King Henry VII of England. He re-instated her, and she was godmother to his first son, Prince Arthur, born the following year.

Elizabeth died of fever six years later, surrounded by all her devoted daughters—except Elizabeth who was about to give birth to her second child, the future King Henry VIII. Her life had been violent and tragic. So many of her family had died yet, through her strength and determination she kept the rest of her children together until the very end. Her love for them could never be questioned. She died penniless. On her deathbed she said she had no worldly goods to bequeath her children. Only her blessing.

ANNE NEVILLE
1456 ~ 1485

The rich married their children off at a very early age in medieval England. Children were used as valuable currency as enormous dowries changed hands to add to the parents' estates. Thus the country's leading families became rich and powerful. Such was the fate of the compliant Anne Neville, daughter of the powerful Earl of Warwick, one of England's most aristocratic families. She had been married, briefly, to Edward, Prince of Wales, the warrior son of Margaret of Anjou, who was killed at Tewkesbury.

The Obedient Queen

At 15 she was a widow. Her father, the Earl, was also dead, killed at the battle of Barnet a month before. She was now heiress to a large part of the Warwick fortunes. Richard, Duke of Gloucester, young brother of King Edward, was waiting in the wings for a share of the inheritance.

Anne had met him in childhood but she knew him now only as her father's enemy. Gloucester had the King's support in the arrangement. He should marry Anne and with her take the family home of Middleham and the surrounding Yorkshire estates. A more headstrong girl might have refused, but the obedient Anne agreed to the proposal. The Princess of Wales became Duchess of Gloucester.

The first ten years of Anne's married life were spent happily at Middleham. While her brother-in-law, King Edward, and his Queen Elizabeth held court in lavish style in London, she lived the life of a châtelaine, presiding with her husband at high table, entertaining and taking part in country pursuits. Whether or not she grew to love her husband is not known, but the birth of her son Edward, at Middleham in 1473, more than compensated for any unhappiness there might have been in her marriage. That same year Richard persuaded the King to release Anne's mother, the Countess of Warwick, who had been kept prisoner at Beaulieu, and brought her to join the family at Middleham.

Anne adored her baby and, with Richard away increasingly, was able to devote herself to her son. He was the very centre of her life and she lived for him. There are touching references in

Ann and Richard as King and Queen,
with heraldic beasts at their feet.

the Middleham household books to some of the little boy's personal effects: 5d for a feather for the boy, 13s 1d for his shoes from Dirick the shoemaker and 100s (a year's wages) for his nurse, Jane Collins.

The Duchess' life changed dramatically from the moment Edward IV died. Richard heard he had been nominated Regent and hurried to London with the intention of intercepting his young nephew.

Anne, who had travelled south with her son, walked barefoot with her husband from Westminster Hall to the Abbey where he was to be crowned Richard III. She wore a gown of purple damask and cloth of gold for the hurriedly arranged ceremony—held not many yards from the Sanctuary, where her sister-in-law, the widowed Queen Elizabeth, and her daughters still lay in hiding.

The day before the coronation, Anne had sailed with her husband and son on the royal barge from Baynard's Castle to the Tower, where young Edward and Richard were made to leave the royal apartments to make way for the Queen and her son. The two little princes were moved to rooms in a tower near the water gate, called ever afterwards the Bloody Tower. That same day, Anne's son was created Prince of Wales.

After the coronation Richard and Anne took their ten-year-old son to Windsor and the boys in the Tower were seen playing less and less in the gardens. By the end of the summer of 1483 they had disappeared and they were never seen alive again. Whether they were smothered in their beds by the orders of Richard, their uncle, as was claimed later, or whether they lived until the reign of Henry VII, then perished, will always remain a mystery.

Anne, too, was soon to face tragedy. She was with the King, holding court at Nottingham Castle in March the following year when she received news that the son she so adored had died 'an unhappy death' at Middleham. Just what happened was not recorded. It can only be assumed, by the wording of the announcement, that the death was sudden and unpleasant. 'You might have seen his father and mother in a state bordering on madness by reason of their sudden grief,' noted a writer at the time. Anne was devastated. She became ill and never recovered. Nothing, from the diversions at court to the friends around her could 'cure the langour or heal the wound in the Queen's breast for the loss of her son'.

Richard grieved too. Not only because he had lost his son; even more important, he had lost his only heir. It was doubtful that his wife, now ailing and approaching 30, would give him another child.

At the outset of their marriage, an Act of Parliament decreed that should Anne ever divorce Richard he would still retain her property. But now it was rumoured that it would be Richard who would be seeking a divorce. By Christmas he was seen casting a favourable eye over his niece Elizabeth, the eldest daughter of the widowed Queen, recently released from her hiding place in the Sanctuary.

Anne grew weaker as she pined for her child and in spring 1485 she died at Westminster. Her death led to more rumours—even that her husband had killed her. But he confounded the gossips by not marrying Elizabeth. Time was running out for him, too. He was defeated and killed by the Lancastrian pretender, Henry Tudor at Bosworth, having reigned for just two years.

*Guests arrive for a celebratory meal after
a child is born. Painted by Massacio.*

The Tudors

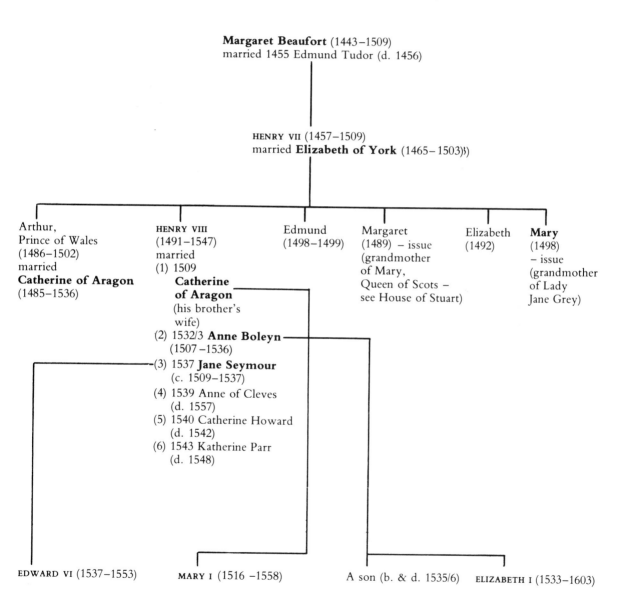

Margaret Beaufort (1443–1509)
married 1455 Edmund Tudor (d. 1456)

HENRY VII (1457–1509)
married **Elizabeth of York** (1465–1503)

Arthur,
Prince of Wales
(1486–1502)
married
Catherine of Aragon
(1485–1536)

HENRY VIII
(1491–1547)
married
(1) 1509
    **Catherine
    of Aragon**
    (his brother's
    wife)
(2) 1532/3 **Anne Boleyn**
    (1507–1536)
(3) 1537 **Jane Seymour**
    (c. 1509–1537)
(4) 1539 Anne of Cleves
    (d. 1557)
(5) 1540 Catherine Howard
    (d. 1542)
(6) 1543 Katherine Parr
    (d. 1548)

Edmund
(1498–1499)

Margaret
(1489) – issue
(grandmother
of Mary,
Queen of Scots –
see House of Stuart)

Elizabeth
(1492)

Mary
(1498)
– issue
(grandmother
of Lady
Jane Grey)

EDWARD VI (1537–1553)

MARY I (1516–1558)

A son (b. & d. 1535/6)

ELIZABETH I (1533–1603)

57

The first Tudor King, Henry VII, was born to Margaret Beaufort, wife of Edmund Tudor, in the troubled years of fear and uncertainty during the Wars of the Roses. When peace came, life for the royal mothers of the new dynasty became more settled. They travelled less and enjoyed increasing comfort in their palaces. More importance was placed on education. Margaret Beaufort and her daughter-in-law, Elizabeth of York, found there was time to spend on the pursuits of learning and pleasure. But old ideas die hard, the wars for succession were recent memories, and every queen was still primarily expected to produce a succession of healthy sons.

It was Henry VIII's fanatical desire for male children that resulted in his six marriages, his break with the Church of Rome—and, ultimately, the dissolution of the monasteries and some terrible martyrdoms.

It is ironic that for all his efforts, Henry's half dozen marriages produced only three children. His longed-for son, the child of his third wife, ruled as the boy King Edward VI but died of consumption in his teens. Henry's elder daughter Mary, determined to restore the country to her mother's Catholic faith, married King Philip of Spain. It would have been a powerful alliance but the marriage did not last and the couple failed to have children.

It was Henry's second daughter Elizabeth, child of the wife he put to death, who, as the great 'Gloriana', led England through the long last years of Tudor rule. But she never married, so left no heir to wear the crown, and carry the family name. From the birth of Edward in 1537 there had been no more children to occupy the royal nursery; no running feet, no childish cries were heard in palace corridors until the turn of the century and the arrival of the new Stuart King, James I.

Royal motherhood in early Tudor times was still influenced by ancient tradition and old superstition. Any device that might keep a pregnant queen and her child safe was employed. Henry VIII obtained an eaglestone (a hollow

A brass rubbing of a Tudor mother wearing a maternity gown, laced at the front.

stone with loose fragments inside that rattled) to help Anne Boleyn through her confinement. It was supposed to induce an easy labour and a safe delivery if worn tied to the left wrist.

The ceremonials of the birth—the lying-in

*A midwife delivering a mother who is
sitting on the traditional birthing stool.*

period and, afterwards, the churching were still strictly adhered to. The lying-in, in particular, was an immensely important time and appropriately rich clothes were worn. Jane Seymour, mother of Edward VI, prepared herself for her lying-in in regal splendour: 'She reclined, propped up with fair cushions of crimson damask with gold, and was wrapped about with a round mantle of crimson velvet furred with ermine.'

Requirements for the confinement and new baby were listed in *The Gentle Craft* by Thomas Delaney: 'Sope and candles, beds, shirts, biggins, wastecoats, headbands, swaddlebands, crossclothes, bibs, tailclouts, mantles, hose, shooes, coats, petticoats, cradle and crickets.' The crossclothes were for the mother, worn across the forehead and supposed to prevent wrinkles. The tailclout was the nappy. The cricket was a low stool for the midwife.

New babies were still swaddled. The baby's arms and legs were tightly bound over a shirt or nightdress. This was supposed to protect the fragile limbs, as well as to make the child an easy bundle to carry about. For protection from evil, babies were often given coral in the form of a necklet or rattle.

Most royal infants were handed straight to a wet nurse, although Catherine of Aragon insisted on breastfeeding her son, Henry. They were brought up apart from their parents in their own households, where they had their own staff, from chaplains down to their own personal meat-carver.

The christening was a particularly splendid occasion. The baby's robe was of cloth of gold, or crimson damask, with a long, heavy train trimmed with ermine and traditionally carried by an earl if the baby was a prince, and by a countess if it was a princess.

Everything was done to make the baby look as important as possible, so it was carried in a rich 'bearing cloth'. Four noblemen held a canopy over the baby, who was then taken behind screens specially erected near the font, and undressed for the ceremony. This area was thoughtfully provided with cushions and sweet-smelling herbs as well as a silver bowl of water in case the baby needed washing. The font, richly hung with cloth of gold, had to be high enough for everybody to see the ceremony.

As they grew older, boys and girls were dressed alike in elaborate frocks of silk and velvet with plumed bonnets. Later, they dressed like their elders—miniature adults, old beyond their years and educated in languages, arts and science, prepared early in life for responsibilities of state. The Renaissance had its effect on England in this period, and Tudor monarchs now had to be as sophisticated as their European counterparts in order to play their role successfully in Church and State, at home and abroad. In this change royal womenfolk were vitally significant in playing a part.

MARGARET BEAUFORT
1443~1509

Margaret Beaufort, Countess of Richmond and Derby, was already tragically a widow when

Mother of a Dynasty

her son Henry was born. His arrival marked the birth of the new Tudor dynasty—the child grew up to be Henry VII, King of England.

For Margaret Beaufort it was a dangerous time to have a child. It was January 1457, the Wars of the Roses were bringing danger and bloodshed to people in high places, and Margaret, who was directly descended from Edward III through his son, John of Gaunt, was particularly vulnerable. She was seven months pregnant when she was widowed, having married Edmund Tudor, Earl of Richmond, less than a year before. She fled to the safety of Pembroke Castle, home of Edmund's brother, Jasper Tudor, Earl of Pembroke.

High-minded, spiritual, intellectual—a well-educated girl of her time—Margaret Beaufort had always shown an independent streak. Her father, the first Duke of Somerset, died when she was three and she was cared for by her mother until she was nine. Then she became a ward of the powerful Duke of Suffolk, who planned to marry her off to his own son; the high-born Margaret was a valuable asset in the marriage market. But Margaret had a vision in which she was told to marry Edmund Tudor, the half-brother of Henry VI. The vision must have made a huge impression on her, for they were betrothed at once and married when she was 13.

After his death plunged her rapidly from carefree youth to the responsibility of lone motherhood in the turbulent years of civil war, Margaret directed all her energies to the care of her child, Henry, and she took on the role of king-maker. Her son's close proximity to the throne made him an obvious target for the Yorkists, so the whole of his boyhood was spent in the security of Welsh strongholds. Henry was a frail child at first but, like many delicate children often confined indoors, he grew up to be studious—one of his tutors remarked that he had never seen a boy so quick to learn. Margaret encouraged in him a love of music and literature that stayed with him all his life and, as he got stronger and spent more and more time out in the hills, he became tall and slim.

Margaret continued living quietly at Pembroke when she married her second husband, Henry Stafford, son of the Duke of Buckingham, and Henry's education continued unhindered. His Uncle Jasper, who was an experienced soldier and an expert on strategy, became his mentor and advisor.

Henry was 14 when the Yorkists had their great victory at Tewkesbury and at once he was in even greater danger. With Jasper Pembroke he sailed to exile in Brittany to await a change in his fortunes. But it was to be a long wait—Margaret Beaufort did not see her son again for 14 years.

Meanwhile, Margaret was married for a third time—to Lord Stanley, later Earl of Derby and a trusted minister of the King. It was a marriage which paved the way for Henry's progress to the throne. The death of Edward IV and the murder of his two sons meant that Richard III was his only rival. Henry was head of the Lancastrian line. The split in the Yorkist party, which had been caused by Richard's move to power, gave Henry the confidence to come out of exile. And Margaret, who had always kept in touch with her son, negotiated his marriage to Elizabeth of York, eldest daughter of the late King Edward and Elizabeth Woodville.

Margaret was, however, involved in one badly-timed, abortive bid for power which resulted in King Richard depriving her of her title and lands. But she was spared further punishment because the King did not want to alienate her husband. Instead she was confined to a 'secret place at home', without servants or companions, so that she would not be able to communicate with her son.

Margaret finally saw her son victorious at Bosworth. Her husband, Lord Stanley, defected from Richard's side. Richard was killed and his crown placed on Henry's head.

The following year, on January 18, 1486, Henry and Elizabeth were married, so uniting the houses of Lancaster and York. Margaret Beaufort's dream was at last realised. Her son, now 28, married and firmly established as king, it was time for her to move quietly into the wings. For Margaret Beaufort was not power-seeking on her own account, she directed her strength towards seeing her son made king. It was her life's work, her driving force, for which she endured hardship, loneliness in remote castles, and constant danger. Once she saw her ambition realised, she took no active part in government and was seldom seen at court except at family gatherings—at Christmas and anniversaries and the christenings of her many grandchildren.

Henry never forgot that he owed his title to his mother. He respected her wisdom and often turned to her for advice on matters of procedure and court etiquette. Mother and son enjoyed a close, loving relationship which was to last to the end of his life. For Margaret Beaufort outlived most of her family—not only Henry, who died just a few months before her in 1509, but her daughter-in-law, Elizabeth, and her eldest grandson, Arthur, Prince of Wales. She actually lived to see her grandson, Henry VIII, take the throne of England, and she was an influential voice once again at court in the first few weeks of his reign.

As, in her later years, Margaret distanced herself from court life, she turned to charitable works and religion. She founded a number of educational institutions, which were called 'Lady Margaret' after her, and still exist today. She finally left her husband to take monastic vows, but although she was a member of five monastic houses, she did not join any of them,

but retired to her manor house at Woking in Surrey. She left a lot of her wealth to the monastery at Westminster and to numerous colleges and charities. Margaret Beaufort was much loved by the nation, rich and poor. On her death it was said 'All England for her death had cause of weeping.'

A portrait of Lady Margaret Beaufort painted by an unknown artist, showing her in her later years when she devoted herself to charitable works.

ELIZABETH OF YORK
1465 ~ 1503

Elizabeth of York was 20 when she married Henry VII on January 18, 1486. Behind her were the tragic

The Humble Queen

years of her youth. There had been good times when, as King Edward IV's daughter, the eldest child in a close-knit happy family, she had dressed in regal splendour and taken her place in royal pageantry. Innocent of the dangers surrounding her father, she knew only the warmth, affection and luxury of the illustrious court. But her young life was soon shattered by poverty and hardship. Her father dead, her young brothers murdered in the Tower, it was she who was left to comfort her mother, Elizabeth Woodville, as she sheltered in the Sanctuary at Westminster. They had fled clutching what possessions they could bundle together —clothes and a few precious jewels, but over the months in hiding they had come to depend on charity. Elizabeth learnt the meaning of poverty the hard way.

Elizabeth of York by an unknown artist. She is holding the white rose of York.

Her marriage to Henry, for which she wore a gown of cloth of gold, with pearls in her hair, was her first public appearance since the death of her father; a celebration that the dark days of her life were over. There was also her coronation— an occasion of great public rejoicing, held separately from her husband's coronation which had taken place earlier. In fact Elizabeth of York, who had been the daughter of a king, the sister of another king, and who was destined to be the

mother of a king—could have been crowned Queen of England in her own right. But she left that glory to her husband. Elizabeth's duties in life were to be a royal wife and mother—and motherhood came quickly. Soon after the wedding, she was expecting her first child.

It was her mother-in-law, Lady Margaret Beaufort, who immediately sprang into action and took charge of the preparations—the elaborate furnishings for the lying-in chamber, the arrangements for the christening and the hire of the nannies to care for the new infant, which Henry had decided should be born not in London but at Winchester, the seat of ancient British kings.

'Her Highnesses Pleasure being understood,' Margaret directed, 'in what Chamber she will be delivered in, the same must be hanged with rich Cloth of Arras, Sides roof, Windows and all, except One Window must be hanged so she may have Light when it pleases her.'

The private chapel was to be 'worshipfully arrayed' and the great chamber also had to be hung with rich arras and was to contain 'a Cloth and Chair of Estate and Quishions thereto', so that when the Queen came from chapel with her lords and ladies she might 'either standing or sitting at her pleasure receive Spices and Wine.'

Between the great chamber and the bedchamber was an anteroom which must also be 'well worshipfully hung'. The bedchamber itself contained a royal bed with the floor 'laid over' with carpets and a cupboard covered in the same draperies as the walls and windows.

When the baby was born, he was laid in a wooden cradle 1¾ yards long and 22 inches wide, within a frame 'fair set forth by the Painters craft', decorated with silver gilt and tongueless buckles on either side for the 'swathing bands'. For showing off to foreign nobility, the baby was transferred to 'a great Cradle of Estate' which was a full 5½ feet long and 2½ feet wide, covered in gold and crimson. This state cradle bore the King's arms at the head post.

Towards the end of her pregnancy, Elizabeth heard Mass, at which she was joined by a crowd of noblemen and ladies. Then, after refreshments, she and her ladies retired to the specially prepared birthing room. But Elizabeth was not confined for long. The baby arrived early, on September 20, 1486—her lusty little son was a month premature.

The efficient Lady Margaret had the christening plans well in hand, for the baptism was held the next day, with all the pomp and ceremony of a royal occasion. Elizabeth Woodville was godmother and the Earl of Oxford, one of the country's greatest soldiers, who had led his men courageously on Henry's side at Bosworth, was godfather. There was a slight hitch—the Earl was away on his estates in the West Country when he had news of the baby's early arrival and although he made a hurried dash to Winchester, he arrived three hours late. After a long delay, the ceremony went ahead without him.

All the family, including the Queen's sisters as well as the noble lords and their ladies, had parts to play in the procession bearing the chrism, the salt, gilt basins and towels. The Earl of Oxford arrived in time to see his tiny, day-old godson, in his robe of crimson trimmed with ermine, laid on the altar and blessed—and given the ancient royal name of Arthur. It must have

been a splendid sight as the whole royal family, nobles of the realm, and clergy, in their fine robes and vestments, gathered by the light of flaming torches. But it was a sight that Elizabeth herself was not allowed to see—for she had to stay out of public view until after her churching ceremony. This stemmed from the early belief that the pains of childbirth were punishment for the sin of Eve and, by extension, a mother should therefore be spiritually cleansed afterwards. Gradually the ceremony came to be regarded as a service of thanksgiving for a safe birth.

Although the new-born prince was lively enough, Elizabeth was unwell that autumn. Before her churching ceremony she received her officers of the household lying on a state bed, then a duchess had to help her down from the bed and lead her to the door, where two more duchesses and a duke were waiting to lead her into the chapel for the ceremony. When, finally, she recovered, she founded a chapel in Winchester Cathedral in thanksgiving for Arthur's birth.

Meanwhile Arthur was cared for by a team of nurses under the close scrutiny of Lady Margaret Beaufort, who also made sure that the strictest security was enforced to protect her grandson. There were nurses to feed him and rock the cradle, but a doctor was always on hand at feeding time, and yeomen and squires guarded the nursery night and day. Everyone with any responsibility towards the child had to swear an oath of allegiance.

Although she was Queen, Elizabeth led a really rather ordinary life as wife and mother, not of a warring consort, as she might have done in the days of her medieval predecessors. Like them she travelled the country, but the cold, stone-built fortresses had given way to comfortable royal palaces. Elizabeth's next child, Margaret, destined to be Queen of Scotland (and grandmother of Mary, Queen of Scots), was born at Westminster in 1489. Then, in June 1491, a fair-haired son was born in the palace at Greenwich and christened Henry in the nearby Franciscan church.

Once out of the nursery, Arthur was sent to Ludlow Castle, the traditional home of the heir to the throne and from where, as Prince of Wales, he could govern his domain. He was a bookish child and there he prepared himself for kingship. Taught by tutors who were specially picked for him by Lady Margaret, he had a classical education, studied languages, music and literature, and practised sports and exercises such as wrestling, hurling and riding.

Elizabeth looked forward to the times when he returned to his family, when she could gather her children around her and they could spend happy hours together. The family lived in the shadow of the plague, a constant fear which hung over them, and by the early 1490s it had taken on a new and virulent form—the sweating sickness. It gripped its victims violently, with stomach and head pains and unbearable sweating, and they died within hours. Thirty thousand Londoners died in two days. So the royal family took their children to the safety of their country homes—Greenwich, Eltham, Windsor, Sheen and Fotheringhay in Northamptonshire.

Together, Elizabeth and her children enjoyed simple, homely pastimes. They danced to the music of the lute and clavichord; they laughed at the antics of jesters and jugglers; they played chess, backgammon and dice, and the little Princess Margaret became a keen card player and loved to gamble. They shot arrows at the butts, played tennis, and enjoyed hawking. The energetic young Henry, who unlike his quiet, studious brother, was an outgoing, extrovert child, was often the ringleader in these family pursuits. And the King, who was fascinated by wild animals, had a collection of big cats and exotic birds which he kept at the Tower.

Christmas was a favourite time, when the

Windsor Castle, about which Edward VI
was to say, at the age of 12, 'Methinks I am in prison.
Here be no galleries nor no gardens to walk in.'

King entertained hundreds of people to lavish banquets, with as many as 60 different dishes on the menu. Celebrations continued throughout the 12 days of the festival, with feasts and pageants, and expensive presents exchanged at court. Elizabeth loved tradition and was keen to preserve the little ceremonies. The formal presentation of New Year gifts was a favourite ritual of hers—they were exchanged between the King and Queen and noblemen who sat in dressing-gowns at the foot of the bed. But one Christmas nearly ended in disaster. It was in 1497, and the family were gathered at Sheen for the celebration, when the palace caught fire. The family escaped with their pet dogs and as many treasures as the servants were able to salvage. After burning for three hours, the building was destroyed.

Elizabeth, while enjoying her years of motherhood, could never forget that her real role in life was to produce healthy heirs. In fact the royal marriage market sprang into action soon after Arthur was born. He was barely a year old when he was betrothed to Catherine of Aragon, the 21-month-old daughter of Ferdinand and Isabella of Spain. The marriage, it was agreed, would not take place before Arthur's 15th birthday. Margaret was betrothed to James IV of Scotland when she was nine, and another daughter, Mary, born in 1498, was betrothed to Charles, son of Archduke Philip of Burgundy. Her brother, Henry, it was decided, would marry the Archduke's daughter.

From a very early age Elizabeth's little sons were initiated into the pomp and ceremony of royal life. When they were only three, both Arthur and Henry were made Knights of the Bath in a ceremony which went on for two days and must have been an ordeal for the little boys. It involved being ceremoniously bathed in a linen-lined bathtub, then dressed in the harsh cloth of a hermit, and spending the night in prayer with other knights before hearing Mass at dawn. After being allowed to sleep until noon, the knights were robed before riding out to receive their stirrups and sword from the King. At the same age, Arthur was also created Prince of Wales and travelled in his own barge to a celebration banquet, at which the tiny child waited upon his father. He had been trained since birth to behave with astonishing self-assurance and maturity in public. At another banquet, held in the Parliament chamber in Westminster, he presided as Prince of Wales, wearing miniature robes and regalia and seated at the high table in a specially-designed high-chair. When his brother, Henry, was three and created Duke of York, he too was the central figure at the festivities.

Elizabeth had other children. There was a daughter, born shortly after the death of her grandmother, Elizabeth Woodville, and christened Elizabeth after her. Sadly, she died when she was four and was buried near the shrine of Saint Edward in Westminster Abbey. She was later joined by a little brother who was too small to survive long after his birth.

In 1499 Elizabeth was pregnant again—it was

The marriage by proxy of Mary,
the 12-year-old sister of Henry VIII.
Early betrothals did not always end
in marriage if political alliances changed.

her seventh confinement in 13 years. To her great joy, she had another son, Edmund, Duke of Somerset. To avoid the risk of the plague, he was sent to the nursery at Hatfield for the summer while Elizabeth, to have a change of air and recover from the birth, went with her husband to Calais to negotiate the marriages of Henry and Mary. It was a happy time for Elizabeth; but her happiness was soon to end. Shortly after her return from France came news of little Edmund's death—yet another to join the little tombs in the Abbey.

Two years later, in May 1501, sixteen-year-old Catherine of Aragon said goodbye to her parents and set sail for England to be married to the Prince of Wales. Her ship was forced to turn back by storms—an ill omen, it was said—but eventually Catherine and her retinue made the crossing and landed at Plymouth in October. Elizabeth communicated with the young girl in Latin—their only common language—and did her best to make her future daughter-in-law feel at home in the strange new country. The marriage of Catherine and Arthur took place a month later in a spectacular ceremony in St Paul's Cathedral, which was followed by a week of public celebrations. There were jousting tournaments, banquets and revels. The whole of London rejoiced. There was another family gathering two months later, when Princess Margaret became the wife of the Scottish King James IV. The marriage took place with the Earl of Bothwell standing proxy for James—a second ceremony was to be held later in Edinburgh. But the dancing, jousting and banqueting went on well into the New Year.

Elizabeth's pleasure at seeing her children grow up and make desirable marriages was soon shattered. In April came the dreadful news from Ludlow that Arthur, the heir to the throne, was dead. Arthur, studious, intelligent, dutiful, but always delicate, had died of consumption. Elizabeth was heartbroken; so, too, was the King, who wept in her arms. Of all her babies, only three, Henry, Margaret and Mary had survived.

The following year, in a restrained ceremony, Henry was created Prince of Wales at the age of 11. And Elizabeth found she was pregnant for the eighth time.

Lady Margaret Beaufort, who was still influential in domestic matters, presided once again over the preparations for Elizabeth's lying-in. This time the new royal home at Richmond, built after the disastrous fire at Sheen, was the chosen birthplace. Lady Margaret, though deeply religious, had a superstitious side to her nature. She believed that the tapestry wallhangings in the room should have a floral design as human figures could have an adverse affect on the unborn child. Furthermore, every window except one should be blackened out with heavy curtains, and the chamber richly furnished with oriental carpets and thick cushions. The bed was to have a feather mattress on top of the wool one, a cloth of gold sheet trimmed with fur, and covers of scarlet velvet edged with fur. Even the chapel was to be refurbished and provided with a new gold crucifix and relics of the saints. It was to be the most splendid setting ever for the birth of a prince or princess.

But the baby was not born at Richmond. The child began to arrive prematurely, when Elizabeth was at the Tower. Maybe she had become bored in her pregnancy, for instead of staying near Richmond, she amused herself by visiting her other homes and travelling by barge on the Thames—even though it was winter. The birth imminent, Elizabeth heard Mass in the chapel in the White Tower, then wearily climbed the steep stone spiral staircase to the royal apartments above. There, on February 2, 1503, in a room hung with blue tapestries decorated with gold *fleur-de-lis*, a little girl she called Catherine was born.

Elizabeth seemed quite well after the birth, but sudden complications set in a week later and she died on Feburary 11. The devoted mother, 'Elizabeth the Good' her people had called her, had lived according to her motto—'humble and reverent'. Having given birth to her eighth child, she died, tragically, on her 38th birthday.

CATHERINE OF ARAGON
1485 ~ 1536

Catherine of Aragon, widowed in April 1502, only four months after her marriage to Arthur, Prince of Wales, must have felt very alone and isolated from the family she had left behind in Spain. As the youngest child of Ferdinand and the formidable Isabella, she had spent most of her life in the warm south of the country, where her parents led a crusade against the Moors. She was six when they captured Granada, and the splendid palace of the Alhambra, with its cooling fountains, courtyards and scented gardens, became her childhood home.

A Royal Pawn

Now a young widow in London, she moved with her servants to Durham House, one of the magnificent palaces which once stood on the Strand, with lawns sweeping down to the Thames. There the dowager Princess of Wales awaited her fate. She was to wait six years, as her money dwindled away and she became the centre of a bitter political wrangle between her father and the King.

Queen Catherine, painted by an unknown artist.

Catherine was to be betrothed to Arthur's young brother Henry. He was only 12 and Catherine was 18. But Catherine, who had never met Arthur before they married—they exchanged letters—now at least would get to know her future husband. No doubt the age gap could be overlooked for the prize of a second chance to be Queen of England. The couple were betrothed at the home of the Bishop of Salisbury in Fleet Street in June 1503, and it was agreed that the marriage would not take place until Henry was at least 14.

Meanwhile, a papal dispensation was needed for Catherine to marry her brother-in-law and there was the all-important question of finance. Only a quarter of her dowry had been handed over when she had married Arthur, so should another dowry be negotiated for her marriage to Henry? Then Queen Isabella died. Catherine lost not only the mother who had given her the education and religious upbringing that was to be her guiding force for the rest of her life, but also her closest friend and ally. Isabella had been the power behind the Spanish throne and on her death relations between Ferdinand and King Henry cooled; hopes of any more dowry payments for Catherine ceased. She was heavily in debt and began selling jewellery and gold and silver plate that she had been allowed to keep from her dowry. Her servants were unpaid and

Nobody seemed to want her but, being a pawn in the royal marriage game, Catherine had no say in her own future. When her mother-in-law, Elizabeth of York, died, King Henry considered marrying Catherine himself, but her parents at once vetoed the idea and prepared ships to bring their daughter and her retinue home. Under such pressure, the King relented and instead her clothes shabby—she later complained to the King that she'd had only two new dresses in four years. Finally, the King had no choice but to let her leave the dower house to live at court.

Meanwhile, Catherine waited for her Prince to grow to manhood. In contrast to his quiet brother, Henry was big and boisterous, an extrovert lover of games and practical jokes, already a keen huntsman who would soon outride the fastest horseman, and become a champion among sportsmen. When Arthur's death made him heir to the throne he had to turn his mind to more academic matters so, while Catherine waited in the wings, his grandmother, Margaret Beaufort, supervised his education. As the future king, he was surrounded by the brightest talent in the kingdom. The poet laureate, John Skelton, was his chief tutor, he became acquainted with Thomas More and he met the famous European scholar Erasmus when he visited from Rotterdam. The young Prince spent his days at Ludlow, studying mathematics, divinity, astrology and Latin.

Despite the formality of a betrothal, Catherine could not be certain of her future. Although she was living at court, she rarely saw Henry and when he reached the age of 14 he protested that the marriage plans had been made against his will. The protest had probably been suggested by his father, wishing to keep his options open in the hope that he might find an even better match for his son. In fact Catherine had to wait until April 1509 when King Henry VII, on his deathbed, made a last wish that his son should marry her. And the new King Henry VIII, by then almost 18, was ready to comply.

Maybe he considered it politically expedient; maybe he really loved her. We shall never know. It was a quiet wedding on June 11, 1509 in the chapel of the Franciscan Observants at Greenwich. He a tall, fair, athletic giant; she petite, with a pale complexion and a little solemn, showing the maturity of her 23 years. Shortly afterwards, on Midsummer's Day, they were both crowned King and Queen in a ceremony surrounded by pageantry.

For the new King who had never been allowed any responsibility, never given a chance to help govern in his father's lifetime, these were heady times of freedom marked with wild celebration. And they were the golden days of Catherine's life.

It was because she had not conceived during her short time of marriage to Arthur that she was given consent to marry Henry. Now she lost no time in becoming pregnant, and happily prepared for the birth of her first baby due the following year. Henry was overjoyed that his dearest wish, to have the all-important heir, was about to come true. And, whether or not there was any doubt before, now their love for one another was obvious. 'The King, my Lord, adores her, and her Highness him,' was the opinion of Catherine's confessor.

Their first Christmas of married life together was an endless round of dances and banquets: Henry's parties went on for days. But his excitement, and Catherine's as they awaited the arrival of their first-born was to end in sadness. The birth, on the last day of January 1510, was two months premature, and the baby—a girl—was born dead. For Catherine it was the first of the terrible disappointments which were to darken her life over the next nine years.

But in 1510, Catherine was still young, in love with her husband, and confident that there were many years ahead to have more babies. Soon she was pregnant again and on New Year's Day, the following year, Henry was in wild good humour. She had given birth to a prince! He was born at Richmond in the early hours of the morning, a fine healthy child. The proud father gave the midwife £10 and the nurse, Elizabeth Poyntz, £30 for their care and attention. When the baby was four days old he was baptised and given the name Henry, after his father; the King of France and the Duchess of Savoy were his godparents— and the tiny child was proclaimed Prince of Wales.

When it came to babycare, however, Catherine, the Spanish-born queen, had her own ideas. She decided to break with tradition and breastfeed the baby herself, rather than hand him over to be reared by a wet nurse. But this did not prevent Henry from appointing a separate household staff for his son—including three chaplains, a serjeant of arms, a clerk of the signet, a cellarman, baker, even a meat carver. The baby's birth had been celebrated publicly with bonfires, church bells and gunfire, and wine flowed in the streets to the delight of people in the city. Then the King rode to Walsingham to give thanks at the shrine of Our Lady.

A more lavish celebration was planned for the following month, when Catherine herself would be well enough to appear in public. It was a wonderful excuse for one of the flamboyant displays Henry loved so much: a two-day fiesta was held in Catherine's honour. It had long been the custom on such occasions for gifts to be donated to charity. This time, the King, feeling generous, hit on the idea of inviting his guests to help themselves to the decorations he and his companions were wearing. The event turned into a royal romp, ending in complete disaster as hordes of excited spectators rushed forward. The sight of the riches proved too much for them as they stripped the bower bare and then moved on to relieve the guests of as many jewels as they could lay their hands on. 'The common people ... ran to the king and stripped him into his hosen and doublet, and all his companions likewise.' Guards took charge of the mob and the merrymaking continued in the King's chamber. Nothing could have worried Henry, such was his elation at the birth of his son.

But the parties were premature. Nine days later Henry, Prince of Wales, not yet two months old, was dead. He died suddenly of an unknown cause. Catherine was heartbroken, and Henry gave his son a princely funeral in Westminster Abbey—974 pounds of wax went into the candles surrounding the hearse. In an age when childhood diseases were often fatal, when doctors were powerless to act against such infections as intestinal viruses and pneumonia, the infant mortality rate was tragically high. Even the wealthiest parents had to stand by and watch

their children die. For Catherine, so desperate to give Henry his longed-for heir, the truth was hard to bear. Henry hid his own feelings and tried to comfort her with the thought that there could still be children.

Henry, putting his disappointment behind him, embarked on campaigns abroad—first in Spain, then France. When he set sail for France in June 1513, he appointed Catherine Regent of England. By then she was pregnant once more. Loyally she spent the long summer days laboriously sewing military badges, banners and standards. Henry was still away, unable to share her grief in September when the baby, another son, was born dead. Heartbroken again, but still not defeated, she became pregnant the following year and in November 1514 she gave birth prematurely to another child—'a prince who lived not long after'. Catherine had lost four babies in five years. But this time Henry was at home to comfort her, and when she had recovered he held a masked ball to try to cheer her.

Catherine did have another baby. It was born at Greenwich, the palace which had become the principal royal home since the old palace at Westminster had been destroyed in a fire only days after the celebrations of the birth of Prince Henry in 1512. The child, a girl, was born at four in the morning of Monday, February 18, 1516, and they called her Mary after her aunt, Henry's favourite sister. And this time, to Catherine's joy, the baby lived. Henry concealed his disappointment that he now had a daughter and not a son and remarked to the Venetian ambassador 'The Queen and I are both young and if it is a girl this time, by God's grace boys will follow.' Mary was baptised when she was two days old, in the adjoining monastery chapel where Catherine had been married. Margaret Pole, Countess of Salisbury, carried her to the font for the solemn ceremony. Princess Catherine, a daughter of Edward IV, and the Duchess of Norfolk were godmothers; Cardinal Wolsey was godfather. After her baptism, Mary was confirmed, and Margaret Pole, a trusted friend of Catherine's, was her sponsor. In fact she became a strong influence in Mary's childhood, for she was appointed head of her nursery suite while her sister-in-law, Catherine Pole, was Mary's nurse. There were also four people employed as rockers of the cradle, and the baby princess even had her own priest, Henry Rowte, who was given the position of chaplain and clerk of the closet.

Catherine could see that Henry was proud of his daughter; he delighted in showing her off. She was two when he took her in his arms to introduce her to his courtiers, among them Wolsey and the Venetian ambassador, who dutifully kissed the small chubby hand. Late in 1517 the little girl was given her own home, Ditton Park in Buckinghamshire. Being close to Windsor, it meant that Catherine could still remain in close contact with her daughter, but she could never forget that Mary was also a pawn in the power game of kings.

In October 1518 Catherine held her in her arms while Cardinal Wolsey placed a diamond ring on the little princess's finger—with all the formality befitting the occasion, she was betrothed to the Dauphin of France. The ceremony was held in the monastery at Greenwich, the scene of her baptism, and she was dressed like a little adult, in cloth of gold, a black velvet cap encrusted with jewels on her head. The solemnity over, Henry then threw himself with gusto into a week of banqueting, masques and parties. A hundred courses were offered to guests at the closing banquet at Greenwich, and afterwards Henry threw sugar plums to his departing guests.

Like all royal mothers through the ages, Catherine was expected to travel abroad, and at Ditton Park, Mary was left in the care of her governess, Lady Margaret Bryan. Not surprisingly, the royal charge was somewhat forward for her age. In 1520, when she was four, and Catherine had gone with Henry to France, her guardian reported that she was 'Right merry and in prosperous health and state, daily exercising herself in virtuous pastimes and occupations.' Catherine, it seemed, had passed on to her little daughter her aptitude for learning and her gift for music. Some French nobles who had

stayed at the court remarked on 'her skill in playing on the virginal, her tender age considered'. When Mary was six, her engagement to the Dauphin was broken off and she was betrothed instead to 23-year-old Emperor Charles V. But that, too, was ended in 1525, and then, at the age of nine, she was sent off to Ludlow. Although Mary was not actually proclaimed Princess of Wales, she was addressed as Princess of Wales and Cornwall, and given the house at Tickenhill in Worcestershire which had been prepared for Henry's elder brother, Arthur. There, as mistress of her own household, the little girl held court. She loved the extravagant Christmas festivities which her courtiers devised for her, but continued to work hard at her lessons. Like her father, she studied science and Greek, mathematics, geography and astronomy, and by the time she was 11 she was able to speak fluently in Spanish and Latin. Spare time was spent on embroidery or music.

Catherine saw less and less of her high-spirited little daughter until 1527 when Mary was engaged for a third time—to Henry, Duke of Orleans, and special celebrations were held in her honour at Greenwich. It was another excuse for Henry's merrymaking, with a round of dancing, banqueting and entertainment, although to all the guests it was obvious that it would be sometime before Mary, a thin, bird-like child, would be married.

By now, though, the storm clouds had gathered round Catherine's marriage; her years of happiness and security as Queen of England were ending. She had had a miscarriage the year after Mary was born and another son was born dead in 1518—all in spite of the efforts of doctors who had come from Spain to treat her. It is possible that Catherine was a victim of toxaemia in pregnancy, or that the Rh factor was involved. But Henry became convinced that his marriage was cursed because he had committed the sin of marrying his brother's wife, even though Catherine had been given a papal dispensation on the grounds that her marriage to Arthur had never been consummated. Henry decided she must have been lying, or why should he be punished like this?

Henry did, in fact, have a son—an illegitimate son born in 1519, whom he called Henry Fitzroy. His mother was Elizabeth (Bessie) Blount, the daughter of a Shropshire knight who had joined the court as a maid of honour when she was 15, and become Henry's mistress. In 1525 when Princess Mary was moved to Ludlow, six-year-old Henry Fitzroy was created Duke of Richmond and given precedence over Mary, with his own household in Yorkshire. Henry did not spare Catherine's feelings about the matter, but although he proudly showed the boy off at court she remained loyal. After so many pregnancies, Catherine was losing her looks and her figure, and the age gap between her and Henry was beginning to show. Around 1525, Catherine was faced with an even greater threat. Henry had fallen madly, passionately in love with Anne Boleyn. And Anne refused to be the King's mistress. She wanted one thing—to be his wife, and Queen of England. Henry's thoughts turned to divorce.

He wanted a male heir to secure the Tudor line, for there were still Plantagenet pretenders ready to claim the crown. The easiest way was to have his marriage declared null and void. But the Pope, who had granted Henry the dispensation in the first place, pronounced the marriage valid. Henry then became obsessed with divorce but Catherine, who had never forgotten the strict religious teachings of her childhood, would not—could not—agree.

When talk of the divorce became public, Henry feared that Mary would gather Welsh support in her mother's defence. He had her household at Ludlow closed down and instead gave her a house nearer home—at Newhall near Chelmsford in Essex. But he needn't have worried. Mother and daughter rarely met. Once, when Catherine asked Henry if their daughter could visit them he huffily replied that she could go and see Mary any time she wished—and stay with her. To which Catherine replied that she would not leave him for her own daughter—or anyone else in the world. In fact, Catherine was

The old palace of Hatfield where the royal children were safe from the risk of plague epidemics.

allowed a visit from Mary for a few weeks in 1531—it was their last time together. In July that same year, when the royal family moved from Greenwich to Windsor, Henry set out early one morning on a hunting expedition to Woodstock with Anne Boleyn by his side. That morning he rode out of Catherine's life for ever.

Henry had left instructions that before his return Catherine was to vacate her apartments and she was forbidden to communicate with him or with Mary. From then on, both mother and daughter, living in reduced circumstances in separate houses, were to suffer agonising shame and humiliation.

Catherine, still refusing to contemplate divorce, sent Henry a New Year's gift in 1532—a gold cup 'with honourable and humble words'. Her message was ignored. In January the following year Henry and Anne Boleyn married in secret and Henry, having denounced allegiance to Rome, declared himself head of the church in England. At a special ecclesiastical court set up in Dunstable in May, Thomas Cranmer, Archbishop of Canterbury, dutifully pronounced Henry's marriage to Catherine null and void. From then on, Catherine would be known as Princess Dowager or Princess of Wales, her 24 years of marriage to Henry ignored. In September 1533 Anne gave birth to a daughter—the future Queen Elizabeth I. And she displayed astonishing contempt for Catherine's feelings by asking Henry to obtain the richly embroidered shawl which Catherine had brought from Spain for the christenings of her own babies. Not surprisingly, Catherine refused.

In fact Catherine steadfastly refused to acknowledge the divorce and Henry's remarriage. Courageously she declared she would only accept the decision of the Pope—and he insisted her marriage was valid. Friendless, surrounded by spies, her health broken, she spent her last days at Kimbolton Castle in Huntingdonshire, a prisoner of the King. There she locked herself in one room, in which she ate and slept, refusing to eat any food that had not been prepared for her by the servant she trusted.

Showing dogged determination, she refused to communicate with servants who had sworn allegiance to the King as supreme head of the church, and refused to accept mail addressed to her by her new title. She had supporters all over the country who acknowledged her as the true and rightful queen. The King knew this and forbade her physician, her confessor and apothecary from leaving the house, for fear they might drum up support which could lead to trouble.

Catherine spent her days doing needlework, and in prayer—praying for her husband and for her daughter, who was never far from her thoughts, for she knew that Mary, too, was suffering, and feared for her safety.

On the birth of her half-sister, Elizabeth, Mary had been declared illegitimate, told she had to give up the title of Princess and had her household closed down. She then had to move to the nursery apartment at Hatfield where, hated by Anne Boleyn, she was made to wait upon the baby Elizabeth. Catherine once remarked prophetically that Anne's marriage would have an unhappy end. Maybe she felt that one day the situation for Mary, if not for herself, would improve, for she wrote to her daughter urging her meanwhile to be discreet and inoffensive to her father. She also sent her two books, and she asked Mary to let her see some of her exercise books. But her request was not allowed.

Mary, in her teens, independent, often headstrong, refused to follow little Elizabeth whenever she was moved from one house to another. Isolated from both her parents—Henry refused to see her—she was kept in seclusion, for it was thought she might try to escape abroad. And at Hatfield orders were given to beat her if she disobeyed the King.

The end came for Catherine on January 7, 1536. There were rumours that she was poisoned but there was no evidence that this was so. Before she died she dictated a letter to the King, in which she forgave him for the misery he had caused her and begged him to be a good father to her daughter. Her final wish, that she should see Mary, her only child, for one last time was never granted. But she was resolute in her beliefs to the end, for she signed her last letter to Henry not 'Princess of Wales' or 'Princess Dowager' but *Catherine, Queen of England.*

ANNE BOLEYN
1507 ~ 1536

The Queen Who Lost Her Head

When news of Catherine of Aragon's death reached Henry, he exclaimed 'God be praised, we are now delivered from all fear of war', and Anne Boleyn declared happily 'I am indeed Queen.' Then, in celebration, the pair dressed from head to foot in bright yellow and Henry put a white feather in his hat. A special Mass was said, to which Henry himself carried their little daughter, and presented her to his courtiers amidst a fanfare of trumpets. A banquet followed; there were yet more celebrations that went on for days . . .

Anne Boleyn, Henry's new queen, was no newcomer to court life. Her father, Thomas Boleyn of Hever, who had been created a Knight of the Bath at the time of Henry's coronation, came from a long line of wealthy London merchants—his grandfather had been Lord Mayor. But Anne's mother, Elizabeth, the daughter of Thomas Howard, Duke of Norfolk, had royal blood in her veins. Anne had been a maid of honour at the French court when her father was appointed Ambassador to France, and stayed in Paris until late in 1521 when, with war imminent, she returned to England. It was not long afterwards, at a court ball in the spring of 1522, that she caught the roving eye of King Henry.

By 1528 it was public knowledge that Anne Boleyn was the King's mistress. She was installed

Hever Castle, Kent, where Henry courted the seductive Anne Boleyn.

in her own splendid apartments at Greenwich and when Henry banished Catherine from court in 1531 Anne took her place at the King's side. They were halcyon days for Anne. The King was madly in love with her and she could happily ignore the unpopularity shown her by the public. Henry showered her with the jewels which Catherine had been forced to hand over to him and lavished upon her gifts of goblets and bowls and chandeliers. In the autumn of 1532, Henry decided to take Anne with him on a state visit to France, and also to give her a title. On the first Sunday in September, in St George's Chapel, Windsor, she was created Marchioness of Pembroke. She knelt before the King who invested her with a mantle of crimson velvet and ermine, placed a coronet on her head and granted her lands worth £1,000 a year. It is not known exactly when King Henry and Anne Boleyn began living together as man and wife, but by January she was pregnant. Clearly a marriage had to be arranged if the heir were to be born in wedlock. The wedding was not the lavish affair Anne must have hoped for, but a simple ceremony held in the utmost secrecy early on January 25—for Henry's marriage to Catherine was still valid. Soon afterwards came Cranmer's pronouncement that Henry's earlier marriage was null and void and Anne was Henry's lawful wife. At Easter, news of the royal wedding was made public. Then, on Whitsunday, Anne was crowned in a spectacular ceremony in Westminster Abbey. She was not known for her beauty, but she had dark, flashing eyes, and her long black hair which she loved to wear flowing loose down her back was her crowning glory. As she rode in a litter to her coronation, it was noted that she was actually sitting on her hair; she wore huge pearls round her neck, and the folds of her heavy robes concealed her expanding figure.

Anne Boleyn was not known for her beauty but clearly her tempestuous nature was attractive.

Henry was confident that the new baby would be a son—the astrologers had told him so. It was agreed that the child should be called Henry or Edward and circulars from the Queen, announcing the goods news to the nobility, were prepared before the event. But again Henry was to experience bitter disappointment. The child, born between three and four in the afternoon on September 7, was a girl. It had been a difficult labour and a complicated delivery in which Anne must have suffered, but Henry did not try to hide his anger. He could hardly bring himself to look at his new, beautiful daughter. She had been born at Greenwich, in a room furnished with a magnificent bed (it had been part of a ransom paid for the release of a French prince taken prisoner in the wars, and brought from the Treasury for the lying-in). The walls of the apartment, called the Chamber of Virgins, were hung with tapestries showing the parable of the ten wise and ten foolish virgins. Anne even tried to appease Henry by making a joke about the suitability of the name of the room, now that a virgin had been born there. But

Henry was so depressed by the whole event that he stayed away from the baby's christening and confirmation held three days later in the chapel at Greenwich. 'God has forgotten him entirely, hardening him in his obstinacy to punish and ruin him,' said one commentator. Nevertheless, the ceremony went ahead, attended by nobles, officers of state, the Lord Mayor and Aldermen of London. The church was hung with rich tapestries for the occasion and a little ante-room, specially screened off and warmed by a brazier, was set aside as a changing-room for the tiny princess. She was baptised by the Archbishop of London with Thomas Cranmer, Archbishop of Canterbury as her godfather and the Duchess of Norfolk her godmother. Trumpets sounded a fanfare as she was held over the silver font under a canopy of crimson satin, and given the name Elizabeth.

Despite her own disappointment, Anne was enchanted with motherhood and her baby. So much so that she begged Henry to let her breastfeed the child herself. Henry refused, not because he felt it unbecoming for a Queen of England to act as a wet nurse, but because his rest would probably be broken by having a baby in the bedchamber at night.

In fact he coldly decided that the child should have her own household as soon as possible. Early in December Elizabeth was taken to Hatfield. There, like Mary before her, she was placed in the capable hands of Lady Margaret Bryan, who was appointed her governess and who was to prove loyal and affectionate in the difficult years ahead.

It was already obvious to royal observers that all was not well with the King's marriage. Shortly after her coronation, only months after their marriage, Henry had begun to lose interest in Anne Boleyn and was seen paying attention to other ladies of the court. When she complained he told her crossly that she must put up with it— 'as one of her betters had done'. While Catherine had quietly accepted Henry's behaviour, had never ceased to be a loyal and devoted wife, Anne, who had been critical, often arrogant even

before her marriage was growing more demanding every day. The King, who even remarked that she was not like Queen Catherine, who never in her life used ill words to him, was rapidly falling out of love. His thoughts were now turning towards one of the young ladies-in-waiting—Jane Seymour.

Henry's disappointment that Anne had not given him the longed-for prince had been intense. She had thought she was pregnant again in the spring of 1534, the year after Elizabeth was born, and Henry cancelled a visit to France to be with her—instead they went on a royal progress together in England. But her hopes had been false. Anne announced she was pregnant again in the autumn of 1535 and all went well until the New Year. Then, in mid-January, Henry had a serious accident while jousting at Greenwich. He fell from his mount, the armoured horse on top of him, and he lay unconscious for two hours. Anne was not among the spectators, but when the news was taken to her she was so shocked that she took to her bed. The stress was too much for her and on January 29 she had a miscarriage. The foetus, it was said, was a male of 15 weeks. Ironically on that same winter day, 1536, Catherine of Aragon, who died three weeks before, was buried in the cathedral at Peterborough. Some said the miscarriage was brought on by the jealousy and rage Anne felt when she discovered the truth about Henry and Jane Seymour.

Anne had dressed in yellow and rejoiced at the news of Catherine's death, for Catherine had been her greatest rival. Likewise, Catherine's daughter, Princess Mary, suffered Anne's scorn and hatred. Declared illegitimate and sent to live at the royal nursery at Hatfield she was forced to wait upon the baby Elizabeth. Having lost her own household she even had her jewels confiscated by Anne who said that her ears should be boxed for the 'cursed bastard she is'.

Anne, her insecurity increasing daily as she failed to have a son, and apparently losing the love of the King, vented her fear, disappointment and anger on the young princess who was a threat to her supremacy. She had been afraid

Mary might persuade Henry to take Catherine back as his wife. With Catherine buried, that fear was gone, but Henry was seriously thinking of ending the marriage all the same.

In the months that followed Anne saw less and less of her husband as he left her alone at court. Ever since her days in Paris she had been a lover of high fashion and spent a lot of time planning her wardrobe, ordering silks and satins and jewels. She loved affection and flattery and she had her admirers. Henry became more and more watchful for the slightest misdemeanor which he could hold against her. There were spies to gather evidence to discredit her. Court gossip travelled fast.

His chance came at the May Day Tournament at Greenwich when Anne dropped her handkerchief for a young jouster in the lists. It was just a trivial act, a lighthearted indiscretion, but it gave Henry the excuse he had been waiting for. The incident led to a trumped-up charge of adultery.

It's not known just how much time Anne had with her little daughter Elizabeth, who was barely three years old when her mother was sent to the block. She obviously spent a lot of her young life apart from her mother and could not have missed her very much when she disappeared from her world altogether. She was much closer to her governess, Lady Bryan, who cared for her from her birth and was concerned with such details as the cutting of the baby's teeth. When she reported that her back teeth were causing her a lot of problems, she wrote 'My Lady hath great pain in her great teeth and they come slowly forth and causeth me to suffer her Grace to have her will more than I would.' Naturally, she was spoiling the little girl, trying to cheer her up, but she complained that Sir Francis Shelton, steward to Elizabeth's household, was letting her have too much of her own way ... 'He would have my lady Elizabeth to dine and sup every day at the board of estate ... Alas, it is not meet for a child of her age to keep such rule yet ... for there she shall see divers meats and fruits, and wine, which would be hard for me to restrain Her Grace from it.' She felt that her small charge was getting far too precocious and, if she were not restrained, she would have digestive troubles to add to her teething problems.

But Elizabeth did sometimes join her parents at Greenwich for family festivities, and she must have been there on that fateful May Day of the tournament. An onlooker at the time, a German Protestant refugee who had been standing in a courtyard at Greenwich, recalled, years later, how he had looked up at one of the windows and seen the Queen cuddling her daughter while she pleaded with the King for forgiveness. But all to no avail. The day after the tournament Anne was taken by barge to the Tower—the same route she had taken on her triumphal journey to her coronation just three years before. On May 15 at her trial in Westminster Hall she was found guilty of adultery which, in Henry's opinion, amounted to treason. Two days later her marriage was pronounced invalid by a court of ecclesiastical lawyers at Lambeth. On May 19, 1536 Anne Boleyn was executed on Tower Green. She wore a grey gown, her hair up in a net, and she met her death with dignity. That evening the King called on Jane Seymour and next day they were betrothed.

*Princess Elizabeth
as a young girl.*

JANE SEYMOUR
1509 ~ 1537

Lady of Virtue

Jane Seymour was the eldest of eight children of Sir John Seymour of Wolf Hall, Savernake, Wiltshire, a knight who had fought bravely with the King in France; her mother was descended from Edward III. She was a quiet, modest girl 'full of goodness' who had been a lady-in-waiting first at the court of Louis XII, then to Catherine of Aragon and afterwards to Anne Boleyn. She had a very fair English rose complexion, but she was not noted for her good looks. Jane had other charms for Henry. Maybe it was her gentle nature that attracted him when he was bored with the volatile Anne. While Anne was flirtatious and frivolous, Jane was direct, honest, a country girl at heart with a maturity beyond her 25 years.

In the early days of his courtship, when Henry sent Jane a love letter and a bag of sovereigns, she handled the situation by returning the letter unopened. Her reply was that as she valued her honour she would not accept the gift. If Henry wanted to send her a present 'let it be when God should send her some good and honest husband'. Henry was impressed. He promised not to visit her unless she had a chaperone, and arranged for Jane, together with her brother and his wife, to move into apartments at Greenwich—where he could walk, unobserved, through interconnecting rooms and visit Jane in secret, but chaperoned nevertheless.

The day Anne Boleyn was executed, Henry wore white for mourning and Cranmer issued a dispensation for his marriage to Jane to take place without banns. Next morning Jane went secretly to Hampton Court for the betrothal ceremony and afterwards the couple left for Savernake, where they were entertained to a grand betrothal feast by Jane's parents. The wedding ceremony was held privately on May 30 in the Queen's Closet at York Place.

Both Hampton Court and the town house of York Place had been handed over by Cardinal Wolsey, and Henry made them his own. Hampton Court became a sumptuous honeymoon home for his queens, with every facility for relaxation—a new banqueting hall, indoor tennis court, a tilt yard for jousting, complete with viewing towers, and an extensive deer park. When Jane Seymour was proclaimed Queen her personal cypher replaced the arms of Anne Boleyn on the gateways and her initials were entwined with Henry's in the heraldic decorations. At Whitsun Jane was presented to the court in the banqueting hall, then Henry took his new wife on a royal tour of Kent, where they were entertained at St Augustine's Abbey in Canterbury. They also toured the city of London and that winter rode across the frozen Thames on horseback. Queen Jane was popular everywhere she went, acclaimed as 'The most virtuous lady and veriest gentlewoman that liveth'.

At first it was rumoured that Jane would never have children; maybe she was known to be delicate. Nevertheless, on July 1, 1536 Parliament declared Anne Boleyn's daughter, Elizabeth, illegitimate and that the succession would now pass to any offspring of Jane Seymour. There was also a clause in the act to the effect that if Jane did not have children, Henry could appoint a successor. This would have left the way open to his illegitimate son Henry Fitzroy, Duke of Richmond. Ironically, that same month, Henry Fitzroy died.

It was obvious from the start that Jane loved children, and she personally set about restoring harmony in the royal nursery. In contrast to the fun-loving Anne Boleyn who preferred more sophisticated pleasures, Jane was happy to play with the little Princess Elizabeth. She also won the confidence and friendship of Princess Mary who, at 20, was confined to her apartments of Hunsdon Manor in Hertfordshire. She was banished from her father and still mourning the death of her mother, Catherine of Aragon, when Henry married Jane. And it fell to the new bride to use her influence to reconcile father and daughter.

Eager to be accepted within the family circle once more, Princess Mary wrote to Henry asking forgiveness, vowing to submit to him 'in all things next to God'. But still that wasn't enough for Henry. She continued, like her mother, to refuse to take the oath of supremacy and for that the King considered sending her to the block. Eventually, in spite of her obstinacy, his ministers persuaded her to submit humbly to all her father's demands, first in writing and later verbally. Having done so, Mary then sent a secret message to Rome, asking the Pope for absolution.

On Mary's return to court, Jane Seymour generously gave her step-daughter a diamond ring as a token of her friendship; and Henry showed his affection by giving Mary a thousand crowns to spend on 'little pleasures'. She told him she would gladly serve his future children and soon found herself back in favour, second only to the Queen. She sat near her at mealtimes while little Elizabeth, who was also allowed to spend more time at court, ate at a table apart.

Henry's happiness was complete in March 1537, with the news that Jane was pregnant. Plans for her coronation were postponed as the King prepared to take every precaution to protect his wife's health. Fear of the plague was ever present, so Jane spent much of her time at Hampton Court, in the comparative safety of the country air. And there she could also indulge her taste for such delicacies as venison and quail.

The scourge of the plague kept Henry away from his wife's bedside; he was at Esher when the baby, a fine healthy son, was born at Hampton Court on October 12, 1537. Wild with delight when he heard the good news, Henry rushed to the Queen at once.

It had been a difficult birth, some historians believe by Caesarean section. When the child was baptised and given the name Edward three days later, the Queen lay on a pallet, wrapped in velvet and fur, to receive the guests. Following tradition, the royal parents did not attend the

Jane Seymour, painted by Holbein. It was said that she was Henry's only true love.

78

This portrait of Prince Edward gives him a more robust appearance than was in fact the case.

actual ceremony of baptism, but waited in their apartments until trumpets sounded at midnight and the procession left the royal chapel for the celebration feast.

The number of guests was limited—a precaution to lessen the risk of infection from the epidemic. But it was, nevertheless, a moving occasion especially as the two sisters, now united, took part. Princess Mary was Edward's godmother, and she was helped by little Elizabeth, aged four, who held the baby's long train.

But while the infant prince flourished, his mother became weaker. She fell ill with puerperal fever and died suddenly on October 24. Jane Seymour, the gentle queen who so loved children and gave Henry the son he longed for, had died after only 12 days of motherhood.

Henry was devastated; stricken with grief that the wife who had, at last, given him an heir had died in doing so. And, for the first time on the death of a wife, he went into mourning. Jane lay in state at Hampton Court for three weeks, her body dressed in a gold robe, a crown on her head. Then she was taken to Windsor for burial in St George's Chapel. Henry was still too distressed to attend and instead sent Princess Mary as chief mourner, but he directed that on his death, his bones should be placed beside Jane's.

The exact reason for the Queen's death is uncertain. If the birth had been by Caesarian section then death was inevitable; there is also a rumour that she caught a chill; others claimed she suffered from the effects of a bad diet. Maybe her weakening condition was tragically overlooked in the excitement surrounding the prince's birth.

Certainly Edward thrived. There are enchanting portraits of him by the prolific court painter Holbein. There is one in which he is dressed in gold and scarlet, complete with plumed bonnet, showing how much tiny children's fashions matched their elders. There is even a Holbein drawing of Edward's wet nurse, Mistress Jak—a very solemn, and apparently much respected lady.

Henry was quick to establish a household for his little son, with Lady Bryan, that well-loved royal retainer, in charge as Lady Mistress. Sybil Penne, the sister of Sir William Sidney, was appointed chief nurse, and the prince also had his own chamberlain and vice chamberlain, comptroller, steward, almoner, dean and physician, as well as a team of rockers.

Princess Mary became a frequent visitor to the royal nursery, but security was strict, not so much for fear of violence but that the child might fall victim of the plague. No member of the household was allowed to visit London in the summer in case infection was carried back to the palace, and even dukes had to have the King's written permission to approach the royal cradle. The baby's feeding, bathing, and the washing of his clothes were all done under the closest supervision, usually with the chamberlain himself in attendance.

As he grew older, Edward's nursery was moved from Hampton Court to Havering in Essex, then to the Hertfordshire establishments of Hunsdon and Ashridge. He was a sturdy child and Henry was proud to show him off. He took him on a round of the royal palaces and once spent a day playing with him at the royal hunting lodge at Royston in Hertfordshire. The little boy seems to have had a lot of toys and he loved music. When he was still a toddler Lady Bryan reported that he 'danced and played so wantonly that he could not stand still and was as full of pretty toys as ever I saw a child in my life.'

Henry died less than ten years after Jane Seymour, having married three more times. Edward was nine when he succeeded to the throne but died of consumption when he was 16. He was succeeded by Mary, then Elizabeth; neither of whom had children. So, in spite of Henry's drastic efforts to ensure the line of succession, there were no grandchildren. On Elizabeth's death, the crown passed to her nearest relative, James VI of Scotland, who became England's first Stuart king—James I. He was the son of Mary, Queen of Scots, whose story is one of the most tragic of royal motherhood.

The Stuarts

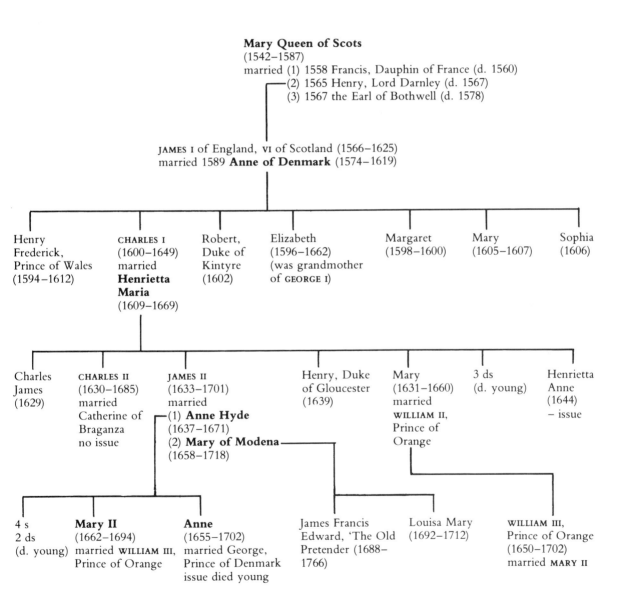

Mary Queen of Scots
(1542–1587)
married (1) 1558 Francis, Dauphin of France (d. 1560)
(2) 1565 Henry, Lord Darnley (d. 1567)
(3) 1567 the Earl of Bothwell (d. 1578)

JAMES I of England, VI of Scotland (1566–1625)
married 1589 **Anne of Denmark** (1574–1619)

Henry
Frederick,
Prince of Wales
(1594–1612)

CHARLES I
(1600–1649)
married
**Henrietta
Maria**
(1609–1669)

Robert,
Duke of
Kintyre
(1602)

Elizabeth
(1596–1662)
(was grandmother
of GEORGE I)

Margaret
(1598–1600)

Mary
(1605–1607)

Sophia
(1606)

Charles
James
(1629)

CHARLES II
(1630–1685)
married
Catherine of
Braganza
no issue

JAMES II
(1633–1701)
married
(1) **Anne Hyde**
(1637–1671)
(2) **Mary of Modena**
(1658–1718)

Henry, Duke
of Gloucester
(1639)

Mary
(1631–1660)
married
WILLIAM II,
Prince of
Orange

3 ds
(d. young)

Henrietta
Anne
(1644)
– issue

4 s
2 ds
(d. young)

Mary II
(1662–1694)
married WILLIAM III,
Prince of Orange

Anne
(1655–1702)
married George,
Prince of Denmark
issue died young

James Francis
Edward, 'The Old
Pretender (1688–
1766)

Louisa Mary
(1692–1712)

WILLIAM III,
Prince of Orange
(1650–1702)
married MARY II

The Stuart line in England did not run smoothly. This was the age of the Gunpowder Plot, the Civil War, the Commonwealth under the rule of Cromwell, and the 'Glorious Revolution'. Political and religious unrest was rife and the monarchy was under close public scrutiny.

When James I, who united the thrones of England and Scotland, married Anne, his Danish queen, it seemed that the succession was secure, but their son, Charles I, died on the scaffold and their grandson failed to produce an heir. His younger brother James was forced into exile.

Two queens, both daughters of James II,

brought stability, if not heirs, to the throne. Mary and her husband, the Protestant William of Orange, reigned jointly but were childless. Mary's sister, Anne, failed to produce a healthy heir, in spite of seventeen pregnancies. The only child to survive infancy, William, Duke of Gloucester, died when he was 11 and Anne knew that with her death the Stuart line would end.

It was still a dreadfully dangerous time for both mothers and babies. Medicine continued to lean heavily on witchcraft and superstition, anaesthesia was as yet unknown and surgery lethal. The poor, unable to afford physicians' fees, often fared better on the homespun

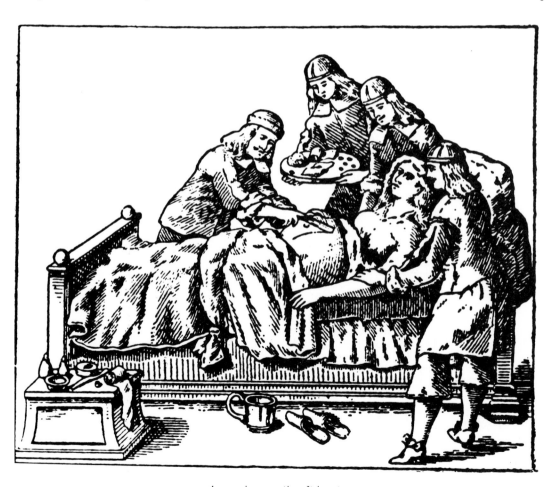

A caesarian operation. It is not
surprising that so many women died.

remedies than the rich, who paid dearly for fashionable treatments that often proved fatal. Miscarriages were common and babies often died shortly after birth. Those who survived were lucky to grow into childhood, for plague epidemics frequently decimated the population. In the summer of 1665, 7,000 Londoners died every week. Many more lives were lost through cholera, typhoid, tuberculosis and smallpox.

The royal way of birth was still a public event, with a ceremonial lying-in and a wet nurse to suckle the baby. Tradition demanded that the little princes and princesses were brought up in their own households, away from their mother whose job, after all, was finished when she was beyond childbearing age.

For the children who did survive, life was becoming less severe. There was a little less work and more play. Toys and games were more plentiful. Those of royal and aristocratic birth were tutored at home. Lower down the scale, wealthy merchants, yeomen and professional men were beginning to discover the merits of boarding schools, but only for their sons. There was a positive decline in education for girls. While in Elizabethan times girls developed an interest in learning to match their brothers, now their studies inclined again towards the feminine

pursuits—embroidery, music, painting and reading devotional books. Amateur theatricals were also popular. Anne of Denmark encouraged her children to take part in elaborate masques for which she commissioned specially-designed scenery and elaborate costumes.

Clothes were freer, lighter and more comfortable, although children were usually dressed formally to have their portraits painted. Babies were swaddled only for the first three months of life, and both boys and girls wore look-alike frocks. At the age of about seven, boys were 'breeched'—put into their first breeches, a big moment that meant goodbye to babyhood.

There were plenty of outdoor games and pursuits. James I listed running, leaping, wrestling, fencing, dancing, playing at catch, tennis, archery, palle-malle (a kind of golf or croquet played with mallets), and 'other such pleasant field pursuits' as being suitable for the training of an heir to the throne. As for indoors, whilst cards and dice were acceptable, chess most certainly was not.

Horn books, an early teaching device for children, were popular and delicious sugary delights became available—marzipan, comfits, candied rose petals and fruit preserves. Wooden dolls were popular with the girls. They were richly dressed and had painted faces and wigs.

MARY, QUEEN OF SCOTS
1542 ~ 1587

Mother of the Stuart line in England was that tragic figure, Mary, Queen of Scots, whose story has captured the imagination of writers ever since. She inherited the crown of Scotland on the death of her father, James V, when she was only six days old, was taken from her birthplace, Linlithgow Palace, to the safety of Stirling Castle, and placed in the care of four Lords—among them Lord Erskine—who were appointed her governors. Two months later she was crowned in the royal chapel.

Queen of Tragedy

Her mother was the French-born Marie de Guise, a granddaughter of Henry VII. As Regent during her little daughter's minority, she was a loving mother, dedicated to securing power for her daughter. But her insistence on supporting the 'auld alliance' with France rather than a peaceful settlement with England only prepared the way for her daughter's troubled reign. When Henry VIII was King of England, he hoped to control and, ultimately unite the two countries by the betrothal of his young son Edward to the infant Queen. Marie de Guise had other ideas. She mistrusted Henry's intentions and instead favoured France—so Mary, Queen of Scotland was betrothed to the Dauphin François, the baby son of Henri II of France and Catherine de Medici. Henry VIII, angered by Marie's rejection, then attempted to subdue the country with a series of violent campaigns, the 'Wars of Rough Wooing'. Even the fortress of Stirling was considered no longer safe enough to hold the young Queen. In the summer of 1548, Marie de Guise wept as she kissed her six-year-old daughter goodbye and watched her sail for France, to grow up at the court of her future husband. It is difficult to imagine the mixture of emotion Marie felt as she stood on the quayside. According to Mary's recollections of her mother, theirs was a close, affectionate relationship, yet, like so many other royal parents before her, Marie felt she had to sacrifice her child for political ends.

Tall for her years, with fair skin and golden hair, the little Queen was adored by her future in-laws. Although she missed her mother's love, she enjoyed a cloudless childhood in the sophisticated atmosphere of the French court. Clever and quick to learn, she loved music and poetry, dancing and hunting. She was a very accomplished young lady when, at sixteen, she and the Dauphin, a year her junior, were married in a splendid ceremony in the cathedral of Notre Dame. Only a year later King Henri was killed in a horrific accident while jousting, and Dauphin François became King. So, in 1559, Mary found herself Queen of both France and Scotland.

But her happiness was tragically shortlived. Just 18 months later, François, who had always suffered delicate health, died after an agonising illness only a month before his 17th birthday. Mary, who had helped nurse him, was grief-stricken. The loss seemed almost impossible to bear, particularly as she was then also recovering from the pain of her mother's death a few months before. Marie had died of dropsy in Edinburgh Castle and Mary, who was heartbroken when the news reached her, had arranged for her body to be brought back to France for burial at Rheims.

The time had come for Mary, Queen of Scotland to claim her throne, but the Scotland she returned to, in 1561, was very different to the country she had left as a child. The country then had been Catholic; now she found the old faith she knew and loved had been outlawed. In her absence religious reformers such as John Knox had led the Reformation in Scotland. Her country was now firmly Protestant. And south of the Border, in England, her Protestant cousin Elizabeth Tudor was Queen.

Mary, raised and educated in the rarified atmosphere of the French court, found life alien, harsh and unwelcoming; the language incomprehensible. But the young widowed Queen knew she had certain duties: to remarry as soon as possible and produce an heir.

In the intervening years Mary had grown tall and willowy, and to the people of Edinburgh she was an eye-catching figure; slim and stately, with fine, delicate features, almond eyes, a pale complexion set off by a mass of auburn hair. Her beautiful hands were also much admired, for they were fashionably pale with long tapering fingers. And apart from her striking good looks, she was intelligent and witty—a lover of life.

For her second husband she chose her cousin Henry Stuart, Lord Darnley, with whom she became infatuated and married against the wishes of her advisers. He, too, was tall, beautiful and gifted; but he was also ambitious, weak and vain—and, at 19, four years younger than the Queen. They married between five and six in the morning on Sunday July 29, 1565 in the royal chapel at Holyrood. Mary made a sombre bride, for she insisted on wearing the mourning black of widowhood, though she changed for the celebrations which followed.

It was a stormy marriage, and the love Mary felt for Darnley soon turned to hate after the horrific murder of her Italian secretary and friend, David Rizzio, the following spring. Mary was six months pregnant when the killing took place, at Darnley's instigation, in her private apartments at Holyrood. Mary even suspected that she could have been an intended victim.

*Lord Darnley and his brother,
painted by Ewort.*

After this terrifying experience it would not have been surprising if she had miscarried. But Mary was resilient and she and her unborn child survived.

It was, nevertheless, a dangerous time to be born, especially for a young prince with so much political and religious unrest. Mary herself posed a dangerous threat to Elizabeth of England. As the Catholic granddaughter of Margaret Tudor, eldest daughter of Henry VII, England's Catholics recognised Mary as their rightful heir.

Such were the conditions when James, son of Mary, Queen of Scots, was brought into the world on the morning of June 19, 1566. Mary had wanted her baby to be born at Holyrood Palace, which was her favourite home, but for safety's sake she was advised to have her child in the bleak but secure stronghold of Edinburgh Castle. In spite of the inhospitable surroundings, Mary was determined to prepare for the birth in the traditional way and arranged for her lying-in chamber to be sumptuously furnished. She chose blue taffeta and velvet for the huge bed and Holland cloth to drape the baby's cradle. Even her midwife, Margaret Asteane, was given a special black velvet dress for the occasion.

The labour turned out to be long and painful— so painful that the Queen declared she wished she had never married. The sister of one of her ladies-in-waiting even tried, by means of witchcraft, to transfer the agony to Margaret, Lady Reres, who was also in labour. It did nothing to relieve Mary's suffering, but, no doubt in gratitude, Lady Reres was afterwards honoured with the position of wet nurse to the Prince.

A fine caul was stretched across the baby's face when he was born, a good omen according to old wive's tales. And, indeed, for a time all the signs augured well. The people of Edinburgh welcomed the news of the Prince's birth with wild enthusiasm. Guns fired in salute from the castle ramparts; there was a thanksgiving service, though Protestant, in St Giles Cathedral, and bonfires were lit on surrounding hilltops. But the childless Queen Elizabeth of England commented sourly: 'Alack, the Queen of Scots is lighter by a bonny son, and I am but of barren stock.'

Although Mary had the customary wet nurse for her baby, she played with James in the nursery and he shared her own room at night. Could she have had some strange presentiment of the separation to come? For the child gurgling in his cradle was destined to spend a sad, loveless childhood, deprived of parental affection. Mary's period of motherhood was to be tragically brief.

Later that summer the royal nursery was transferred to Stirling. Surrounded by 500 armed guards, the baby was handed, like his mother before him, into the care of the Erskine family. There Mary planned the decoration and furn-

The Queen's bedchamber at Holyrood, from which
Rizzio was dragged to his death.

ishing of his nursery suite and once again she chose blue. She ordered blue fabric to cover and drape the cradle, a new mattress and blankets and bolster, tapestries for the walls and buckets of gold and silver. The wet nurse, Lady Reres (followed by one Helen Little who, it was said, had a liking for drink), was given a new canopy and cover for her bed. At Stirling the Prince had his own household which included a team of nurses to rock his cradle and courtiers to keep him amused. Even this sheltered, caring up-bringing did not prevent him catching smallpox, which left him scarred for life. He also suffered so badly from rickets that he always had weak legs

and his right foot turned outwards, giving him a permanent limp.

For the early part of his life, James was a strong, sturdy infant and a great joy to Mary, who loved small children. Once he was installed at Stirling, she enthusiastically began to plan his christening, which took place with great cere-mony in the Chapel Royal in December. She chose the King of France, the Queen of England (as a safeguard for her son, perhaps) and the Duke of Savoy as godparents; all, of course, rep-resented by proxy. They all gave the most lavish presents, the most impressive of which must have been the magnificent gold font which weighed two stone, the gift of Queen Elizabeth. Mary herself paid for all the rich clothes worn by the leading nobles, the expensive fabrics and cloth of gold and silver. Her half brother, Moray, was resplendent in green, her cousin, the Earl of Argyll, wore red and Bothwell, Mary's lover, was in blue. They made a dazzling spectacle as they walked in procession with the clergy by the light of flares and torches. Later came the feasting, the masques and the fireworks appropriate to such an occasion. But Mary's days of happiness were numbered. Soon Darnley, not yet 21 years old, was dead—murdered at Kirk O'Field, and Mary, headstrong, volatile, ill-equipped to help herself, began making one mistake after another. Her enemies were blaming her and Bothwell for Darnley's death.

In April Mary saw her son—at ten months playing happily in his nursery at Stirling—for the last time. A month later the Earl of Bothwell was divorced and he and Mary married in the Great Hall at Holyrood, just three months after Darnley's death. It was the beginning of the end. First her Lords and the Reformers, then the whole population seemed to be turning against her. She was mobbed by angry crowds who called her an adultress and demanded that she divorce Bothwell. Her life was suddenly in terrible danger. After her royalist supporters were defeated at Carberry Hill and she resisted demands that she divorce, she was taken under guard to the Douglas stronghold, the lonely island fortress of Lochleven Castle.

There, in a state of shock following her rapid change in fortune, the young Queen pined for her child. It is said that she had other pregnancies; that there might have been twins by Darnley, had she not miscarried, and a daughter too, by Bothwell. But James was her only surviving child. Incarcerated in her island prison she worried over his fate. Would he be safer in England? Or better still, in the care of her relatives in France? But it was not her decision and she was helpless to intervene. On July 24, 1567 she was forced to abdicate and five days later

13-month-old James was crowned King of Scotland. It was a Protestant ceremony this time, performed by the Bishop of Orkney in the Church of the Holy Rood, close to the walls of Stirling Castle, and John Knox preached the sermon. Afterwards came more firecrackers and gunfire and public festivities, but for Mary there were no celebrations.

Less than a year later, on Sunday, May 16, 1568, she left Scotland for ever. After a hair-raising escape from Lochleven, she sailed in a fishing boat from Dundrennan on the Solway Firth. At one point she considered making for France, but the tides were against her and with a small band of supporters she landed in England—at Workington on the Cumberland coast.

Her freedom was shortlived. Considered a threat to the English crown, Mary, Queen of Scots was held prisoner for the remaining 19 years of her life, mainly in Sheffield but also at Chatsworth, Carlisle, Tutbury and Chartley—all of them steps towards the last terrible scene: her execution at Fotheringhay.

All her life she had hoped for a reunion with the son who did not know her. Separated from him for so many years, she kept an unrealistic image of him in her memory as she longed for the baby she had cradled in her arms at Stirling. She frequently pleaded with Queen Elizabeth to let her correspond with her son, and to think of her as a 'desolate mother, whose solitary child had been torn from her arms'. To no avail.

Mary wrote many affectionate letters to James and sent him gifts, too, including some walking reins she embroidered in gold and silver thread. The red silk straps were stitched with the words: 'God hath given his angels charge over thee: to keep thee in all thy ways.' She also made a book of verses for him, embroidering the cover. When he was three and a half, Mary sent him a pony and saddle and a touching note saying: 'Dear Son, I send three bearers to see you and bring me word how ye do, and to remember you that ye have in me a loving mother that wishes you to learn in time to love, know and fear God.' Sadly,

A rare portrait of Mary with her son James.

James was rarely permitted to receive his mother's gifts or messages and, in reality, he grew up with little affection for her. Her very absence would have had an untold influence on his early life and, anyway, his opinions were formed and reinforced by his tutors, who were his mother's enemies and who poisoned his young mind with tales about her wicked ways. He never knew the truth; how desperately she missed him and agonised over his situation.

The days of innocence, playing with the bats and balls, drums and hobby horses which were the simple pleasures of a sixteenth-century childhood, ended early for James. Life in the Erskine household followed a strict regime. The Earl of Mar and his wife Annabelle, Countess of Mar, were highly respected and considered most suited to the job of moulding a future king but,

alas for James, the Countess was a firm disciplinarian and his life lacked the love and reassurance of a mother figure. There was little time for love and laughter. Over the Border in England lived his paternal grandmother, the old Countess of Lennox, who sent him books and loving messages but they never met. His only other close relative, his grandfather Lennox, who was Regent, died a violent death when James was five. In fact, the little boy watched horrified as his grandfather's wounded body was rushed past him on a stretcher into Stirling Castle after an attempted coup by his mother's supporters. It was his first confrontation with violence and it gave him a distaste for war which was to last all his life.

Burdened with so many cares, it is not surprising that he grew old before his time. Early portraits show him to be a frail, grave-faced child

The Earl and Countess of Mar.

dressed, according to the fashion of the day, like an adult, in sombre colours relieved only by white ruffs at his neck and wrists. Life was sombre indeed at Stirling. As he grew older the blue decor of his nursery was replaced by dark damask drapes and when he was just five, James left his childhood behind and made his first public appearance as King.

Mary would have been proud of her son, had she ever really known him, for he resembled her in many ways. He was a forward child with a keen intellect and was quick to learn. His normal day at Stirling began with prayers followed by breakfast, a meal of meat washed down with ale or wine. Dinner was taken at midday and supper was served early in the evening. Between came lessons in the castle schoolroom which he shared with other boys, the sons of nobles, of his age. For recreation there was music, falconry, archery and golf. In spite of his handicap, caused by rickets, James grew up to a keen sportsman.

From his early lessons at the knee of the Countess of Mar who, it is said, hated Mary, James graduated to the tutelage of George Buchanan who taught Latin, Greek and French. As an avowed enemy of Mary, he also launched a smear campaign against her. He wrote a book of scurrulous gossip about her private life, de-

*James spent his boyhood
at Stirling Castle.*

signed to make the King despise his mother. Another tutor, Peter Young, who was much more suited to the job, later took over James's education, but some of Buchanan's views stuck in the mind of the young King.

Surrounded by such an overbearing influence and deprived of parental love, it is hardly surprising that James sought affection elsewhere. The bright spark of his life was his cousin Esmé Stuart whom he first met when he was 13.

Esmé, from the French court of Henri III, was 36 and like an exotic bird, a miracle to the boy who had spent his life with plain-speaking Scots warlords. It is likely that the young King, who was not exactly worldly, did not know of the homosexuality that surrounded the French court. Rumours spread that the two were deeply involved, fuelled when James showered Esmé with such titles and appointments as Privy Councillor, First Gentleman of the Bedchamber and Lord Chamberlain, with the appropriate incomes and gifts of diamonds and gold. The affair ended abruptly in 1582 when James was kidnapped and Esmé was sent back to France, where he died shortly afterwards.

James, who had spent the first 12 years of his life at Stirling, and then at 13 had made his first triumphal visit to Edinburgh, riding through the city in silver and white satin, had grown up fast. It was his tutor and confidant, Peter Young, who stepped in to negotiate the King's marriage. But the wedding to Princess Anne of Denmark did not take place until 1590, and by then Mary, Queen of Scots was dead.

Exactly how James reacted to news of his mother's execution is unknown. Nor do we know his true thoughts or feelings towards her. He was then 21, and she had been a stranger all his life. Some said he remarked happily: 'Now I am sole King.' Other observers at court noticed that he was sad and went to bed without eating.

Eventually, when the truth about his mother was revealed to James, it was too late. Then he condemned and totally rejected the teachings of Buchanan that had robbed him of any natural feeling for his mother in his early years. It had been Mary's dying wish that he should unite the kingdoms of England and Scotland. And in 1612, as King of England and Scotland he had her body brought at last from Peterborough to be laid in a marble tomb in Westminster Abbey.

ANNE OF DENMARK
1574 ~ 1619

The Fun-Loving Queen

Anne of Denmark, tall, blonde and stately and one of the seven children of King Frederick of Denmark and Norway seemed a good choice as a marriage partner for James, bringing fresh blood into the Stuart line.

In contrast to James' solitary childhood, she enjoyed a warm, loving family life, so cosseted, in fact, that there is an extraordinary story that court etiquette did not allow her to walk until she was nine years old, and throughout her childhood she was carried around by courtiers. True or false, she grew up to be strong and energetic and her greatest love was dancing.

She married James first by proxy in the summer of 1589 and that autumn he sailed to Norway to meet her. It was a dangerous journey, made just as the winter storms were setting in, and the weather forced him to stay abroad until spring. He eventually joined his 15-year-old bride in Oslo where, after a formal marriage ceremony, there was a celebratory banquet, followed by a third ceremony at Kronenborg in Denmark. Indeed, the couple were well and truly married when the citizens of Edinburgh welcomed them home with processions and bands, in May 1590, and later celebrated as Anne was crowned Queen.

There was even greater public rejoicing when Anne gave birth to her first child, a son, on February 19, 1594. Following tradition, he was born at Stirling, and named Henry Frederick after the royal parents' fathers. The rejoicing came not only because an heir to the throne had been born, but because conditions in hygiene and sanitation and medical care generally were still so primitive that *any* child was lucky to survive. The Queen was to have seven children, but only two of them lived to become adults.

Although by Anne's time the old lying-in customs were dying out, wet nurses were still employed and a rather unpleasant-sounding habit—feeding an infant pap—was accepted practice. A mixture of gruel and milk was first chewed by the nurse, then put into the baby's mouth. Compared with today's methods of food preparation, the old ways sound lethal.

Swaddling was still carried out because it was firmly believed that a baby would develop

The fashion-conscious Anne of Denmark.

deformed bones or a bent spinal column if not rigidly bound almost from the moment of birth. French historian A. Leroy described swaddling as follows: 'On his head is placed a child's cap, a wool skull cap and a cone-shaped headdress. A band passes under his chin to hold back the ends of the three hats and forces the ears to be flattened against the head. Pieces of linen applied on the ears add the finishing touch to the obstruction of their natural development and take away any means of communication with the outside world.

'Other pieces of linen are placed in the armpits and at the groin to absorb the excessive perspiration caused by the clothes which are too warm. Then comes the shirt, camisole, and cloth which wraps up the shoulders and is crossed over the chest. The child with his arms laid against his body and his legs which are kept straight, is then wrapped up in a swaddling cloth, then in a second one which is softer and it is all kept together by wrapping up the baby tightly with linen bands. A last band is wrapped to keep the head still.' This following account is of the young Louis XIII of France: '*November 11, 1601:* baby is 15 days old. His head is wiped off for the first time. *November 17, 1601:* his forehead and face were wiped off with fresh butter and almond oil to clean off the building up dirt. *July 4, 1602:* he was combed for the first time, enjoyed it, and turned his head according to the areas which itched. *October 3, 1606* (seven years old): he was given a bath for the first time, and with his sister.' Is it strange that so many children died of infection in their early days?

But Queen Anne, as the 19-year-old mother who so clearly loved children, had a terrible disappointment immediately; the realisation that her baby, like his father before him, had to be handed over to the care of the Earl of Mar and brought up at Stirling Castle. Following the law of Scotland, the heir to the throne had always been raised there for safe-keeping and King James was adamant that the custom should continue with his own son. In spite of her constant pleading, Anne was allowed to see her baby only on occasional visits. He was a beautiful child and as he grew older their partings were more and more distressing. When he was 15 months old he was taken to see his mother at Linlithgow Palace, and she tearfully declared that she didn't think she could live without him. Indeed, for the young Queen, who was reputed to have a somewhat frivolous outlook on life, to be separated not only from her far-away family but from her baby son as well, was heartbreaking.

The King remained unmoved. From his attitude one can assume that either his own childhood at Stirling must have been a good deal happier than has been supposed, or that he felt the severity of the regime was beneficial to a future king. Nevertheless, Anne continued to fight for the right to have her son with her. She tried to persuade James to refer the matter to his council, after she had canvassed supporters on her side. She even made a desperate bid to have him kidnapped and returned to her. But although the King allowed her to make frequent visits to Stirling, spending all her time with the child while she was there, he would not give in.

It was her second child, Elizabeth, born at Falkland Castle, Fife, on August 19, 1596, who brought Anne some measure of consolation. She was named Elizabeth after the Queen of England, who was her godmother, with the English ambassador standing proxy at the baptism ceremony in August 1596. A second daughter, Margaret, was born at Dalkeith in December 1598, and it was recorded that the fond father ordered a new cradle with four matching stools for the four rockers and a chair and a footrest for the baby's nurse. There were also warm flannel nightcaps, decorated with embroidery—no doubt to keep the royal head warm on cold December nights—as well as silk stockings for the Queen. And for the two-year-old Princess Elizabeth, to quell any feelings of jealousy on the arrival of a baby sister, there were two baby dolls to play with, a new hairbrush and a tiny satin mask.

However, Margaret died in infancy, but on November 19, 1600, another son was born at Dunfermline Palace. James remarked on the fre-quency that the date, 19, brought good fortune into his life. 'I first saw my wife on November 19 on the coast of Norway; she bore my son Henry on February 19, my daughter Elizabeth on August 19. And now she has given birth at Dunfermline to my second son on the anniversary day on which we first saw each other. I, myself, was born on the 19 of June.'

The happy father rushed to Anne's side but found his wife and son weak and ill. It seemed unlikely that the baby would survive, so baptism was hurriedly arranged and he was given the name Charles. The fact that he began to thrive surprised everyone, but as he grew older it became evident that he had a speech impediment and, like his father, he suffered badly from rickets. The poor diet fed to him in babyhood left him so crippled that he was almost four before he could walk. Another son, Robert, was born a year after Charles, but he died in infancy.

Following the custom of the time, the young princes and princess had their separate households—Henry with the Earl of Mar, Elizabeth with the Earl of Linlithgow and Charles with the Earl of Fife at Dunfermline. But Anne and James were loving parents who kept in close touch with their children as they travelled frequently between their royal residences. Anne also took a personal interest in the restoration and decoration of the palaces and entertained lavishly. But she still nursed a passionate longing to have her first-born son, Henry, with her, and she never gave up the struggle.

Her chance came in April 1603, after Queen Elizabeth's death and James' succession to the English throne. Once again Anne was pregnant, but when she received a touching letter from nine-year-old Henry, congratulating her and the King on their peaceful possession of the English throne, she became even more determined to have him with her. James had already left for England, accompanied by the Earl of Mar; Anne had to wait in Scotland until after the old Queen's funeral, when the ladies of the court would be available to welcome her. It was then she saw her opportunity, and with a party of

Anne in hunting dress with Oatlands
in the background.

nobles who supported her cause, she travelled to Stirling to plead with the Countess of Mar for her son's release.

Without the authority of the King, the Countess was powerless to grant Anne's request. In the stormy scene which followed, the Queen became hysterical. She was carried to the royal apartments where, shortly afterwards, she gave birth to a stillborn son. Anne, although her own life was now in danger, had at last won her case. The King, naturally shocked when the news reached him, at once relented and ordered that Prince Henry should finally be handed back to his mother. And so Henry and his sister, Elizabeth, travelled south with their mother when she left for England on June 2, 1603. It was a journey of great pomp and splendour, a triumphant royal progress—which ended with the coronation of the new King and Queen in Westminster Abbey in July.

Once the celebrations were over, Queen Anne was again troubled by thoughts that her family was not complete. Charles had been left behind in Scotland and, moreover, he was ailing. She persuaded the King to allow him to join her, and in the summer of 1604 appointed Lady Carey to help care for him. The methods of treatment designed by James in an attempt to cure the young prince's speech problems and help him to walk more easily seem astonishing, in the light of modern medicine. He suggested that Charles' tongue be cut to help him to speak, and that he be made to wear iron boots to strengthen his legs. Happily for Prince Charles, Lady Carey had much more enlightened views. She vigorously refused to allow such drastic treatments and the Prince eventually flourished.

The Queen had two more children, both daughters—Mary, born at Greenwich in April 1605, and Sophia in June the following year. But Sophia lived only long enough to be christened, and her birth left Anne weak and ill. Her tiny coffin was carried up the Thames from Greenwich to Westminster on a funeral barge draped in black velvet, and she was buried in a private ceremony in the Abbey. A year later Princess

The tomb of Princess Sophia in Westminster Abbey.

Mary, who was in the care of Lord and Lady Knevet, was taken ill with catarrhal fever and also died. The sorrowing Queen went into seclusion at Hampton Court, while King James ordered memorials to be erected for his daughters in Westminster Abbey. Mary, wearing a laced bodice and bonnet, appears to be rising from her bed while her baby sister is shown asleep in her cradle. They are touching reminders of the fate of so many children of their time.

For much of her life in England, pleasure-loving Anne lived apart from her more high-minded husband, although they always remained on good terms and were seen together at many royal banquets, balls and masques. Whitehall was still the royal family's official London residence. Until it was burnt down in 1698 it was the centre of the court. With over 2,000 rooms, great reception halls and chambers. Anne made Somerset House her official London residence, while Inigo Jones began to build a riverside retreat for her at Greenwich (she died before it was finished). When she wanted to take the country air she went to Oatlands, the favourite royal home in Surrey.

Anne spent lavishly on fine furnishings and decorations for the houses; she also entertained extravagantly, loved banquets and balls, and often danced in the gorgeous dresses which once belonged to Queen Elizabeth I. Not surprisingly, both she and her husband were soon in debt. But Anne was never happier than when she was with her children. She showered them with affection and when she began taking part in amateur dramatics she encouraged the children to join in. Writers of the day, among them Ben Jonson, were suppliers of royal scripts. There is a record of a masque, a variety show of music, dancing and poetry, staged in 1610, in which Charles, then aged ten, played Zephry, in a green satin costume embroidered with golden flowers. He also wore silver wings and a halo, and danced by a waterfall with twelve little girls in blue satin dresses. Elizabeth was there, too, as a river nymph. But while it was considered acceptable for children to take part in such frolics, there were raised eyebrows when the Queen blacked her face and arms and, with a party of noble ladies, played the roles of Moors in a Christmas entertainment.

One of the proudest times in Anne's life came when her favourite son Henry was created Prince of Wales. It was a great delight to her to be able to stage-manage the festivities herself, not just because the occasion allowed her to use her creative talents, but because there was a special bond between mother and son. In the event of any dispute or misunderstanding between her and her husband, it was often Henry who played the diplomat, the peacemaker.

The year 1612 was a turning point in Anne's life; the year when the family togetherness, her whole happiness, came to a tragic end. That was the year King James arranged for the remains of his mother, Mary, Queen of Scots, to be brought to London and placed in a new tomb in Westminster Abbey. And in doing so he ignored an old superstition 'that the grave was never disturbed of a deceased member of a family without death claiming one or more of that family as prey.'

At once, it seemed, Anne's beloved Henry fell ill and, as his cough and fever grew worse, she became increasingly alarmed. A rainbow was seen in the sky, suspended for seven hours over the very room where Henry lay in St James's Palace, and it was read as a very bad omen indeed. The fever was diagnosed as highly contagious and the Queen, although devoted to her son, was afraid to visit him. His sister, Elizabeth, however, disguised herself in an effort to get into his room, even as he lay dying, and he asked to see her; but her way was barred.

When Henry died at midnight on November 5, 1612, Anne took the news with a mixture of rage and grief. Only days before she had sent him medicine which had proved beneficial. Now she was sure someone had poisoned him and she demanded a post mortem. It showed, however, that he had died of natural causes, from a fever that had claimed thousands of lives that year.

Anne was not the only one who grieved for Henry. He had been a popular young man, tall, fair and good-looking, both intelligent and athletic; an ideal future king. Now the nation mourned their prince. But Anne was soon to lose Elizabeth, too, not through death, but through marriage. She was engaged to Frederick V, the Elector Palatine, and the wedding took place shortly after Henry's funeral.

Not long after, the once light-hearted Anne sank into a depression. She began to travel widely, to visit friends and take the waters at Bath in an effort to restore her spirits. But an attack of dropsy followed by gout lowered her, and then a cough set in. The King, himself ill at Newmarket, was too weak to be with her at the end. She died at Hampton Court in March 1619, with her only surviving son Charles at her bedside.

Anne, the tall, fair, princess from Denmark had not made her mark on the political scene, nor had she made a lasting impression on the life of the country; maybe she had been frivolous, spendthrift, too. Such were the comments made against her in her day. But her warmth and affection, her loving concern for her children, and the fun she brought into their lives gave a fresh aspect to royal motherhood at the start of the seventeenth century.

HENRIETTA MARIA
1609 ~ 1669

La Reine Malheureuse

Henrietta Maria, the petite, dark-haired daughter of Henry IV, King of France, and Marie de Medici, was the next Queen of England. She married Charles I shortly after he became King on the death of his father, James I in 1625. She was only 15, he 25, when they married by proxy at Notre Dame in Paris. Then Charles travelled to Dover to meet her. She disembarked on a wet Sunday evening in June and was carried in a chair from the ship, up the steep cliffs to the castle where she spent the night. Next morning at 10 o'clock she met Charles for the first time, then came a second marriage ceremony at Canterbury.

It was not love at first sight. The young Queen was miserably homesick and there were disputes over the vast number of courtiers, priests and servants she had brought with her from France under the terms of her marriage treaty. After a stormy scene when the King ordered them out of the country, his relationship with the Queen began to improve, and by 1628 she was expecting their first child.

Childbirth was becoming a little safer, and midwifery techniques improving. In 1610 surgeons were licensed to assist at a birth if the need arose, something totally unheard of before. (In Germany, in 1522, a doctor was actually burned at the stake for simply attempting to study the process of birth. He had disguised himself as a woman to be present at the confinement.) So Henrietta Maria had one of the leading surgeons of the day standing by to attend her. He was Peter Chamberlen, a Huguenot, and it was he who invented obstetric forceps (although the secret was kept in his family and not made public until 125 years later). The Queen also arranged for a French midwife, Madame Peronne, to attend her—but her well-laid plans went very wrong. Her first son was born prematurely at Greenwich, his arrival, it was said, hastened by the Queen's terror as one of two dogs fighting in a palace gallery snatched at her dress. Madame Peronne had not arrived from France, so a local midwife from Greenwich was called to the royal presence instead. The poor woman was so overcome by the importance of the occasion that she fainted and Peter Chamberlen had to take charge. But the tiny child could not survive. He was quickly baptised, given the name Charles, and died shortly afterwards.

The following year, when Henrietta was again pregnant, she decided against being at Greenwich for the birth and chose instead St James's Palace. Apartments were set aside for her on the sunny south front of the building, overlooking the gardens, and she ordered green satin covers for her bed. These were to be worked by her embroiderer, Charles Gentile, at a cost of £670. This time she took no chances with her midwife and she sent her dwarf, Jeffrey Hudson, to France to fetch Madame Peronne. But Madame Peronne and her escorts were captured by pirates. The new baby, another boy, was born safely at the end of May 1630. He was big and bouncing and dark haired—the Queen thought him quite ugly—and 'so dark that I am ashamed

Henrietta Maria painted by Van Dyck.
She had her first baby when she was nineteen.

of him'. But at least he was healthy. Church bells chimed the news across the City and the nation rejoiced. The country had a new Prince of Wales and future King. Holy water from the river Jordan was used for the baptism at St James's Palace and the ceremony was carried out by Laud, the future Archbishop of Canterbury. The month-old prince, wearing a tiny white robe with an ermine train, and lying in a ceremonial jewel-studded crib, was also called Charles. Months later his mother was still worrying about her little son's looks, his black hair and dark complexion—and he seemed to be putting on too much weight. Writing to her sister, she said: 'He is so ugly, I am ashamed of him, but his size and fitness supply the want of beauty. He has no ordinary mien; he is so serious in all that he does that I cannot help fancying him wiser than myself.'

The following year Henrietta had a daughter, the much-loved Mary, Princess Royal. She, too, was born at St James's Palace and baptised by Archbishop Laud the same day. For the birth, it is recorded that the Queen ordered a bed of tawny velvet, even though she had not yet paid for the green satin one from Gentile. Mary was joined two years later by James, Duke of York, destined to succeed his brother as James II, then came Elizabeth, followed by Anne, and Catherine. Catherine, born in Whitehall, the Queen's seventh child, lived less than an hour. There was heartbreak, too, when Anne died of tuberculosis before she was three, but by then Henrietta was pregnant again and Henry, Duke of Gloucester, was born at Oatlands in 1639. Henrietta had had eight children in ten years, and then her last baby, the adored Henrietta Anne, affectionately called 'Minette', was born at Exeter shortly before the Queen fled to France.

The early years of family life were idyllic for Henrietta Maria. Young and attractive, adored by her husband, she and her children made a pretty picture at court. Lively, energetic and light-hearted, she loved riding and dancing and she spent lavishly on beautiful clothes. Although court life was more formal than it had been in the

reign of James I, there were still glittering parties and spectacular masques. Old traditions continued. The King and Queen could often be observed by the public dining in state at Whitehall—there was a gallery on which they could stroll. No wonder the Queen liked to escape to more private places, such as her house at Greenwich, which Inigo Jones had started for Anne of Denmark, or to St James's with its extensive gardens, Hampton Court, or Oatlands.

Royal nurseries were still staffed by numerous servants; the wet nurses and dry nurses, rockers, maids, footmen and governesses. It was a world which Queen Henrietta, with all her many interests, not to mention her mounting anxieties, did not have much time to share. Nevertheless, she delighted in the growing family, taught them manners, instructed them in her religious faith, gave them advice and encouragement. The children's early years were peaceful and happy. Gone were the strictures of earlier times; children were behaving more like modern children. The formal silk and satin clothes so beloved of the royal portrait painters were replaced by comfortable cotton smocks at playtime. Like generations of little boys before and after him, the Prince of Wales was bored with toys and preferred, instead, to go to bed clutching a block of wood, ignoring the model ships and animals, toys and games of his playroom. He was only eight when he was made a Knight of the Garter and, that same year, given his own court at Richmond. There, in the care of William Cavendish, Earl of Newcastle, he learned about kingship. He was a determined child. Once, when he resolutely refused to take some medicine, the Queen was asked to persuade him but even she couldn't make him change his mind. Instead, the Prince wrote to the Earl, who was away at the time, saying: 'My Lord, I would not have you take too much physic, for it doth always make me worse, and I think it will do the like with you.' The Prince and the Earl were the best of friends. Life at Richmond was relaxed and, away from the schoolroom, there was fun out of doors with the

*The model ship that was made for
the young Prince Charles in 1634.*

church forms of worship while ignoring the demands of the Puritans and the Presbyterians. Meanwhile, Henrietta, a devout Catholic, was obviously anxious to bring up her children in the old faith. When the King forbade her to take them to Mass in her Chapel at St James's, she instructed them secretly and gave them rosaries and prayerbooks, which made her and the King unpopular with their Protestant subjects.

To placate their feelings, Henrietta reluctantly agreed that her eldest daughter Mary, although still only a child of nine, should marry William, the young Protestant Prince of Orange. It was arranged that the little Princess should stay in England until she was 12, then the wedding took place quietly at Whitehall on May 2, 1641. It was followed by the traditional ritual, the public 'bedding'—although the couple were surrounded by their family and courtiers, and after a few kisses they separated to go to their own beds.

Ten days later the Earl of Strafford, one of the King's ministers who had been charged with treason, was executed on Tower Hill. The King and Queen and two of their children had attended his trial weeks before, and tearfully the King had signed the death warrant—and afterwards sent the ten-year-old Prince of Wales to the House of Commons with a letter begging for clemency. The Prince was turned away, the petition unopened. After Strafford's death, the King tried to arrest five of the leading dissenters and organise his army against the Parliamentarians. It was one more fateful step towards his own downfall. Soon Henrietta heard angry mobs surrounding the palace.

On a cold January day in 1642, the Queen and her daughter Princess Mary hurried to Dover and boarded a ship for Holland. The King was there to see them off. It was an emotional farewell as he kissed his little daughter goodbye. She was leaving to live at the court of her new husband in Holland, and Henrietta, it was said, was travelling with her for companionship. In fact, the Queen had in her luggage the crown jewels, which she intended to sell or pawn to raise

dogs and horses, games of golf or bowls, and learning archery.

While the young princes and princesses enjoyed their childhood, their vivacious and witty mother shone at court. She had her blackamoors, dwarves and monkeys to amuse her and, on a more serious level, she found herself surrounded by the leading painters, poets and writers of the day. Under Charles' patronage, the arts flourished. And if there were not enough pastimes at court, the Queen sometimes went to the theatre—a very daring entertainment in those days.

But Henrietta's untroubled years were soon to end. As the storm clouds gathered, her family scattered and the country erupted in a state of civil war. The seeds of trouble had been sown early in his reign when the King, wishing to be an absolute ruler, dissolved Parliament. It did not meet for 11 years, and Charles, though intending to rule through his council, was not equipped for the job. Ill-advised and unprepared; deaf to the demands of his people, and badly in debt, he faced disaster. There was the question of religion, too. He enforced High

*A Van Dyck portrait showing Charles,
Henrietta Maria and two of their children.*

money for arms. She also planned to ask for military support from Holland.

Henrietta was still overseas in August when civil war broke out between her husband's royalist supporters (commonly referred to as 'Cavaliers') and the Parliamentarians ('Roundheads'). The King took his two eldest sons, 9-year-old James and 12-year-old Charles, Prince of Wales, into battle with him and in October, as cannon balls flew around them, the two young princes watched the first great battle of the war at Edgehill.

The brothers survived their adventures unscathed, to be reunited with their mother at Edgehill when she returned from Holland four months later. It had been a successful mission.

Not only did she have a large sum of money from the Prince of Orange, she also had a shipload of munitions, bought with money raised from the sale of the jewels.

For three years Oxford was the Royalist capital and Queen Henrietta came home not to a royal palace but to the warden's lodgings at Merton College where apartments had been prepared for her. Her younger children, Henry and Elizabeth, were cared for by the Countess of Dorset and lived as normal a life as possible at St James's Palace or in the country at Oatlands. The King and the Prince of Wales were heavily involved in the war, but James continued his studies at Oxford.

The following winter the Queen was unwell. She had a cough which would not go away and she was in pain. She was sure she was going to die, but in fact she was pregnant for the ninth time. In April, with the war turning against the Royalist cause, the King decided Henrietta should go to the West Country for safety. He went with her as far as Abingdon and they kissed goodbye, little knowing that they would never meet again. The baby, a healthy girl, was born at Bedford House in Exeter on June 16, 1644 and christened Henrietta Anne in an Anglican ceremony in the cathedral. Four weeks later, as Parliamentary troops surrounded the city, the Queen, though seriously ill with puerperal sepsis, escaped to Falmouth and from there sailed to France.

Her new-born infant was left in the capable care of Lady Dalkeith and the King, on his way to Cornwall, eventually saw his new daughter for the first time on July 26. He set up a household for her and asked Lady Dalkeith to promise that she would never leave her. For years after, Lady Dalkeith remained a loyal and loving servant to the little princess, far more of a mother to her than the Queen.

The Prince of Wales, meanwhile, had also made his escape to France, but James joined Elizabeth and Henry, first at St James's, and then at Syon House, where they were placed in the care of the Earl of Northumberland. As the King was now living in Hampton Court, the children were allowed to meet him occasionally. They were sad little gatherings, any one of them could have been the last. The King warned his sons not to accept the crown should it be offered to one of them instead of their elder brother. They were to keep faithful to the Church of England and always obey their elder brother. And he told James that if things got any worse, he was to try to escape to his sister Mary in Holland.

The situation did deteriorate when the children were returned to St James's and forced to live under strict supervision. Now helped by one of the King's supporters, James planned his daring escape. As he played hide and seek with his sister and brother one evening, he slipped down a back staircase and out into the park, where a waiting coach took him to freedom in Holland—disguised as a woman.

The Commons then ordered that Henrietta Anne, still living with the faithful Lady Dalkeith at Oatlands, should join the other children at St James's. Remembering her promise to the King, Lady Dalkeith asked permission to accompany the two-year-old toddler, but her request was never acknowledged. Sensing danger, Lady Dalkeith dressed as a poor servant, disguised the princess as an urchin boy and travelled to Dover. From there, undetected by guards, the pair took an ordinary passenger boat to France and had a tearful reunion with Henrietta Maria in Paris.

Only Elizabeth and Henry were still in England when their father went to his execution. Together they went to see him on the eve of his death, January 29, 1649, for a last sad farewell. Elizabeth never really recovered from her sorrow. She became ill soon after the execution, requests to Parliament to allow her to join her sister in Holland failed, and she was found dead on her bed in Carisbrooke Castle, her head resting on her father's bible. She was just 13.

The war had changed Henrietta Maria from a light-hearted young wife to a determined supporter of her husband's cause. Her advice to the King was not always sound, but she showed tremendous courage and daring on her mission to Holland, and she endured hardship and danger at the height of the Civil War. But although she had given birth nine times, her children had never figured large in her life and were certainly no match for her relationship with her husband. Her son, Charles, often referred to her as 'the best of mothers', but to the children, growing up in the care of governesses and tutors, she must have seemed remote and distant. The only one who ever meant anything to her was the youngest, Minette.

Now, with the King dead, Henrietta Maria was a tragic figure—*La Reine Malheureuse*, as she came to call herself. Living in near poverty in

*The execution of Charles I
in Whitehall.*

Paris with Minette, she waited as, one by one, her children joined her. She became bossy and matriarchal in her attitude to them, and they, independent and used to coping without her, found her difficult and argumentative.

When he was at last King, Charles II arranged a family banquet for Henrietta Maria and the children at Dover. Of her original large brood, only four—Charles, James, Mary and Henrietta-Anne—had survived to celebrate at the feast. Not long before the Restoration, Henry died of smallpox. And on Christmas Eve 1660, Mary, too, died of the dreaded disease.

The following year, Henrietta left England to live in Paris with Minette. A home in England had been prepared for her, but she returned only to collect her pension. She considered France her home, with or without her children.

Charles II succeeded his father, Charles I, on the Restoration of the Monarchy in 1660, after the death of Cromwell. From exile on the Continent, the King returned to London in triumph on May 1. 'The happiest May Day for many a year' wrote the diarist Samuel Pepys. It was, indeed, a glorious beginning of a new reign; but there was no heir. Although Charles II fathered several illegitimate children, his wife Catherine of Braganza was childless. When he died in 1685 the crown passed to his brother, James, Duke of York, whose first wife was Anne Hyde. By James's succession she had been dead 14 years but as a mother she had done her duty well.

ANNE HYDE
1637 ~ 1671

Anne Hyde was the eldest daughter of Sir Edward Hyde, later Earl of Clarendon, who from being a Cavalier leader in the Civil War, rose to be Chancellor in the reign of Charles II. Anne, like her father, seems to have had the same aptitude for promotion. She went with her mother, brothers and sisters to Holland, where she attracted the attention of Mary, Princess of Orange, sister of James, Duke of York. Although her rapid rise in favour was unpopular with both Queen Henrietta Maria and with Sir Edward Hyde, Anne became a favourite at court. The Princess made her a maid of honour, she was seen at glittering court gatherings at the Hague, and travelled with the Princess to Paris to meet Queen Henrietta Maria. There, James, Duke of York, and Anne Hyde met for the first time.

The Unacceptable Bride

It was an unpopular match from the start. Strongest opposition came from Henrietta Maria who did everything in her power to prevent her son's marriage with a commoner. It was totally unacceptable. She even made a hurried journey to England to try to stop the wedding taking place, and reprimanded her son for 'having such low thoughts as to wish to marry such a woman'. But James was unmoved. She also sought the help of his brother, Charles, 'to prevent, with her authority, so great a stain and dishonour to the crown ... and to urge that the highest remedies be applied for the prevention of so great a mischief'.

Indeed, if Charles II were to die without an heir, Anne, a commoner, would be Queen. The situation was unthinkable. But Henrietta's pleadings did nothing but strengthen James' resolve—and, anyway, Anne was already pregnant.

They were married by the Duke's chaplain, privately, at around midnight on September 3, 1660 at Worcester House, Anne's father's residence in the Strand. But for some reason, no sooner had the wedding taken place than James began to have misgivings about his wife and looked for ways to reverse the situation—and there were rumours, intended to give James grounds to break the marriage, that the child was not his. Princess Mary, who not long before had welcomed Anne into her household, was also less than amused and pressed her brother to end the marriage. Even Anne's father, Edward Hyde, refused to support his daughter. He felt that to incur the wrath of the royal family could easily endanger his own position in the government and he even suggested to the King that he should send his daughter to the Tower and have her executed by act of Parliament for such behaviour. He himself offered to propose the act.

Charles, having reluctantly given his consent to his brother's marriage, would not go back on his word. The marriage had taken place and the child, which James had agreed was his, was about to be born. Nothing could be changed, and Charles himself visited Anne during her lying-in. The baby, a son, was born six weeks after the wedding. He was christened Charles and given the title Duke of Cambridge. But he lived only seven months and with him died any questions that might have arisen over the succession.

Eventually Anne Hyde, now Duchess of York, came to be accepted at court. As well she might, for no one could deny that as a royal wife she did her duty. She had only 11 years of marriage during which she was pregnant most of the time. Of her eight children, only two survived beyond babyhood, but both became Queens of England.

Although she was not an acknowledged beauty, the Duchess had a likeable personality; she was sociable and witty. She always loved her husband, in spite of his unfaithfulness throughout their married life. She found solace in her interest in the arts—she commissioned

*Anne Hyde, James, Duke of York
and their daughters Mary and Anne.*

the leading painters to portray her; she herself also had literary talent, and enjoyed writing. Her other interest was eating—her love of food made her grossly overweight.

Her babies—four boys and four girls—were born with such regularity that the events were barely noteworthy. Indeed, when her second child, Mary, was born at St James's Palace in April, 1662, Samuel Pepys, said, 'Her birth, by reason of her sex, pleased nobody.' What was wanted was a son and heir. When the Duchess gave birth to a boy, James, 15 months later, to family and public rejoicing, the presence of the little Princess Mary was completely overshadowed. But James died when he was barely four years old and Anne lost two more sons, Edgar and another Charles, within months of their births. Only one other child, Princess Anne, born in 1665, continued to thrive.

Anne, like her sister Mary, was born at St James's, the York's London home. The Duchess loved the palace with its surrounding gardens and parkland. During the Civil War it had been used as barracks for Cromwell's troops and the splendid staterooms and private apartments had become run down, but the Duchess had them modernised, refurbished, gilded and painted to her own taste. And, like Queen Henrietta, she chose her own apartments overlooking the gardens where the children loved to play.

In their very early years the Duchess' daughters divided their time between the palace nursery, where they were cared for by the usual team of royal nannies lead by the capable Mrs

*St. James's Palace, birthplace
of both Mary and Anne.*

Danvers, and the home of their Hyde grandfather at Twickenham. Mary grew into an attractive child, with a happy temperament and tall for her age. When her parents had recovered from the disappointment of their child's sex, they enjoyed her company. Pepys noted that he watched James playing with her 'like an ordinary private father'. Anne, three years younger, tended to be plump like her mother and rather more serious. She also suffered from a complaint which made her eyes weak and watery, and at four she was sent to

France to consult a leading specialist.

But their mother could not have foreseen the future that lay ahead for her little girls. They were aged only six and nine when she died, aged 34. Worn out by childbirth and in agony with breast cancer, she passed away only a month after her last confinement. Mary and Anne were moved to Richmond, where they were placed in the care of their governess, Lady Frances Villiers.

When she died in 1671, Anne Hyde, the unwelcome bride of eleven years before, had in fact given the nation two future Queens.

MARY OF MODENA
1658 ~ 1718

The widowed Duke of York wanted to remarry as speedily as possible, and the bride suggested to him was Mary Beatrice of Modena. He was 40, she just 15, the only daughter of Alfonso IV of Modena. Yet the prospect of a young Italian wife, plus the promise of a generous dowry from

Mother of a Scandal

Louis XIV of France, thoroughly appealed to James. The marriage treaty was quickly drawn up—and Mary Beatrice was devastated. Her one wish since childhood had been to become a nun in a religious order founded by her mother. She had no wish to marry, and certainly not to a stranger. Unworldly and innocent, in her sheltered life she had never even heard of James, Duke of York, nor even of England. In desperation she appealed to Pope Clement X, but he told her that by marrying she could lead England back to the Catholic faith.

Her marriage took place at Modena in September, 1673, with Lord Peterborough standing as proxy for the Duke. Afterwards, with her mother, the widowed Duchess Laura and court attendants, the reluctant bride headed for England. It was a splendid royal progress across France and the Duke of York was waiting to meet them when they landed at Dover in November. He must have been delighted by what he saw, for Mary Beatrice was pretty and slim with jet black hair and dark Italian eyes.

In her innocence, poor Mary Beatrice could not have guessed the wave of hatred that was soon to be unleashed on her and her husband. The Earl of Shaftesbury, as Lord Chancellor, called for the proxy marriage to be declared void. The marriage was unpopular not only because it had the backing of France, at a time when French popularity was at its lowest ebb, but her religion, rather than encourage conversions, only inflamed anti-Catholic opinion.

Mary must have felt very much alone when her mother finally left her at St James's at the end of 1673. The Queen, Catherine of Braganza, did not approve of her, and her husband was still little more than a stranger. She had met him tearfully, and the great love she was eventually to feel for him was yet to grow. But, at 15, Mary

Mary of Modena by Wissing.

Beatrice also found herself in the strange position of being stepmother to Mary and Anne, aged 12 and 9, and became very attached to them. She was able to sympathise with Mary when she, too, at the age of 15, was told with just a fortnight's warning that her wedding had been arranged to her cousin William of Orange, and afterwards Mary Beatrice took Anne to Holland to visit her sister and brother-in-law.

When it came to producing healthy heirs, the new Duchess Mary Beatrice had little more success than her predecessor. Her babies died with the same tragic regularity. But the Protestant public were in no hurry to be told that the Duchess had given birth to a Catholic boy child. With the Princesses Mary and Anne, the Protestant line of succession was quite safe.

The Duchess's first pregnancy ended in miscarriage, but in the afternoon of January 10, 1675, when she was still only 16 years old, she gave birth to her first child at St James's Palace. The baby was a girl, and the mother's happiness must have been somewhat dampened by her husband's obvious disappointment with the sex of the baby. He said to his nephew, 'I believe you will not be sorry to hear of the Duchess being safely delivered; it is but a daughter, but, God be praised, they are both very well.'

In her marriage treaty, Mary Beatrice had been promised the right to exercise her religion. Now she wanted her daughter baptised according to the Catholic rite. James, evidently feeling that this would add further to their unpopularity, refused. Nevertheless, the Duchess, conscience-stricken, had the child, Catherine Laura, baptised secretly by her priest, Father Gallis, who was called to her bedside. When the King began arranging his niece's christening, and Mary Beatrice told him what she had done, he nevertheless went ahead with his plans, and the baby went through a second, Protestant ceremony.

Despite the problems over religion, which the Duchess appears to have accepted as the sacrifice which was expected of her, her marriage was happy. But the sorrow and heartbreak which had already dogged the Stuart line was to recur before long. In October 1675, Catherine Laura, aged nine months, had convulsions and died. And Mary Beatrice, pregnant again, suffered a miscarriage the following day.

Her second child, born at St James's Palace a year later, was again 'but a daughter'. She was baptised Isabel, and the Duchess, no doubt thinking how lucky she was to have a thriving child of whatever sex, appears to have kept the little girl close to her. When Isabel was three, Mary took her, together with her own mother, the Duchess Laura, and stepdaughter Anne on an extensive round of travels to Brussels and The Hague. It was a troubled time in England and James felt it would be safer for his family to be abroad.

Mary Beatrice, like Anne Hyde before her, was pregnant for most of the early years of marriage. In November 1677 there was much private rejoicing in the family, when the longed-for son arrived; a male heir. He was born just three days after the marriage of Princess Mary to the Prince of Orange, which meant Mary Beatrice could not attend the wedding; nor could Princess Anne who was ill with smallpox which had spread through the palace. The new-born Prince Charles, Duke of Cambridge, did not escape. Mary Beatrice was still in her lying-in chamber with her baby when spots appeared on his body. He died on December 12, little more than a month old. James and Mary were heartbroken. There was another baby, a daughter, Elizabeth, a year later, but she, too, died in infancy. And in March 1681, when the Duke and Duchess were

living in Scotland to escape the political heat in England, their precious only daughter Isabel died. Mary Beatrice had given birth to four children in five years. Now she was childless.

By the following year she was pregnant again and returned to London for the confinement. She also asked to have her mother with her, and King Charles agreed. It was seen by the anti-Catholics as a plan by James and Mary Beatrice to assure the birth of a son by *any* means. And so the wild rumours began—that the Duchess's mother was on her way with a newborn boy baby, ready as a substitute should the child be a girl. Rumours mounted when Mary Beatrice went into labour two weeks early, before there was time to call the necessary witnesses to the birth. Had the baby been a boy, the parents would have been hard pressed to prove its legitimacy. Happily, in this case, another daughter was born, Charlotte Maria. But she, too, died in infancy. The Duchess had yet two more miscarriages, in 1683 and 1684, and was seriously ill as a result.

James became King in 1685, on the death of his brother, Charles II, and the birth of a healthy male heir became urgent. His Protestant daughters Mary and Anne did not agree, for they would be displaced by the birth of a half-brother. Although both sisters were by then married, they had, so far, produced no heirs.

Her health declining, Mary Beatrice, now Queen, went to the spa town of Bath to take the waters, hoping she might conceive, and the King made a special journey to St Winefride's Well in Wales to pray for a son. Only two months later rumour spread that she was, indeed, pregnant. While the Queen's Catholic supporters rejoiced—to them the news was nothing less than miraculous—the rest of the population became increasingly suspicious. It was six years since the Queen's last confinement, and she was now 30 years old. Mary Beatrice had never been popular with the English; back in 1682 London mobs had vandalised shops that bore her coat of arms. Now there were more rumours of plots, and accusations. Even her stepdaughter Anne turned against her, afraid that she would urge the King to make her change her religion.

In December the news was publicly announced; Queen Mary Beatrice was pregnant. In January there was public thanksgiving. Her stepdaughters were scornful, disbelieving. Anne tried to be in the room when the Queen was changing, so that she could see the royal stomach with her own eyes; the Queen angrily tossed a glove at her. Denied positive proof, the two sisters, exchanging letters, concocted stories of a phantom pregnancy.

Plans were made for the baby to be born at Windsor then suddenly changed when the Queen said the baby might be due a month earlier, and instead chose St James's Palace for her confinement, so that witnesses could reach her more easily.

So began the historic scandal of the warming-pan baby. The arrival was even earlier than expected, on June 9, 1688, and took everyone by surprise. The Queen had been sitting up late, playing cards at Whitehall when she felt that the birth was imminent and impatiently enquired whether her apartments were ready—workmen had been finishing some decorations. Told that there was little chance of the chamber being ready, she insisted: 'I mean to lie at St James's tonight, even if I lie on bare boards!'

So the Queen was carried by sedan-chair to St James's and arrived as the clock struck midnight. Ten hours later, James Francis Edward, Prince of Wales, was born. Years after, he would be recorded in history books as the 'Old Pretender', destined to spend his life in exile, the father of the Jacobite heir Bonnie Prince Charlie. But the scandal that surrounded his arrival that June morning was to change the way of royal birth for many generations to come.

Although it was celebrated with official rejoicing, and his father wept and prayed for joy and thanksgiving, the arrival of a prince to Catholic parents met with only a cold response from the public. As stories about the birth spread, so did the rumours that the child was simply a substitute rushed into the palace in a warming-pan. The King was forced to call witnesses—all 67 of those who were present at the confinement. And it is thanks to the detailed descriptions from nurses, courtiers and onlookers, that we have such a vivid account of the Stuart style of birth.

The Queen, worried that her room had not been prepared, was found by one of her women of the bedchamber, Mrs Margaret Dawson, sitting on a stool, waiting for the bed in the next room to be made up. But the quilts were not yet aired, so Mrs Dawson persuaded the Queen to get back into the bed she had just left, while a pan of hot coals was ordered to warm it for her. Then her midwife, Mrs Judith Wilkes and her nurse arrived to take care of the Queen. These events were timed at around 8.30 a.m.

Witnesses grouped around the end of the bed included the widowed Queen Catherine of Braganza and 18 members of the Privy Council. The Queen was understandably embarassed by the crowd of men necessary to witness her at such an undignified time and begged the King to hide her face in his wig.

She also asked for a pre-arranged system of signals to announce the baby's sex, afraid that she would laugh or burst into tears in front of everyone. Only the King would know. Just before 10 a.m. the Queen was heard to cry: 'I die, Oh you kill me, you kill me!' And the baby was born. 'I didn't hear the child cry,' said an agitated Mary. And at that moment it did. The King, forgetting all the arrangements for discretion, asked: 'What is it?' And was told: 'What your majesty desires.'

The delighted father knighted the Queen's physician, Dr Waldegrave, on the spot and gave Mrs Wilkes 500 guineas. Whether or not the Queen herself felt such elation we do not know. So many of her confinements had come to nothing. That very night the baby was accidentally given an overdose of Dr Goddard's drops, a medicine prescribed as being good for babies. Fortunately it did no harm.

The King wrote to his daughter Mary to give her the good news, and she at once wrote to her sister, Anne, with a list of questions. They asked and gave detailed accounts of the birth. When he was three weeks old, the baby was dressed in a purple robe trimmed with ermine to receive the Lord Mayor of London and other dignitaries, but so much scorn was heaped on the event, with cartoons and cruel jokes, that the Queen decided to keep her baby in seclusion. This led to yet more rumours, this time that the child had died.

Because Mary Beatrice had lost so many babies in infancy, her doctors decided to experiment with the little prince's diet. Instead of employing a wet nurse, they prescribed a gruesome-sounding concoction of barley flour, sugar, currants and canary wine mixed into a gruel. He was also dosed with 30 different medicines. Not surprisingly, his health began to fail and in August he almost died. He was sent to Richmond, where it was hoped the fresh country air would help, and the Queen went too, to be near to her 'dearest boon of Heaven'. There she decided to revert to the time-honoured tradition of the wet nurse and hired the services of the village tiler's wife. The prince made a remarkable recovery—for which the nurse was well rewarded.

Meanwhile the King's enemies had not been silenced by the deposition. The mistrust and disbelief that surrounded the birth of his son continued. Pamphlets questioning his birth were circulated—the Queen herself even found one concealed inside her glove. There was a rapidly-growing fear that the birth of a Catholic heir would lead to the enforcement of Catholicism. When seven Anglican bishops banded together and asked the help of William of Orange, husband of Princess Mary—who, until the birth of the prince had been James' Protestant heir—they found he was already preparing to invade.

William of Orange landed at Torbay on November 5, 1688, with a force to defeat James's army. James, accompanied by Prince George of Denmark, consort of Princess Anne, left London to meet the invading forces. But at Salisbury Prince George deserted the King, and James returned to London. Queen Mary Beatrice, who at first had regarded her stepdaughters with affection, as friends and allies, must have felt be-

James, The Old Pretender,
as a boy.

who saw the Queen's face during labour, who was present in the room, and who had actually ever felt the child move—evidence of the hatred and suspicion the two now felt.

There was not a shred of evidence to support the changeling theory, but the King still had to set up an inquiry, call all the witnesses of the birth and produce a deposition to prove that the Queen had, indeed, given birth to Prince James Francis Edward. Some eye-witnesses recalled seeing damp stains of breast milk on her smock, trayed and trapped by the sudden turn in events; most of all, she feared for the safety of her son. Less than 40 years before, her mother-in-law, Queen Henrietta Maria, had been forced to flee to France. Now, Mary Beatrice had to escape.

With two nurses and attendants she and her six-month-old baby left Whitehall on the night of December 9. Travelling in a coach and six, they crossed the river at Horseferry and drove to Gravesend where a yacht waited to take them to Calais. It was a rough crossing. On landing, Mary Beatrice went to Mass in thanksgiving for her safe arrival, then sent a message to Louis XIV asking for his protection.

James was finally defeated by William at the Battle of the Boyne in 1690 and joined his family in exile in France. At their little court at St Germain, near Paris, they surrounded themselves with other English expatriates, hoping and praying that one day they would be able to return to England. Mary Beatrice, who had asked the Pope to protect her son, doubtless cherished a hope that one day he would accede to the English throne, but, as the years went by, these hopes diminished. She found consolation more and more in her religion. Whenever James was away she stayed at the Convent of the Visitation at Chaillot. She found consolation, too, in her youngest child, Princess Louisa Mary, born to her when she was 34 years old. Remembering the furore which surrounded the birth of the Prince of Wales, James wanted his privy council to be present at the birth, but none came. Only the wife of the Danish ambassador went to St Germain to witness the birth on behalf of the English people. Christened Louisa after Louis XIV who was her godfather, she grew into a lively, much loved child. And she was a great comfort to Mary Beatrice when James died following a stroke in 1701.

She spent her retirement at St Germain and the convent at Chaillot. Having sold most of her jewellery, and given her money to support needy English exiles, she lived on a pension paid by the French. To her great sorrow, her daughter, who had been so close to her, died in 1712 at the age of 20. Only her son, Prince James Francis Edward Stuart, survived her, and married Clementina, granddaughter of the Polish King John Sobieski.

Queen Mary Beatrice herself died in 1718, aged 60.

MARY AND ANNE
1662 ~ 1694   1665 ~ 1714

Queens Without Heirs

William and Mary were summoned to take the throne on February 13 1689, when James II and Mary Beatrice had fled to France. Mary, the elder daughter of James and his first wife Anne Hyde, had dutifully obeyed her father's wishes and married William of Orange, her cousin, when she was only 15 and he 27. It is said she cried for a day and a half when she heard of her father's plan: they had absolutely nothing in common. He was short and thin with a serious outlook on life; she was four inches taller and had an outgoing personality. Yet by the time of her death from smallpox at the age of 32 she had grown to love him, although it was a love rarely reciprocated.

Throughout her short life, Queen Mary longed to have a baby. By the attention she gave to her little nephew, it was obvious that she would have been a loving mother, but it was not to be. She became pregnant for the first time 11 years after her marriage, but suffered a miscarriage in the third month—brought on, it was thought, by bumpy journeys she had unwisely taken on the rough roads between The Hague and Rotterdam. She miscarried a second time in the same year, and later had a strange phantom pregnancy—doubtless the result of her intense longing for a child. Although she continued to hope for a baby, she never became pregnant again.

Waiting in the wings for her time to inherit the throne was Mary's sister Anne, just three years her junior and married since the age of 18 to Prince George of Denmark. As they grew older, sisterly affection turned to dislike, until there was a rift between the two. While Mary was extrovert, Anne was silent, often moody. They rarely spoke except when friction led them to quarrel. But the one thing the two Stuart sisters had in common was a tragic inability to bear healthy children. Anne's record was appalling. She had 17 pregnancies in 16 years. Of these, ten ended in miscarriage and only one child survived beyond infancy.

After their marriage in the Chapel Royal at St James's, Anne and her husband moved into apartments made available to them at White-hall Palace. Within a year the Princess was pregnant, but the child was stillborn, due, it

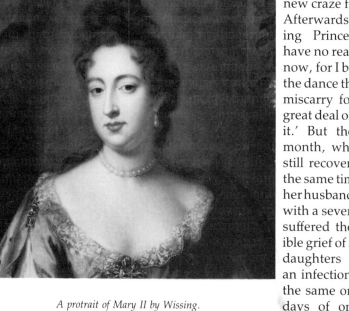

A protrait of Mary II by Wissing.

was thought, to Anne's fall from a horse. Although she must have been deeply disappointed to lose her first child, birth in the late seventeenth century was still a hazardous business. Confinements frequently ended in the death of the child or the mother, or both. Anne, who at that stage in her life was quite robust, had no cause for concern.

In 1685 when her father inherited the throne as James II, she attended his first opening of Parliament, accompanied by all the pomp of the occasion, although she was heavily pregnant. Just a fortnight later, on June 2, the child was born;

a little girl, christened Mary by the Bishop of London next day. Exactly a year later, on June 2, 1686 she had a second daughter, baptised Anne Sophia by the Bishop of Durham, with Lady Churchill as her godmother. It was, at last, a happy time for Anne, with her two infant princesses installed in the royal nursery.

Her happiness was all too brief. The New Year of 1687 began tragically enough with yet another miscarriage, triggered off, it was suspected, by all too energetic dancing of the rigadoon, a new craze from France. Afterwards, the sorrowing Princess said: 'I have no reason to like it now, for I believe it was the dance that made me miscarry for there is a great deal of jumping in it.' But the following month, when she was still recovering, and at the same time caring for her husband who was ill with a severe fever, she suffered the most terrible grief of all. Both her daughters died from an infection—probably the same one— within days of one another. The first to die was the baby Anne Sophia, aged just eight months, then her elder sister, not yet two. And within the next twelve months Anne had two more miscarriages. With such a heartbreaking succession of disappointments, it is easy to understand the mixed emotions of anguish, disbelief and jealousy she felt towards her stepmother, Queen Mary Beatrice, when she gave birth to Prince James Edward.

Anne at last had a son of her own in July 1689, in the first year of the reign of William III and her sister Mary. The baby was born at Hampton Court and christened William after the King, who bestowed on him the title of Duke of Gloucester. Right from the start it was obvious that he was a weakly child. Family rejoicing could only have been restrained as Anne could not have expected him to live. He was slow to feed and the nipple of his wet nurse, a Mrs Shermon, was blamed for being too big. So another wet nurse, Mrs Wanley, who had suckled one of Anne's earlier babies, was brought back to service. All went well and the little boy thrived until he was six weeks old, when he began to have convulsions. Doctors ordered a change of milk and young mothers, potential wet nurses, flocked to Hampton Court to apply for the job.

It was Prince George, the baby's father, who made the final choice when he spotted a Mrs Pack waiting in the crowded Presence Chamber for her turn to be interviewed. The wife of a Quaker, she looked strong and healthy and, after a few feeds, the young prince showed signs of recovery. But all was not well. His head was large in proportion to his body and as he grew older and began to walk he had trouble keeping his balance. He was obviously handicapped. His mother, doubtless embarrassed by his strange appearance, kept him very much to herself, hidden away from public view and referred to him touchingly as 'my poor boy'.

Nevertheless, in spite of his frailty, William's upbringing developed on the traditional lines so loved by royalty. With his own staff of servants, his everyday care was first in the hands of his wet nurse and nursery attendants. Later his governor, Lord Fitzharding, and the kindly Lady Fitzharding, who was appointed governess, had charge of him. But as time went by the little boy's disabilities became more pronounced. When he sat on the floor he had difficulty getting up again and although he could walk on even ground, stairs worried him. He insisted that two people helped him up and down. Doctors today disagree as to the exact cause of the problem. It could have been a form of hydrocephalus, which would have accounted for his illness at six weeks, and could have caused the deaths of some of his brothers and sisters. Or it could have been a severe case of rickets.

Although William had a sympathetic doctor, his father's attitude, in today's enlightened times, seems little less than brutal. In fact, it was ignorance more than cruelty that prompted his behaviour. Thinking his son was difficult and simply seeking attention, he actually whipped him for his actions while Anne simply looked on, seemingly frightened but uncertain how to act.

Although the poor child's handicap was so misunderstood, he was shown warmth and kindness, often over-indulgence, by relatives and friends. His parents' feelings seem to have veered from cold disregard for his failings to over-protection, as they struggled against all odds to mould their treasured son and heir to become a future king. As a child he was showered with gifts fit for a prince; the Duchess of Ormonde gave him a miniature carriage drawn by dog-sized ponies, and the Duke of Marlborough, who was later appointed his governor, gave him the command of a Dutch regiment of footguards. Even the childless Queen Mary swallowed her pride when she wished to enjoy the company of her young nephew. She displayed a 'statue-like coldness' whenever she communicated with her sister Anne, but overcame the rift between them to channel her frustrated maternal instincts towards William. She visited him often and sent him gifts of toys.

When it came to play, the little boy showed few signs of being an invalid. He loved war games and when he was taken to Kensington to benefit from the country air, he played with a crowd of village boys. In November every year, the anniversary of the birth of Queen Elizabeth I was still celebrated in England and the young William of Gloucester liked nothing better than to assist in the firing of a gun salute.

Anne, as a mother, was overwhelmed with feelings of pride and hope when she saw her son, on his seventh birthday, installed as a Knight of the Garter at Windsor. The little boy, his slight figure weighed down by the robes and regalia of the occasion, appeared fragile indeed to onlookers at the Windsor ceremony; but to the young prince who obviously enjoyed pomp and

Queen Anne with her husband,
Prince George of Denmark.

pageantry, it was the most perfect birthday of his life. And as a precious memento, King William presented him with a diamond and onyx jewel to attach to his Garter chain.

Much of William's boyhood was spent at Windsor where he began the usual grooming for kingship with the study of languages, history and law. He was there for his 11th birthday celebrations in 1700 when the whole family gathered to celebrate with dancing and fireworks.

The next day he became ill and by evening he was delirious. It was thought he had smallpox, for which he was bled, but later—too late— scarlet fever was diagnosed. A week later, the boy who had danced so joyfully was dead. Anne, who had tenderly cared for him during those last days accepted his death with resignation and piety. At his funeral she was quietly composed and it was said by some that she believed her loss to be a punishment for the way she had turned against her father when he was forced from his throne. Anne also knew that at 35, she would be unlikely to be a mother again. In the 11 years since William's birth, she had had two more babies—Mary, born two months premature, survived only two hours and George, born at Syon House, who lived just long enough to be baptised. From then on, her eight further pregnancies ended in miscarriage.

The years of constant pregnancy, miscarriage and childbearing had taken their toll. At 35 Anne had, not surprisingly, lost her figure. Always overweight since, like her mother Anne Hyde, she adored food and ate far too much, she now suffered chronic ill-health and was almost constantly in pain.

When she succeeded William III to the throne in 1702 she was crippled with gout and was frequently ill. Visits to the spas of Bath and Tunbridge Wells to take the waters were the more harmless cures she tried. Medical care in those days called for such drastic treatments as bleeding (sometimes with the application of leeches), and opium (often in the form of laudanum), quinine, and just plain gin were commonly prescribed. They usually did more harm than good. Nevertheless, Queen Anne survived her husband, Prince George, who died in 1708. She, herself, passed away at Kensington Palace on July 31, 1714, aged 49. She died without an heir; and as the young Catholic Prince James Edward was unacceptable to the English, she was the last of the Stuart line.

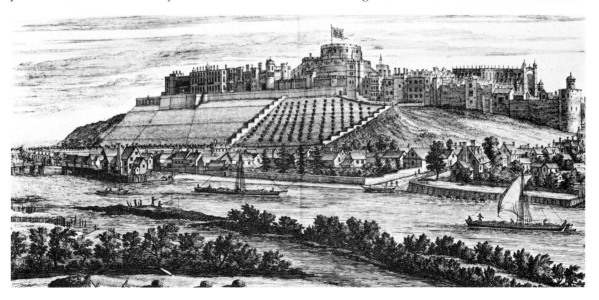

Windsor Castle in the period.

The Hanoverians

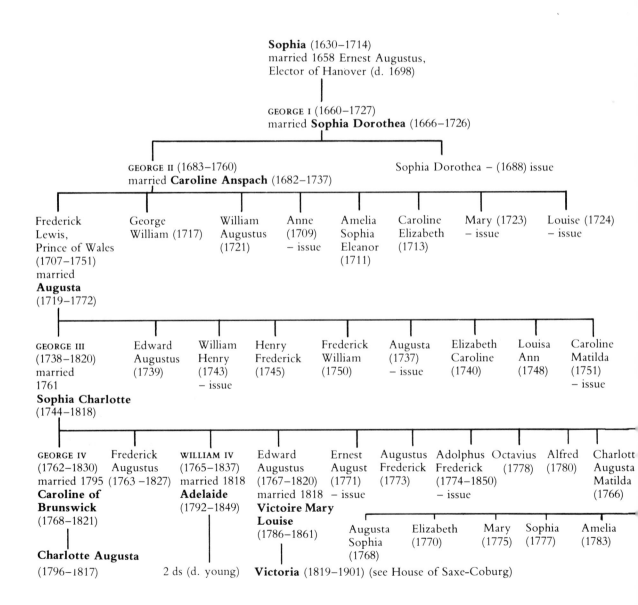

Sophia (1630–1714)
married 1658 Ernest Augustus,
Elector of Hanover (d. 1698)

GEORGE I (1660–1727)
married **Sophia Dorothea** (1666–1726)

GEORGE II (1683–1760)
married **Caroline Anspach** (1682–1737)

Sophia Dorothea – (1688) issue

Frederick
Lewis,
Prince of Wales
(1707–1751)
married
Augusta
(1719–1772)

George
William (1717)

William
Augustus
(1721)

Anne
(1709)
– issue

Amelia
Sophia
Eleanor
(1711)

Caroline
Elizabeth
(1713)

Mary (1723)
– issue

Louise (1724)
– issue

GEORGE III
(1738–1820)
married
1761
Sophia Charlotte
(1744–1818)

Edward
Augustus
(1739)

William
Henry
(1743)
– issue

Henry
Frederick
(1745)

Frederick
William
(1750)

Augusta
(1737)
– issue

Elizabeth
Caroline
(1740)

Louisa
Ann
(1748)

Caroline
Matilda
(1751)
– issue

GEORGE IV
(1762–1830)
married 1795
**Caroline of
Brunswick**
(1768–1821)

Frederick
Augustus
(1763–1827)

WILLIAM IV
(1765–1837)
married 1818
Adelaide
(1792–1849)

Edward
Augustus
(1767–1820)
married 1818
**Victoire Mary
Louise**
(1786–1861)

Ernest
August
(1771)
– issue

Augustus
Frederick
(1773)

Adolphus
Frederick
(1774–1850)
– issue

Octavius
(1778)

Alfred
(1780)

Charlott
Augusta
Matilda
(1766)

Augusta
Sophia
(1768)

Elizabeth
(1770)

Mary
(1775)

Sophia
(1777)

Amelia
(1783)

Charlotte Augusta
(1796–1817)

2 ds (d. young)

Victoria (1819–1901) (see House of Saxe-Coburg)

The eighteenth century was a period of tremendous change for Britain, one that saw the country transformed from a predominantly agricultural one into an industrial one, and British merchants and manufacturers prospered. But there was unrest abroad; the French Revolution and Napoleonic Wars in Europe, and the American War of Independence, which lost Britain her American Colonies.

There was marked change, too, as a foreign family took the throne. When Queen Anne died in 1714, leaving no heirs, George of Hanover was invited to become George I of Great Britain, being the next Protestant in line. But George never learned to speak English and made no secret of the fact that he much preferred Hanover to Britain. Perhaps not surprisingly, the people felt very little enthusiasm for him as King. However, his son, George II, found popularity through his wife, Caroline of Anspach, who was much loved. George III, who came to the throne in 1760, was brought up as an Englishman and was much closer to his people.

This new blood to the throne did little to change the traditions, though. The publicity surrounding royal birth in Georgian times makes exposure by the media today look positively restrained. Little was left to the imagination as all the royal births took place before an audience of witnesses including the Archbishop of Canterbury, the Chancellor and the Prime Minister. Afterwards, intimate details of the birth were spread like wildfire; news was circulated by onlookers, the ladies of the court, the attendants and others surrounding the royal bedside. Then there were the receptions for noble ladies from Britain and the Continent, who came to view the new-born infant. As many as 40 at a time would crowd into the bedchamber.

Wet nurses were still the fashion as it was still not the done thing for high-born ladies to feed their babies themselves—it interrupted their social life and spoilt their fashionable figures.

But there were some changes. While the custom of swaddling babies still continued, once past babyhood the royal mothers chose beautiful clothes of soft rich silks and brocades, satin and velvet for their offspring. Little princes wore breeches and their coats were trimmed with lace frills; princesses had long coats, hooped petticoats, fans and muffs and embroidered gloves.

Although the Hanoverian age saw stirring events overseas, Britain was at peace with herself, and the well-to-do led leisured lives. Parents and children enjoyed gentle pursuits such as singing, chamber music, poetry-reading, walking and riding. They relaxed at the newly fashionable spas and began to appreciate the benefits of the sea air as well. It was a time for royal mothers to begin to enjoy their many children and share their interests.

A mother, dressed in the height of fashion—with slits in her gown for suckling her infant.

SOPHIA, ELECTRESS OF HANOVER
1630~1714

When the only surviving son of the future Queen Anne died in 1700, it was left to Parliament to proclaim a successor. James Francis Edward, exiled son of the deposed James II, was precluded by the Bill of Rights which barred the throne to Catholics. Instead, Parliament looked to Sophia, Electress of Hanover and granddaughter of James I, and by the Act of Settlement of 1701 she was named as Anne's successor. In fact her son was to succeed as Sophia died just before Anne.

Sophia was the youngest daughter of Elizabeth of Bohemia, sister of Charles I, who married Frederick V, the Elector Palatine and King of Bohemia, and who became known as the Winter Queen— Frederick having lost his crown soon after marriage and after one winter's rule. They spent the rest of their lives in exile, often in hardship. Sophia, the youngest of their twelve children grew up, like the rest of the family, in a household apart from her parents. Elizabeth had little time for mothering and Sophia complained, touchingly, that her mother enjoyed her pet monkeys and dogs more than her many children.

The exiled family lived for most of the time in Holland, and while the children missed out on mother love, boys and girls alike shared an education which was to make Sophia one of the most intellectual and well-read women of her time. She studied modern languages as well as Latin

Doting Mother

*Sophia, Electress of Hanover,
in later life.*

and Greek, law and mathematics. Then, at an early age, she showed her independence by moving to Heidelberg. She was 28 when she married Ernest Augustus, Elector of Hanover, and made her home there. It was an arranged match, but love grew and their first child, George Lewis, was born in 1660, the year of the Restoration of Charles II in England. Ernest Augustus stayed at Sophia's side throughout the three days of her labour and when George arrived— a big, bouncing boy—she declared that her baby was as 'beautiful as an angel'. When he was a year old Sophia took him by boat down the Rhine to Rotterdam to show him off to her mother, and later that year George Lewis was joined by a baby brother, Frederick.

Sophia's pregnancies over the next five years ended sadly, in still-births and miscarriages until the arrival of Maximilian, who was one of twins. From then the nursery expanded rapidly. Maximilian was followed by Sophia Charlotte (who was to be the only daughter), then Karl, Christian and, last of all Ernest—born when elder brother George was 14.

Sophia was a doting mother. She appears to have set out to give her babies all the affection she lacked in her own childhood and her two elder sons travelled with her from a very early age, not only on the Continent but also in England when their grandmother, the widowed Elizabeth of Bohemia, returned home after the Restoration.

She was destined to mourn the death of three of her sons—Frederick, Karl and Christian—all of whom died in battle. Of her remaining children, George Lewis, on whom she doted, was to become her favourite and closest, particularly after her husband's death in 1698. She was 70 when she was named heir to the English throne in 1701, an incredibly tough, determined woman, still capable of fiercely guarding her son's interests. She had at one time urged him to seek the hand of the future English Queen Anne in marriage, but Anne had not been impressed.

The witty, intellectual Sophia was remarkable by any standards. Historians claim she would have made an outstanding queen. But she died suddenly, while walking in her castle grounds, at the age of 84, less than two months before the death of Queen Anne. Sophia, having just failed to become Queen of England, passed into history instead as the mother of England's first Hanoverian monarch. It was left to George Lewis, aged 53, with no interest in and little knowledge of England, to take the crown.

SOPHIA DOROTHEA
1666~1726

The Captive Queen

George I, son of the ambitious Sophia, was duly proclaimed King of England and arrived in the summer of 1714, six weeks after the death of Queen Anne. George's wife, Sophia Dorothea, the mother of his two children, was left behind in Germany.

Sophia Dorothea, daughter of George's first cousin, had been only 16 when they married. But it was a marriage destined for failure. George Lewis, an accomplished horseman and warrior was a difficult man, a heavy drinker, slow thinking and lacking in social graces. He was ill-matched with the pretty, high-spirited young bride who felt homesick and bored with court life. But outwardly all went well at first and in December 1683 Sophia Dorothea gave birth to the requisite son and heir—the future George II of England. However, there was a gap of more than five years before their daughter, also christened Sophia Dorothea, was born, in March 1688, and by then the couple were openly drifting apart. Indeed, early in their marriage George Lewis was unfaithful to his wife to such an extent

Sophia Dorothea—sadly romantic

*Sophia Dorothea with her two children, George and Sophia.
They were parted shortly afterwards.*

*Sophia's love affair with Count Philip of Konigsmarck
scandalised the family.*

that she felt moved to complain. He reacted so violently he nearly strangled her.

Her life changed irrevocably at a court ball, shortly after the birth of her daughter. There, at the invitation of her family and in-laws, was the Swedish Count Philip Von Konigsmarck, a colonel in the Dragoons. Tall, handsome, charming, he could not fail to have attracted her. They fell in love and the story that followed is one of unbelievable cruelty.

As their meetings became less secret, letters passed between Sophia Dorothea and Philip and the affair grew into a scandal until the summer of 1694 when the family moved swiftly to finish the affair once and for all. George Lewis himself was away on the July night when Count Philip went to Sophia's apartments, and was never seen again. Countess Von Platen, mistress of Ernest Augustus, Sophia's father-in-law, was strongly suspected of having engineered the Count's murder, but it was never proved, and the body never found.

Sophia, aged 28, was tried for adultery and her marriage dissolved. Then, forbidden to remarry and denied access to her children or even the companionship of her lady-in-waiting, she was sent into exile at Ahlden Castle. There she was to remain until her death in 1726—only six months before her husband's.

Sophia was never allowed to see her children again—they were brought up by grandparents—and for the rest of her life their portraits were her dearest possessions. That she had been a loving mother to her two young children is supported by the fact that her son George always remembered his mother with affection. He was nine when she disappeared from his life, just old enough to have definite recollections of her, and throughout his life he always carried a picture of her. These early memories of a mother he barely knew may have been enhanced by childhood fantasy, but he was naturally resentful of his father's cruel treatment of her, and father and son were always on bad terms. It was left to his young sister, the future Queen of Prussia, who was only four when she last saw her mother, to become her father's closest confidante.

CAROLINE OF ANSPACH
1683～1737

Royal couples can have mother-in-law problems just like their common counterparts, but this was not the case for George, Prince of Wales, and his young wife Caroline of Anspach. With poor Sophia exiled at Ahlden, it was father-in-law George Lewis who caused the problems in the domestic royal circle.

Orphan Queen

The blonde, beautiful and statuesque Caroline of Anspach was orphaned as a young girl and raised in the cultured atmosphere of the court of her guardian, Elector Frederick of Brandenburg. She was 22 when she married her prince, George Augustus, in 1705 and she was soon to discover the pressure of problems within the royal family circle. Six months after they were married, George wanted to go to war, but his father, doubtless fearing for his son's safety, refused to allow him to do so until Caroline had produced an heir. She was so harassed by constant enquiries from members of her family and court officials that, when she *was* pregnant, she cut herself off and lived in complete secrecy from everyone except her closest relations. The child was born late—or the Princess miscalculated its arrival time—and, after such a long wait, the Electress Sophia was outraged because she was not allowed even to glimpse the baby until the christening, which was held in private in Caroline's bedroom. It would have made the perfect case for another warming-pan scandal!

The baby born in such secrecy in Hanover in 1707 was baptised Friedrich Ludwig—although he was to become known in England as Frederick Lewis. With his safe arrival, his father was at last allowed to go to war, and in the years ahead, Caroline was to have seven more children. The Hanoverian line looked secure for the future.

Frederick—a sickly child at first, who was prescribed asses' milk by his doctors—was followed by a succession of girls—first Anne, then Amelia and Caroline.

Family life changed dramatically in 1714 when George and Caroline, as Prince and Princess of Wales, followed George I of England, to London for his coronation. It is hard to imagine the feelings of a mother who could be so detached from her seven-year-old son as to agree to distance herself from him by hundreds of miles and leave him behind in Germany, but this is what Caroline decided for her first-born son, little Frederick

*Queen Caroline and her son William Augustus,
Duke of Cumberland.*

Lewis. While his three young sisters joined their parents in England, he stayed in Hanover in the care of his great-uncle Ernest Augustus, to be educated by tutors in the German tradition. This decision was made to please the people of Hanover, who took pride in court life and would have felt deprived if the whole of their ruling family had moved away.

Caroline soon had her mind on other matters. By the spring of 1716 she was preparing for her next baby, the first to be born in England, and she insisted on bringing her own midwife from Germany. She also alarmed her attendants when she insisted on the rather un-English practice of going for long walks while pregnant. When she went into labour at Hampton Court, Sir David Hamilton, one of the country's leading exponents in midwifery, was present as well as

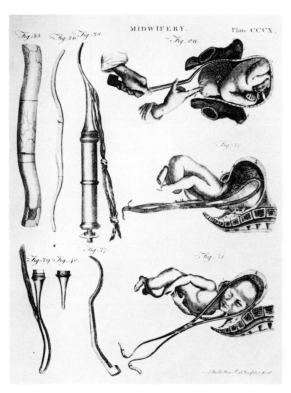

Midwifery instruments and some period textbook illustrations of methods of delivering babies with forceps.

the German midwife, and Caroline was urged to allow him to take charge. The midwife was outraged and, as she spoke no English, the Secretary of State, who was also near the royal bedside, had to squeeze her hand and smile kindly at her in an attempt to calm her down. It was in this highly charged atmosphere that Caroline laboured from Sunday until Friday when, tragically, the baby, a son, was born dead.

Caroline was pregnant again by the spring of 1717 and a son was born in October. But this child, whose birth was the cause of great family jubilation, also sparked off a historic rift that was to shatter the already strained relations between the King and his son.

First there was a dispute over the baby's name. Caroline, who wanted him to be called William, was told that as the King was to be the godfather, her child would be called George William. But the row that caused real breakdown between the King and the Prince of Wales flared up at the St James's Palace christening. The Prince had wanted great-uncle Ernest, the Bishop of Osnabruck to be the second godfather, but it was pointed out that it was customary for the Lord Chamberlain to be given the honour. Although the Lord Chamberlain of the day was the Duke of Newcastle, whom the Prince strongly disliked, he eventually gave in to his father's wishes, but after the ceremony, the Prince spoke to the Duke who *thought* the Prince, in his broken English, said 'I shall fight you out', meaning he was being challenged to a duel.

It turned out to be more than a storm in a Hanoverian tea cup. For the Duke reported the matter to the King who angrily called for an investigation. The Prince and Princess were put under house arrest and shortly afterwards the Prince of Wales was evicted from St James's Palace. It was an astonishing act, even for a father known for his authoritarian ways. And when Princess Caroline loyally followed her husband, leaving her children behind at the palace, the King reacted by taking over responsibility for the children—the three little daughters aged nine, seven and five and their baby brother—and placed them in the care of the Countess Schaumburg-Lippe.

Princess Caroline, who was told that she would be allowed to visit her children only once a week, acquired a new home, Leicester House in Leicester Square. With the Prince, who was more socially inclined than his father, she helped set up an alternative court, a centre for glittering gatherings of up-and-coming politicians, artists, musicians and leading members of the new young society. Robert Walpole was a frequent visitor; Handel's music was all the rage.

There came a slight thawing in family relations early in 1718 when the seemingly healthy Prince George William became ill, with 'choking and coughing' symptoms. The smoky winter air was probably blamed for the attack and the Countess of Schaumburg-Lippe took her tiny charge to the more rural palace of Kensington. There, away from the pomp and protocol of St James's, the Prince and Princes of Wales were allowed to visit their little son. But in spite of careful nursing, the baby gradually weakened and died in February 1718, when he was little more than three months old. It was later discovered that George William, the child who had been at the centre of the royal feud, had in fact been born with a growth on his heart.

The Princess went on to have three more children—William Augustus born in 1721, Mary in 1723 and Louise in 1724, when Caroline was 41. And after the death of baby George William, the Countess of Schaumburg-Lippe began making frequent visits to Leicester House to give Caroline news of her daughters' progress. The Prince and Princess also started to call on their daughters at St James's, always apparently avoiding any chance meeting with the King. Nevertheless, as time went by, the family became reconciled, at least at an official level.

Meanwhile Caroline's eldest son, Frederick, was still living in Hanover. Disinterest in her son, whom she had not seen since childhood, had somehow grown to active dislike, and when William Augustus was born it was actually suggested that he should be declared heir to the throne and Frederick should remain in Germany and become Elector of Hanover. Only his grandfather, King George, on his frequent trips back to Hanover, visited the growing prince.

The King was actually on one of his journeys home when he died of a stroke in 1727 and for the Prince and Princess of Wales, leaders of the 'Leicester House set', it was time to take up their roles of King and Queen. At last the royal parents were able to live as a family, joyfully reunited with their three eldest princesses, Anne, Amelia and Caroline. But the girls had doubtless been affected by their ten-year separation from their parents and took a long time to settle down. Their brother, poor Frederick, now Prince of Wales, was doomed to stay in Hanover. His parents, who had had complaints from his governor about his addiction to drink and cards when he was only nine, preferred to leave him there for a bit longer. Frederick was almost 22 when he arrived in London at last in 1729.

Life for George II and Caroline was orderly, almost humdrum. The court continued to be based at St James's, but the new King and Queen spent a lot of their time, as had George I before them, at Kensington in the spring and at Hampton Court in the summer, where the old King had made a lot of improvements. They sometimes went to Richmond, but rarely travelled far, except to Hanover every three years.

Caroline, who was intelligent and clever and loved meeting people, particularly liked Hampton Court. She knew that only the very young or active would trouble to travel so far from London, so she felt sure that when she held a drawing-room, she would be surrounded only by the people she really wanted to meet. She also loved the outdoor life which could be enjoyed to the full at Hampton Court—summer breakfasts of fruit and chocolate in the garden; time spent with the King, hunting or walking or riding together in the park. Dinner was served at three in the afternoon, and lasted for two hours; then it would be the children's turn to ride or walk with their mother. When the weather was bad they often had a musical evening, with Princess Anne playing the harpsichord while the others sang or read poetry.

Caroline, who read widely, was very knowledgeable on a lot of subjects. At a time when gin was commonly given to children as a sedative, when laudanum was an everyday medicine, when bleeding by applying leeches or cutting veins was a popular treatment for a number of ills, Queen Caroline had a surprisingly modern approach to medical matters. It is largely through her influence that innoculation for smallpox was introduced, inspired by a friend who had been to Constantinople and seen the practice. Caroline, who once had smallpox herself, was determined to put the idea to the test. As a safety check, the King allowed five criminals to be pardoned on condition that they had the innoculation. Seeing the guinea pigs survive unharmed, the Queen decided it would be safe to innoculate the children.

Caroline was an energetic woman who made

Frederick and his sisters, Mary, Louise and Caroline in the Banqueting House at Hampton Court.

sure that her children's quarters were run smoothly. For them it was an ordered existence. Lady Portland was governess to the youngest, but there was also a French Huguenot, Lady Charlotte de Roucy, who was the Princesses' companion, and Mrs Howard, later Lady Suffolk, who was in overall charge. Mrs Howard ran things with meticulous care, keeping note that small items, such as tuning the harpsichord and food for the pet birds amounted to £50 a year.

The Queen herself kept a watch on her daughters' wardrobes, and sent regular orders to lacemakers who were paid between £20 and £60 for pretty lace-trimmed bibs, aprons, caps and ruffles. For special occasions, such as birthdays, little dresses and suits were made entirely of lace. The custom of swaddling infants still continued until the end of the century and older children dressed like their parents. So the princesses wore petticoats spread over hoops, dresses and coats that were long and full, made of rich brocade, flowered silk, damask or velvet. They wore stylish hats and wigs that were the fashion for children and parents alike. The royal children had a new set of underclothes every two years and the old ones were given away as perks to their maids. Their shoes, which could not have been very hardwearing, had to be replaced every week, and fans cost eight guineas a year.

The Queen made sure the children were kept occupied every day. The fact that they didn't go to school, but had their own tutors, did not mean they had an easy time. Every minute appears to have been accounted for. On a typical day, the children got up at seven a.m., said their prayers, washed, dressed and had their breakfast by eight. For the next hour they took a walk, followed by an hour's reading and another hour of reading aloud. Learning by heart took another hour and the children spent a further hour at prayer before lunch—which also lasted an hour. They were allowed just an hour of recreation—a game of shuttlecock, a walk, or a talk about 'sensible things' before an hour of music practice, and then more study—and so on, at hourly intervals throughout the long day. Caroline, herself a woman with an enquiring mind and a love of learning, obviously expected her children to follow her example.

Walking was another great love, although the young princesses found it rather dull, and Caroline was responsible for the planting of a lot of new trees in the royal parks—Hyde Park, Kensington Gardens, St James's and Richmond—and for creating the Serpentine. In later years Kensington Palace became Queen Caroline's favourite home. She always stayed there when the King was away and in the gardens she kept a collection of small animals—tortoises sent to her by the Doge of Venice and a number of squirrels.

Yet despite the time and love Caroline gave to her children, her dislike for her eldest son grew more intense as the years went by. 'My first-born', she once remarked, 'is the greatest ass and the greatest liar and the greatest canaille and the greatest beast in the whole world, and I most heartily wish he was out of it.' She and her husband often wondered how they came to have such a son, and the King wished somebody could prove he was a changeling! He refused to let his son, the heir to the throne, have any responsibility. He would not make him a privy councillor, or appoint him Regent when he went to Hanover. Even Frederick's marriage to a most suitable bride did nothing to improve the relationship. Yet quite what the hapless Frederick had done to provoke such wrath is a mystery.

AUGUSTA
1719~1772

Possessive Mother

Augusta, who married the unloved Frederick Lewis, Prince of Wales, was the daughter of the Duke of Saxe-Gotha-Altenburg. They married in 1736 when he was 29, she 17. She, at least, had been approved by his parents as a suitable bride when she landed at Greenwich on the morning of Sunday, April 25. She then drove to Lambeth where the royal barge was waiting to take her to Whitehall to be presented to the King and Queen at St James's. It was a stately arrival for the new Princess of Wales, though she came with no servants and she spoke no English.

The wedding, an evening ceremony held in the chapel at St James's two days later, was quiet by royal standards. But although there were no processions, the shy teenage bride dressed in a silver gown and crimson robe was so overwhelmed by the occasion that she was sick. It could have been in anticipation of that most embarrassing tradition, the ceremonial bedding of the bride and groom, which followed the wedding supper. The Queen accompanied the Princess to her apartments, where she changed from her wedding gown into ceremonial nightclothes and was put to bed beside the groom—then all the guests filed through the bedchamber to see the newlyweds in bed.

A year later, when Frederick announced his wife was pregnant, Queen Caroline refused to believe him—in fact she refused to believe that the son she hated so much was capable of fathering a child. Amid rumours that this might be a changeling birth, the King and Queen insisted that Augusta should be at Hampton Court for the confinement. They were spending the summer there and they wanted to be present at the birth. The King refused to let Parliament grant Frederick an increased allowance, and he would not give him a residence of his own. Instead he had to make do with apartments in St James's Palace. Now it seemed the very existence of Augusta's baby was in question.

Queen Caroline decided that, come what may, she would witness her grandchild's arrival. Her son was equally determined to outwit his mother. But his foolhardy plan could have cost

Augusta her life. The couple obeyed his parents' command and moved into Hampton Court, but when Augusta went into labour late one evening Frederick put his plan in motion. It was a hot Sunday night in July 1737 when Augusta, her waters already broken and in great pain, was half dragged, half carried down the long corridors of Hampton Court, into a waiting carriage. With the help of Prince Frederick, assisted by Mr Donoyer, the dancing master, and Mr Bloodworth, an equerry, she was secretly smuggled at great speed along the bumpy road to London.

With the Princess went her dresser, two ladies-in-waiting and a man named Vried, the Prince's valet who was also a surgeon and mid-wife. The nightmare journey ended at St James's Palace, where the Princess, wrapped in two tablecloths, gave birth 45 minutes later to a daughter. She was a 'little rat of a girl, about the bigness of a large toothpick case' said one witness.

The King and Queen at Hampton Court were woken with the astonishing news of the birth at 1.30 in the morning. Caroline and her two eldest daughters at once set out for London. They arrived at St James's at 4 a.m. and Caroline kissed and congratulated her daughter-in-law saying 'Apparently, Madam, you have suffered terrible', to which the Princess nonchantly replied 'It is nothing.' And when Caroline saw the baby—'the poor little ugly she-mouse', she was completely satisfied that this was really the Princess's own child and not a substitute. 'It was a miracle', said the Queen 'that the Princess and her baby survived.'

The Princess was still confined to bed when her daughter was christened Augusta a month later. She watched the ceremony propped up on lace pillows in her huge state bed. The royal baptismal font was brought from the Tower for the ceremony but the King and Queen, who were godparents, were represented by proxy. Little Augusta lay in an ornamental cradle under a canopy of state, then she was placed on her nurse's knee on a silver-embroidered cushion.

In spite of the successful birth of the baby Princess, the King and Queen were still angry with their son. And history was repeated when King George, like his father before him, banished his son from St James's Palace. So Frederick and Augusta moved to the country air at Kew which was to become their family home.

It had been a difficult year for Queen Caroline with the anxiety surrounding the birth of her grandchild and ever-increasing tension between Frederick and the King. Before long her health broke. She had suffered a hernia at the birth of her last child several years before but, reluctant to give in to ill-health, she struggled on without complaint. She was taken ill while visiting her library in the Green Park, collapsed and had to return to the Palace. The King wanted to cancel the court that morning, but Caroline insisted that it should continue, as she did not want anyone to know she was ill. She actually went into the reception for a while, but the strain was too much and she retired in severe pain. In an attempt to

Augusta, Princess of Wales.

save her life, she was operated on for a strangulated bowel. During the operation, an elderly assistant, who was holding a candle, set fire to the surgeon's wig!

Caroline succeeded in keeping the cause of her illness a secret, even from the King, and she died in agony eleven days later, on November 20, 1737. On her deathbed she urged the King to marry again, but he said he would not. 'I shall have mistresses' he replied. And Frederick, the unloved son, was refused permission to see his mother before she died.

Banished from court, the Prince and Princess of Wales spent much of their time at Kew, but the Duke of Norfolk's house in St James's Square became their London home. It was the birthplace of their second child, the future George III. He was born two months premature—in June 1738 before any preparations had been made for the confinement, and within hours of the Princess's morning walk in the park. He was so small and frail and obviously not expected to live that he

was baptised shortly after his birth, and a gardener's wife, a Mrs Mary Smith, was hurriedly appointed to be the wet nurse. She was so successful that he grew into a plump well-rounded infant and, years after, the grateful King appointed her royal laundress, a job which was later passed on to her daughter.

Augusta had seven more children—Edward, Duke of York, Elizabeth, William, Duke of Gloucester, Henry, Duke of Cumberland, Louisa, Frederick and Caroline Matilda. Family life at Kew was well ordered, almost humdrum, but Frederick, whom Augusta called Fitz, who was so deprived of family life in his own boyhood, seemed determined that his own offspring should have a happier time. It was, in any case, a more relaxed period in which to grow up. Children in royal circles were treated less like adults and given a little more time to play and be free. Frederick planned the children's education—an arrangement with which the compliant Augusta was only too happy to agree. In addition to the classics, languages and mathematics, they were encouraged to dance, join in amateur theatricals and play the flute and harpsichord. Frederick also enjoyed playing outdoor games such as cricket and rounders with his children, and it was a game of cricket that cost him his life. He was hit on the head by a ball which knocked an abcess. It burst, and led to blood poisoning and he died only two months before the birth of Augusta's ninth child, Princess Caroline Matilda.

Augusta, suddenly a widow at 32 and mother of the 13-year-old heir to the throne, ignored the old family feud. The quarrel had been, after all, between her husband and the King, and she had only supported her husband as a loyal wife. Now, in her distress, she wrote to the King, commending herself and her children to his protection. He responded willingly and showed kindness and generosity towards the bereaved family. Little changed in the royal nursery, where stern but capable nurses and governesses ruled over their small charges and kept to a daily routine of a plain diet, regular exercise and less-

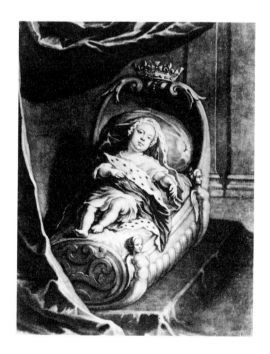

George III as a baby.

*The Earl of Bute, rumoured
to have been Augusta's lover.
A portrait by Reynolds.*

be groomed for kingship. The King, at the age of 67, realised that his teenage grandson had to be prepared for his succession, an event which could happen within the next few years.

Augusta, who was to be appointed Regent if the King died before her son reached his majority, also turned to John Stuart, Earl of Bute, a long-standing friend of her husband, for advice and support. She won too the support of William Pitt when the Regency Bill was put through Parliament, and in so doing defeated the wishes of her brother-in-law, the hated Duke of Cumberland, who had also claimed Regency rights. It was Cumberland, nicknamed 'Butcher', who six years earlier had crushed the Jacobite rebellion of 1745 and mercilessly slaughtered the Highlanders at Culloden. Augusta feared him, and she fiercely protected her son's right to the throne. A new Augusta emerged. The once timid, obedient wife developed into a forceful, matriarchal personality. And in spite of the King's overtures of friendship and the interest he now showed in his grandchildren's future, it was Augusta, the possessive, over-protective mother who remained in firm control of the family.

After the Prince of Wales' death, Augusta continued to live with her younger children at Kew and Leicester House in London, while Savile House next door was taken over for the household of the older children. Shielded by his mother from any bad influences, Prince George was isolated from society and denied, in his formative years, any practical training for kingship. And except for the company of his brothers and sisters, he lacked any companions of his own age. Augusta urged him constantly 'to be a king', but reared in such sheltered circumstances, he naturally grew up to be intensely shy, modest, and innocent of the outside world. Meanwhile, there was a growing belief, popular though unproven, that Augusta and the Earl of Bute were lovers; some gossips even said the couple were scheming against the prince.

In an effort to wean him away from his mother's influence, the King tried to turn the boy's thoughts towards marriage. He was 18

ons in the three R's. But the King reorganised the eduction of the elder children, particularly the princes'. The teachers who had been appointed by Frederick were replaced by tutors of the King's own choosing—for now George had to when his grandfather pointed out to him the attractions of a certain German Princess, Sophia Caroline Maria—a young lady the King himself admired, declaring that he would marry her himself if he were 20 years younger. Not surprisingly, it was Augusta who put her foot down, and persuaded her son that Sophia was not the girl for him: (in fact marriage plans were shelved until George was 23 and King of England, and the question of choosing a bride had become a matter of urgency). Meanwhile, the suggestion of marriage rejected, the old King made another attempt to push his grandson towards independence by offering him a separate establishment in one of the royal palaces. The offer met with a polite but predictable response. The Prince refused, saying it was his duty to stay with his mother.

George never forgot his duty to his mother who outlived her husband, her beloved Fitz, by more than 20 years. He became King on the death of his grandfather in 1760, and after his marriage at the age of 23 to Sophia Charlotte of Mecklenburg-Strelitz the couple visited Augusta every Saturday evening for the next 12 years. In the last months of her life, when it was obvious that she was dying of cancer of the throat, they called on her at her Carlton House home every night and her eldest daughter, Augusta, was called over from Germany to nurse her at the end. She died in 1772, unmourned by the majority of British people who accused her of being the domineering power behind the throne during the first years of her son's reign. She had certainly been autocratic and narrow-minded; over-zealous in her protectiveness of her children—who, except for George himself, largely blamed her for their unhappy marriages and misfortunes in later life.

Many of her nine children were frail. Princess Elizabeth died at the age of 19, in 1759, and her younger sister, Louisa, who had never been a strong child, died of consumption in 1768; Prince Frederick William died at 15 in 1765. Two years later his elder brother, Edward, Duke of York, who had always been Prince George's closest friend and who had been educated with him,

died in Monaco after catching a chill. Their two surviving brothers caused their mother a lot of pain by making socially unacceptable marriages: William, Duke of Gloucester, fell in love with the illegitimate daughter of a milliner and married her in secret, while Henry, Duke of Cumberland, settled down with a widow and commoner by the name of Anne Horton. But at least royal dukes had brides of their own choosing. They did not experience the terrible unhappiness endured by their sisters.

Augusta, whose dramatic birth had caused the final break between her father and the King, made a seemingly suitable marriage, but the high-born husband chosen for her, Charles, Prince of Brunswick, turned out to be cruelly unfaithful. Two of her children were born badly handicapped, one blind, the other insane; her eccentric daughter, Caroline, married her nephew, the Prince of Wales, and thus became the unpopular Queen of George IV. For years Augusta tried to hide the truth of her unhappiness from her family, but when her husband died of wounds in battle, leaving her almost penniless at the age of 70, her brother, George III, brought her home to England. He settled Augusta and her sons in a house at Blackheath where she lived until her death in 1813.

While Augusta, Duchess of Brunswick, had bravely endured her unhappy marriage into old age, her youngest sister, the high-spirited, attractive Caroline Matilda, the last of Augusta's children, had the most tragic life of all. She was married at 15 to her half-mad cousin, Christian VII of Denmark, and her story almost mirrors that of Sophia Dorothea, the mother of George II. Unwisely, the young Queen involved herself in politics and had an affair with a young doctor and reformer by the name of Struensee. He was executed and, but for the intervention of George III, Caroline, too, might have faced the same fate. She was released from Denmark, and taken to the castle at Celle in Hanover. She was forced to leave her little son and baby daughter behind and she never saw them again. Her health by then was breaking and she died at the age of 24.

SOPHIA CHARLOTTE
1744~1818

Sophia Charlotte, daughter of the Duke of Mecklenburg-Strelitz, married George III in 1761. George and his mother picked the bride from the eligible princesses listed in the New Berlin Almanac when a need for a consort became urgent, for he wanted to be married before his coronation in the autumn. They certainly chose a successful wife and mother, for Charlotte was destined to have 15 children before she was 40. She was also to prove as possessive and domineering as her mother-in-law.

At 17, a well-educated and independent girl, Charlotte was only too ready to break from her sheltered existence in Germany and take what-

Farmer's Wife

ever life offered in the exalted position of Queen of England. She had known nothing of her impending marriage until the day she went through an odd little ceremony, symbolic of marriage, with a British diplomat, a certain Mr Drummond, standing as proxy for the King. A week later she was on her way to England. Even nine gale-lashed days at sea did nothing to dampen her spirits.

George, it seems, was somewhat disappointed when he first saw his bride; a plain, thin girl with an upturned nose and unfashionably large mouth. They were married that same evening at St James's Palace and eyebrows were raised as her already lowcut bridal gown was revealingly

*Sophia Charlotte, known to her subjects as
Queen Charlotte, with her two eldest sons.*

dragged down even further by the weight of her violet velvet mantle secured on one shoulder by a large bunch of pearls. The effect, remarked Horace Walpole, was that 'the spectators knew as much of her upper half as the King'. But Charlotte had poise all the same. Even on her wedding night, in the interval between the supper and the ceremony at 10 o'clock she was relaxed enough to entertain the guests by singing and playing the harpsichord.

Any dreams Charlotte had of being queen of a glittering court must have quickly faded as she settled down to become the wife of George III. 'Farmer George', as he was affectionately known by his subjects, was a man of very simple tastes, modest, shy sometimes to the point of rudeness, and deeply religious. He was a faithful husband in an age when fidelity in court circles was rare, and he was devoted to Charlotte and their children. They were, in fact, a well-matched couple. The marriage was a long one and, until the King's illness made normal life impossible, extremely happy.

A year after their marriage, the King bought Buckingham House, which became known as the Queen's House—and, today, Buckingham Palace. Although close to St James's, it was regarded as a country retreat and all but the first of Charlotte's children were born there. Childbearing came very naturally indeed to Charlotte. Her children became her life. Two of her sons, George and William, became kings of England. Another son, Edward, was destined to be the father of Queen Victoria. And so we have the remarkable long-running record of Charlotte, her husband, sons and grand-daughter on the throne of England, spanning the years until the twentieth century.

The Queen's first child, the Prince of Wales, christened George Augustus Frederick, was born at St James's Palace and arrived easily in the care of the royal surgeon, Caesar Hunter, and midwife, Mrs Draper. 'The Queen scarce cried out at all,' said one of her attendants. The Prince was a beautiful baby. 'We examined him all over and found him perfect, with every mark of health and of a large size,' recorded Mr Hunter.

Although much of the old ritual surrounding a royal confinement had died out by this time, it was considered essential for a mother to stay in bed for a month after the birth. Although royal etiquette did not allow her to breastfeed, Charlotte chose to feed the infant herself with pap. The baby was also prescribed a soothing mixture of sweet almonds, rose syrup and rhubarb—a spoonful to be taken every hour.

The Queen was unwilling to eat solid food for a few days after the birth and preferred caudle (a mixture of warm eggs and wine), warm broth and tea. But chicken, a popular diet then for new mothers, seems to have been forced upon her. By the eighth day she had her appetite back and ate almost a whole chicken. She was also spending a little time out of bed each day. The custom of holding receptions during the lying-in period continued, so every day crowds of noble ladies, not only from Britain but from the Continent as well, called at the palace to view the new-born prince. They filed into the room in groups of up to 40 at a time to see the child, resting on a velvet cushion on the lap of his wet nurse, a Mrs Margaret Scott. She had just had her 12th child and was, therefore, very experienced at breastfeeding. She sat with the Prince by his cradle, sheltered behind a light latticed screen so the visitors couldn't get too close, and the guests were served with huge quantities of cake and caudle. Five hundred pounds of cake, at a cost of £40, and eight gallons of caudle went in a single day.

Charlotte's second child, Frederick, Duke of York, was born the following year, and by then Buckingham House was ready. It was more modern, better ventilated and, therefore, better for the Queen's confinements. But the baby arrived so quickly that Mr Hunter could not get to the royal bedside in time. Only Mr Hawkins, the obstetrician, and Mrs Draper, once again the midwife, were there. It was August, a time of intense heat and thunderstorms which caused the Queen a lot of discomfort in an otherwise uneventful birth.

The Queen had a miscarriage the following year, then another son, William, Duke of Clarence (the future William IV). He was born quickly in the early hours of August 9, 1765, not long after his mother had returned from dinner in Richmond feeling vaguely tired.

Baby number four was born the following September—at last a daughter. She was christened Charlotte Augusta Matilda, but she became known as Princess Royal, while her mother nicknamed her 'Michaelmas Goose'. A year later came Edward, Duke of Kent, the son who was to be the father of Queen Victoria. His weight was unrecorded, but he was the largest baby the Queen had ever seen.

And so the pattern continued, with Charlotte taking her pregnancies so much in her stride that when she was expecting her second daughter, Augusta, she went to a birthday ball in her 33rd week of pregnancy and danced four times with the King of Denmark. Charlotte was pregnant every year for the first eight years of marriage. She had a break in 1769, but was pregnant again by the following year. The baby, Elizabeth, was followed by Ernest, Augustus, Adolphus, Mary, Sophia, Octavius, Alfred and Amelia, and her confinements got easier and easier. Before Ernest's arrival she attended a reception in the morning and gave birth to him in the afternoon, after only 15 minutes labour.

She was so successful at motherhood that when one of her sons, Octavius, the most attractive of all her children and a favourite of his parents, was suddenly struck down with a severe illness and died within 48 hours at the age of four, it was remarked that by losing a child, Charlotte had become 'a proper mother'. Such was the mortality rate in the past that the grief of losing one's children was an accepted part of motherhood.

In fact Charlotte, like Queen Caroline before her, was keenly interested in medical matters and often over-zealous in regard to her children's health. They were often made to undergo drastic treatments of the day, such as blistering and bleeding, quite needlessly for mild childhood complaints, and little Octavius is thought to have died as a result of smallpox vaccination. (Another son, Alfred, had also died in infancy after a long illness the year before.) Amelia, the youngest of Charlotte's children and the King's favourite daughter, was always delicate. In her teens she had tuberculosis of the knee and finally died of consumption at 27. Her lifelong ill-health was always blamed on early weaning, because her wet nurse had been called hurriedly out of service.

It was not long before Buckingham House was too small for the fast increasing family. They began to spend more time at Windsor and their home at Kew was extended. The eldest sons were moved into their own residences, with their tutors and staff, in houses overlooking the Green at Kew. Their lessons began at seven each morning, and they were instructed mainly in English literature, languages, mathematics and religion, and their sisters, particularly the tomboyish Augusta, joined them in cricket, hockey and football. But they proved to be rebellious young pupils, hard for their tutors to handle. Their father, who made himself responsible for his sons' upbringing, sent the boys abroad around 1780: Adolphus to university at Gottingen at the early age of 12, Augustus at 14 and Ernest at 15. William, who became the sailor prince, was sent to sea at 13. After academic studies came military training in Hanover from the age of 17. The King, it seems, was content to keep his sons away from home.

Only the Prince of Wales, the darling of the nursery, was exempt. His position as heir to the throne precluded him from taking risks, although he was part of the social scene at a very early age. He was installed as a Knight of the Garter at three and from the age of ten he and his brother Frederick were seen at their father's levées. Then, in addition to their own house at

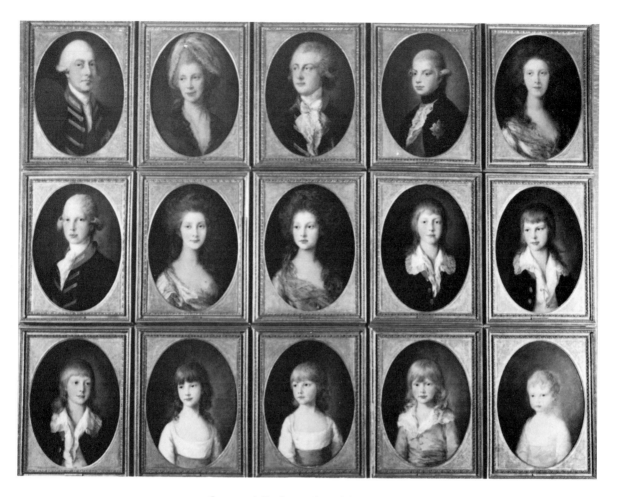

George and Charlotte and 13 of their children.

Kew, they had their own apartments at Buckingham House. But the wild ways of the Prince of Wales were soon becoming evident, so at 17 his companion Frederick was sent to Hanover to escape his brother's bad influence.

Charlotte's daughters, meanwhile, were growing up in what was described by one of the princesses as the atmosphere of a nunnery, under the complete domination of their well-meaning but prim and possessive mother. Their education was in the hands of their governess, Lady Charlotte Finch, a woman of considerable intellect who was appointed to her position on the birth of the Prince of Wales and stayed with the family for 30 years. Her assistant governesses were equally devoted to the royal children; some gave their lives to the job, teaching the princes until they were old enough to be educated by tutors, then becoming important influences in the lives of the princesses— eventually intimate companions and lifelong friends.

It was the King who set the pattern of life in the royal household; it was a rigid routine. He rose at 5 a.m., called his daughters, then set and lit his own fire and made tea before morning prayers. He had the simple tastes of a country gentleman. In the morning he went walking or hunting; he rode his horses hard. In an age when the rich ate vast meals he dined frugally—leg of mutton was a favourite dish—and he was quick to stop any sign of extravagance in the royal kitchen. Fruit, unless grown on the estate, was banned from the table. The children ate in relays according to age, and the King and Queen rarely entertained. When they did, hospitality was far from lavish.

Unless they were away, attending a special function, the family spent the evening at their own pursuits. Literary and artistic interests were encouraged. Often one of the family read aloud from the extensive library, or the Queen summoned a specially-auditioned reader for the evening. They were a musical family; Bach was a favourite, and on some evenings there was a royal rendering on the flute, clavichord or harpsichord. Meanwhile the princesses worked on their drawings or watercolours. Elizabeth was a particularly gifted artist. But they were monotonous evenings for the young princesses. Conversation was limited because Charlotte's strict code of etiquette made any normal exchange of talk virtually impossible. No child was allowed to speak unless first spoken to; everyone had to stand in their parents' company until offered a chair, and always walk backwards when leaving their presence. The children had impeccable manners from a very early age, but such rigid rules did not encourage warm relationships.

The King loved all his children in babyhood; he even made frequent early morning visits to the nursery. But he failed to see eye-to-eye with his young sons when they began to develop what he considered to be rebellious tendencies, and that's when he decided they should finish their education abroad. His daughters he loved dearly all his life, and the affection was mutual. Charlotte, however, seems to have had little true maternal love. Certainly she was thought incapable of showing outward affection towards her children. She loved them in her own way; she was proud of them; she lavished time on them and fussed over their education. She protected them from all outside influences which she considered might harm them in any way. But she remained cool in her affection, and some of her daughters actually said in later years that they felt deprived of her love. As a family, they were often just as much exposed to the public gaze as the royal family today. In spite of several assassination attempts on the King's life, they continued to move among their subjects who flocked in their thousands at holiday times to glimpse the family walking on Kew Green or in the botanic gardens. There was also the quaint custom of terracing at Windsor—when the Queen could be seen on certain days walking with her family and attendants in crocodile formation around the terraces. They were a good-looking family, attractive, tall and blond with rosy cheeks. With some of the younger princes, as well as a baby or two, they must have made a pretty sight for royalty watchers. But sometimes the open spaces of Windsor were too public for the Queen, and she and her daughters were forced to seek some seclusion in the garden of a gamekeeper's cottage.

Birthdays were the highspots of the year for the children. Gifts were presented after morning prayers, an orchestra played at breakfast and everyone had a new outfit for the occasion. Sometimes the birthday treat was a river trip or a ceremonial drive complete with military band escort. When the Prince of Wales was four a fancy dress party was held for him at Richmond. The birthday Prince went as a sailor, his brother, Frederick, as a clown and William, the baby, as a 'mademoiselle'. Older children were taken to the opera or the theatre and given a breakfast or garden party until in their late teens, when a grown-up ball or banquet was held in their honour. With such a large family, these celebrations came round frequently, and the children looked forward to them with mounting excitement since they broke up the monotony of the daily routine at Kew.

In 1788 came what was to prove the turning point in Queen Charlotte's life. The King fell ill. It was described as a serious bilious attack, and when he was able to travel he went with the Queen and their three eldest daughters to Chel-

*It was a regular custom for George III and his family
to parade on the terraces at Windsor.*

tenham to take the waters. The attack was, in fact, the first sign of the distressing illness the King was to suffer during the last years of his reign. The exact diagnosis is uncertain. It is thought to have been a rare inherited disease, porphyria, caused by a disturbance of the breakdown products of the red blood pigment but the true nature of his illness still baffles doctors today.

The King's doctors advised him that the newly fashionable sea-bathing therapy would be beneficial. And so in 1789 the King and Queen and their daughters began the habit of taking seaside holidays, a custom which they were to continue for the next 16 years. They chose Weymouth, where the Duke of Gloucester had a house in which they stayed for three months every summer. Sea-bathing then was a serious business. It took place in the early morning, involving all the paraphernalia of bathing machines and attendants, and the whole town turned out to see the royal party take to the waves. Charlotte was not an enthusiastic bather, but Augusta and two of her sisters, Sophia and Amelia, went for a dip under doctors' orders. Sea-bathing in those days was practised mainly for medical reasons, not for fun.

When the King and Queen and their daughters were not jumping in the waves they were sailing on them. Almost every day, even in the roughest weather, they cruised in the bay on a warship on loan from the Navy. In the evening the royal party often patronised the local theatre and sat through concert party entertainment. It must have been a delightful and exciting experi-

A formal family group
at Buckingham Palace.
A painting by Zoffany.

ence for the princesses: their first chance of travel. For most of their young lives their world was strictly bounded by the royal houses in London, Richmond, Kew and Windsor, and they rarely moved beyond the Home Counties.

For the rest of the year, the same humdrum life continued, and as time went by Charlotte became more and more possessive. She held her daughters' purse-strings, chose their clothes, decided which books (mostly the improving kind) they were allowed to read. They reached their twenties, even thirties, waiting in vain to be freed by marriage into the arms of suitable husbands, but offers they received were vetoed. The

King and Queen could not bear the thought of parting with their daughters. The Princess Royal eventually won her cause, and Charlotte herself stage-managed the wedding, to Prince Frederick of Würsternberg, and even made her daughter's dress. Meanwhile the other sisters waited; everything had to be done according to seniority.

The princes and princesses were loyal to one another, supportive and affectionate. The princes, when young, were treated severely—the King gave permission for them to be beaten, if necessary, but they nevertheless grew up to be boisterous larger-than-life figures who mainly lived abroad, far from the disapproving eyes of their parents. The princesses were barred from corresponding with their brothers although, with the aid of friends, letters were smuggled between them, and they remained firm allies.

In spite of all the chaperoning, Charlotte's daughters contrived to indulge in illicit love affairs. Sophia and, it is rumoured, Elizabeth as well, gave birth to a child. Sophia was 23 when she married an equerry, shortly before her confinement at Weymouth. Elizabeth's pregnancy as a young girl was treated as a mysterious 'illness' and it is thought she went through an illegal marriage service. She was almost 50 when, still against the warnings of her mother, she married Frederick, Prince of Hesse-Homburg, and settled down to have 11 happy years with him until his death in 1829. Mary married her cousin, the Duke of Gloucester, Augusta had a relationship with an equerry until his death 28 years later. Even Amelia, Charlotte's youngest child, the invalid of the family and the King's most precious daughter had a poignant little love affair with a general before her death.

While Charlotte's daughters were conducting clandestine relationships, her sons were less discreet. For a mother who had tried so hard to bring her children up to be correct, they must have been a great disappointment. And with the King's health deteriorating she sought solace at Frogmore, her own retreat at Windsor. In 1811, when she had to acknowledge that the King would not recover, George, Prince of Wales, Prinny, as he was known, was being particularly troublesome to his parents. He had extravagant tastes, a love of rich living, a fondness for gambling and an eye for the ladies—altogether a way of life which was not compatible with the sober round at his father's court. But for all his faults, Charlotte loved her eldest son and she forgave him when he gave in to his sisters' request for their own allowance. They had patiently waited until they were in their thirties and forties before making their bid for a little freedom. Once their brother was proclaimed Regent they saw their chance and appealed to him for an independent allowance to be granted through Parliament (until then their money had been doled out to them like pocket money). He also gave his sisters the use of apartments at Buckingham Palace, which meant they could visit the capital when they chose. The bonds had finally been broken—or so they thought. In fact Queen Charlotte was so distressed by her daughters' rebellion that they had to reassure her that she would still be notified about their plans.

Dropsy that had originated with the birth of Prince Alfred in 1780 worsened over the years and Charlotte came to depend more on her family for support. She lived on to see the marriages, in middle age, of her daughters Mary and Elizabeth, and the birth, marriage and death of her granddaughter Charlotte. By then she had lost her hold over the daughters who had so patiently accepted her dominance over them for the love of their father.

She faded away at the age of 74 in November 1818. She sat in her armchair, the Prince Regent holding her hand, Augusta and Mary dutifully at her side. The King, solitary in his dementia, outlived her by two years. He died aged 81 in 1820, five years after Waterloo, and closed a reign of 60 years.

CAROLINE OF BRUNSWICK
1768~1821

The Unwanted Queen

Caroline Amelia Elizabeth, daughter of the Duke of Brunswick and Augusta, a sister of George III, married George, Prince of Wales in April 1795, 16 years before he became Regent. It was a disastrous marriage, doomed from the start. For George, it was a marriage of convenience—and for money. He was hugely in debt because of his enormous extravagances, and he had no intention of cutting down on his pleasures. He loved to entertain lavishly in the splendour of his pleasure palace, the Royal Pavilion at Brighton, and he spent vast sums on his huge art collection; on racing and hunting and on his numerous mistresses. He had already been married for ten years to Mrs Maria Fitzherbert, a Catholic widow some years older than himself, but the marriage, which had taken place secretly, had been declared illegal by Parliament.

The first meeting between George IV and Princess Caroline.

In 1795, at the age of 33, he decided that marriage to a suitable Protestant wife would solve his financial problems. Parliament would grant him money and he would be able to pay off his debts. When he told his parents, King George III and Queen Charlotte, of his intentions, they were delighted, and looked forward to the additional benefit of the birth of an heir. By this time George had, in any case, lost interest in Mrs Fitzherbert and despite his marriage arrangements, he had turned his attentions to the Countess of Jersey, who was nine years older and a grandmother. He found her captivating, and decided that nothing—including marriage—would prevent him from enjoying her company. He ensured that she would become part of the royal household by appointing her one of Princess Caroline's ladies of the bedchamber, and it was Lady Jersey who travelled to Greenwich to meet George's bride-to-be.

The Prince knew very little about Caroline of Brunswick. Although first cousins, they had never met and he sent a friend, Lord Malmesbury, to make the negotiations and accompany the Princess on her journey to England. It is a pity he did not make more searching enquiries about her himself, because it seems that everyone else knew the shortcomings of the King's eccentric niece. Even Queen Charlotte hinted darkly that all was not well with Caroline. But no one wanted to offend the King, her uncle, so the wedding went ahead.

So what was wrong with Caroline? And why was she the cause of so much concern, so many whisperings and rumours? For a start, her appearance was described as short, thick-set and graceless, her behaviour coarse, her conversation tasteless—and her dress slovenly and dirty! Before she arrived in England, she had to be coached in the elegant ways of the court; she was told she would have to wash more often—all over—and be far more particular about changing her underclothes.

Queen Charlotte, her future mother-in-law, heard even worse reports: that Caroline was in love with a commoner and she was over-sexed to such an extent that she had to be chaperoned from room to room. Her governess even had to follow her at dances for fear she would get into indecent conversations and make an exhibition of herself. Clearly the Prince had chosen badly, yet no one had troubled to warn him.

The couple disliked one another on sight. When they first met, Caroline was shocked to find the Prince much fatter than she had expected; and Caroline failed to follow the advice about her underwear so that the Prince, overcome by the smell, had to ask for a glass of brandy. At this late stage, though, he had no choice but to go ahead with the marriage, which took place at St James's Palace. The bride, given away by the King, was happy, the groom morose, and the Archbishop of Canterbury looked worried when, during the service, he had to ask if anyone knew of any impediment to lawful marriage.

The service over, the Prince consoled himself with so much brandy that when the newlyweds retired for the night, he fell into the hearth of the bedchamber and slept there until early morning. It is not known how often they slept together as man and wife, but Caroline was very soon pregnant and, once this was confirmed, the Prince coldly informed her by letter that he no longer intended to treat her as his wife. Although they tried to keep up appearances for the sake of the King and Queen, their relationship was strained from the very first few days of married life at Brighton. Their dislike for one another was mutual and soon grew to hatred. To the Prince, accustomed to the opulence he had created at Brighton, grace, elegance and dignity were everything. He truly despised poor Caroline for her gauche manners, her rough exuberance and lack of good taste. She, while listening patiently to the criticism and advice which was heaped upon her, objected to the presence of the Prince's

mistress. The couple were soon living separate lives and rarely spoke, but Caroline spent most of her pregnancy at Brighton.

Queen Charlotte, with her own long experience of motherhood, was ever ready with advice for the mother-to-be. She persuaded the Princess to choose a cradle without rockers and assisted in the appointment of a wet nurse named Mrs Smith. When the Princess developed a particular craving for pork the Queen arranged for milk-fed piglets to be sent to her. It seems that in spite of her shortcomings, Caroline was on good terms with her mother-in-law.

The baby, a big beautiful girl, arrived almost exactly nine months after the wedding on the morning of January 7, 1796 in the presence of the Archbishop of Canterbury, the Chancellor, the Dukes of Gloucester, Devonshire and Leeds and several other nobles. The birth, at Carlton House, the Prince's London residence, was not an easy one. The labour was long and the baby, noted Queen Charlotte, was immense. There was slight disappointment that the baby was not a boy, but she was received by the Prince of Wales with 'all the affection possible'. The King, who preferred girls anyway, said, quite truthfully, that he 'always wished it would be of that sex'. And told his son, 'You are both young and I trust will have many children.'

But it was not to be. The baby, christened Charlotte after her grandmother, the Queen, was to be Caroline's only child. The Prince of Wales moved out of Carlton House when his daughter was born. Three days after the birth he made his will, bequeathing everything to Maria Fitzherbert, 'who is my wife in the eyes of God and who is and ever will be such in mine.' To Caroline he left one shilling. The marriage which had broken up as soon as it began was at an end and Caroline asked the King for protection.

Soon the secret was out. Newspapers printed every twist and turn in the royal rift and public sympathy supported the wronged Princess, who seemed, at first, to be living an exemplary life. The King appointed her Ranger of Greenwich in

Caroline with Princess Charlotte.

1798, and she moved with her little daughter to a house in Blackheath. She took an interest in gardening, and vegetables from the estate were sold at Covent Garden; she learnt to play the harp, studied to improve her English, painted a little and gave time to charitable works. Caroline also entertained leading personalities of the day; artists, writers, and politicians began visiting Blackheath, where she attracted a glittering circle to rival Prinny's set at the Pavilion.

Ever since Charlotte's birth, Caroline had quarrelled with the Prince of Wales over their daughter's custody. Caroline's lifestyle, now increasingly the subject of conjecture, did little to help her cause. When, in 1802, she adopted one William Austin, the son of a dockworker, as a charitable act, rumour spread that he was her own and, in 1806, the King set up an enquiry. The Royal Commission, which became known as the 'Delicate Investigation', proved the rumours unfounded, but the royal family had lost confidence in Caroline's ability to bring up the heir to the throne. When little Charlotte was eight, the King became her guardian, and took responsibility for his granddaughter's education. He appointed governesses and tutors to instruct her in languages and literature, history, geography, religion and music. She lived at Carlton House when her father was in residence, at other times at Windsor or Kew with her grandparents. Meetings with her mother were strictly limited.

And so Caroline lost any influence she might have had over her daughter. Instead, Charlotte became the darling of her grandparents, the King and Queen, and the Princesses who, as adoring aunts, showered her with gifts and attention. They loved the bright, quick-witted little girl. But in spite of the old Queen's influence, her careful training and love of decorum, Charlotte was rude and unruly. She had inherited her mother's rebellious streak.

As Caroline's way of life became even more unseemly in the eyes of the royal family, the Prince of Wales announced that the time his daughter spent at his wife's Kensington Palace apartment would be limited still further. The once-a-week meetings for dinner that Caroline enjoyed with her daughter—always with approved companions—were cut to once a fortnight. Although the rules were, in reality, disregarded, the King eventually banned all contact between mother and daughter.

Life at Windsor, with elderly grandparents and middle-aged aunts, probably represented security at first to the little girl caught in a tug-of-war between quarrelling parents. But by the time she reached her teens she must have found the quiet, cloistered atmosphere at the castle very tedious indeed. It is thought that she preferred her father's company to her mother's. Caroline, who saw her daughter so rarely, did not—possibly could not—give her all the affection she might have done under normal circumstances. Caroline was in fact much closer to her adopted son, William Austin, who went everywhere with her, even sharing her bedroom as a child.

In spite of Charlotte's careful chaperoning, Caroline actually contrived to encourage her daughter in a relationship with a captain in the Hussars. It is a curious story, which shocked the Prince of Wales when Charlotte told him how her mother let the admirer into the palace by a garden door and then locked the pair in her bedroom. Caroline's motives have never been explained; it was rumoured that she wanted to discredit Charlotte in favour of William Austin. Fortunately, the Captain behaved with dignity and restraint.

The Prince of Wales certainly found his daughter hard to handle. As a teenager she grew to detest the sheltered life at Windsor, where the once loving aunts were now sternly critical. When at 16 she asked for her own household and servants, and actually begged the Prime Minister to intercede on her behalf, the Prince was furious. In 1811, when the Prince became Regent and Caroline was barred from his presence, in public or private, Charlotte was struggling for her own identity. The solution, though, was obvious. Marriage.

She was a determined young lady who wanted

George IV—'A voluptuary under the horrors of digestion.'
A cartoon by Gillray.

meant living abroad—something to which she was bitterly opposed. In the family row which followed, she fled from her apartments in Warwick House, hailed a hackney cab at Charing Cross and dashed across town to seek her mother's sympathy. But Caroline was not at home when Charlotte got to Connaught Place and had to be fetched from Blackheath. Throughout that evening there came a constant stream of visitors. The Lord Chancellor, the Bishop of Salisbury and several other advisors argued all night. Eventually Charlotte was granted her wish not to marry the Prince of Orange, but this did not mean she could marry the Russian prince either. Back in her father's custody, Charlotte stayed first at Carlton House, then in strict seclusion at Cranbourne Lodge.

Although Charlotte was now barred from any contact with her mother, she felt deserted when Caroline, now banned from official functions in England, sailed for the Continent in 1814. For her travels, she assumed the title of Countess of Wolfenbuttel; and her grand tour of Europe was to keep her away from England for the next seven years. And Charlotte, now threatened by the very real possibility that her parents might divorce, knew that if her father remarried and had an heir, she would no longer be in line to the throne.

a say in the matter. She was attracted by the young Duke of Devonshire, but he was not of royal blood, so marriage was out. The Regent suggested the Prince of Orange, and at first Charlotte agreed in a half-hearted way, until she set eyes on Prince Augustus of Russia and, to her father's anger, broke off the engagement. Marriage to the Prince of Orange, she discovered,

CHARLOTTE
1796~1817

Princess Charlotte, boisterous, outspoken, headstrong, one of the few princesses in history who said 'no'—and meant it—was now once again reconciled to her father and married a man of her choice, and of whom her father also approved. He was Leopold, Prince of Saxe-Coburg, the future King of the Belgians. And it was a real love match. The marriage took place on a May evening in 1816 and the bride, wearing a silver gown with diamonds in her hair, was cheered by

The Tragic Princess

waiting crowds of Londoners who stood for hours to watch her leave for the ceremony. It was a simple, moving service in the Crimson Room at Carlton House. The Regent, no doubt relieved that his difficult daughter was now off his hands gave her, according to one of the guests, 'a good hearty, paternal hug.'

The couple spent their honeymoon at Oatlands, the home of the Duke and Duchess of York near Weybridge, then settled down happily to married life at the country house which had been acquired for them—Claremont, near Esher in Surrey. Charlotte was a popular princess and the public eagerly waited for news of a royal baby. After two miscarriages, Princess Charlotte naturally began to worry that she would have difficulty having a baby, so when she became pregnant a third time her doctor, Dr Baillie, called in a highly regarded specialist, Sir Richard Croft, for advice. He prescribed regular bleeding and a light diet and the birth was forecast for early October.

October came and went and the doctors appeared unworried by the baby's failure to arrive. But Charlotte herself was deeply depressed. She seems to have had a foreboding, a premonition that all was not well. Although officially forbidden to do so, she wrote to the one person she obviously needed, her mother. In a sad, dramatic letter, she poured out her feelings.

Charlotte was one of the few royal princesses to die in childbirth.

'Why is not my mother allowed to pour cheerfulness into the sinking heart of her inexperienced child? . . . I have but one mother and no variation of place or circumstance can remove her from my mind . . . Not for myself but for my mother a pang of terror shoots across my bewildered brain . . . Believe me, my adored mother, I fear less to die than to live.'

She eventually went into labour on November 3 with her obstetrician, Sir Richard Croft, in attendance; the labour lasted for 50 hours. But Charlotte's longed-for baby, a boy, was born dead. Her doctors tried desperately to save him. Brandy was poured into his mouth in an attempt to revive him, his lungs were inflated, he was given a warm bath—and even rubbed with salt and mustard—all to no avail.

Charlotte herself appeared to recover from the ordeal, but she fell ill later that night and complained of severe pain. Her doctors were recalled and tried to ease her agony with large quantities of brandy and hot water. They fought to save her but by morning she, too, was dead. She was 21 years old.

Her mother, Caroline, was far away on the Adriatic coast of Italy when news reached her that her daughter was dead. She, like the rest of the family, reacted with shock and disbelief; Charlotte's father, the Prince Regent, and her husband, Prince Leopold, were heartbroken. The future hope for the Hanoverian line, the girl who married for love, was gone.

Blame for the tragedy was placed on Sir Richard Croft. It became a subject for debate and controversy among the medical profession. Although he was exonerated by the Prince Regent and by fellow doctors, Sir Richard broke under the strain and shot himself three months later. The exact cause of Charlotte's death remained a mystery. Some suggested the Princess had porphyria, the mysterious blood disorder said to have killed George III, while others believed that the use of instruments earlier in the delivery might have saved her. Whatever the truth, it is a tragic story.

ADELAIDE
1792 ~ 1849

The Good Stepmother

Of all Queen Charlotte's many children, the Prince of Wales was the only one to have fathered an heir. If Charlotte's son had lived he would have inherited the throne. Instead the Prince, later George IV, was succeeded by his younger brother, the Duke of Clarence, who became William IV (the Queen's second son, the Duke of York, having died before him).

In 1817, after the death of Princess Charlotte, there was an urgent need for her uncles, the royal dukes, to marry and produce legitimate children. Persuaded by the incentive of an increased allowance if they married, the Dukes of Clarence, Kent and Cambridge all made a dash to the altar, having chosen for themselves legal wives of royal blood. The 53-year-old William, Duke of Clarence, who for 20 years had lived at Bushy, near Windsor, with an actress Mrs Dorothy Jordan, by whom he had ten children, married

Adelaide longed for motherhood but was a generous stepmother.

Princess Adelaide of Saxe-Meiningen; Edward, Duke of Kent, aged 51, who for 29 years had travelled round the world with his French Canadian mistress, Madame de St Laurent, settled down to married life with Princess Victoire of Saxe-Coburg, sister of the widowed Prince Leopold; and Adolphus, Duke of Cambridge, was married to Augusta of Hesse-Cassel.

Both the Duke of Kent and the Duke of Clarence chose to marry at Kew on the same July day in 1818. The new Duchess of Clarence attracted little admiration when she was launched into London society. Princess Adelaide of Saxe-Meiningen, 25 years old was, by all accounts, plain, mousey and prim. Outwardly she had few assets. But she was eagerly looking forward to motherhood. She was patient, kind and loved children, and with great generosity she promised to welcome William's surviving nine children as her own. She proved to be the ideal wife for she had a settling influence on the slightly eccentric sailor prince who once counted Nelson amongst his friends.

William was disappointed to find that his allowance on marriage was not as much as he had hoped so the couple settled in Hanover, where they could live quietly, away from the excesses of the English court, and by the following year Adelaide was expecting her first child. Sadly she became ill with pneumonia during the pregnancy and the treatment she received led to a premature birth. The baby, a daughter named Charlotte Augusta, survived only a few hours. Adelaide was heavily pregnant for the second time when the Duke and Duchess travelled back to England to attend the wedding of William's eldest son. But the long drive over rough roads proved too much for Adelaide. She collapsed as they were approaching the coast near Calais and the pregnancy ended in miscarriage. Bravely Adelaide crossed the Channel and spent the next six weeks recovering at Walmer Castle.

Still the couple continued to be indefatigable travellers, constantly on the move between her family in Bavaria and his in England. They were back in London for the wedding of another of William's children when Adelaide gave birth to another girl. Although premature, Elizabeth Georgina Adelaide was a healthy baby and seemed to thrive, but the Duchess' happiness was shortlived. Four months later her daughter suffered inflammation of the bowel and died. Adelaide's next pregnancy also ended in bitter disappointment when she miscarried twins. Although there were rumours of other pregnancies, this was the last recorded.

Destined never to have children of her own, Adelaide nevertheless became a devoted step-mother and grandmother. Her husband's brood, the Fitzclarences, were not always easy to handle. Although his five pretty daughters were all married off easily into noble families, the sons quarrelled endlessly with their father as they pressed him for titles and appropriate allowances with which to keep up their status in life. But by 1830 when William had succeeded to the throne, he and Adelaide delighted in the company of numerous Fitzclarence grandchildren, whose laughter was frequently heard echoing through those once sombre halls at Windsor.

Although obviously saddened by her inability to bear healthy children, Queen Adelaide was not embittered. When a baby called Victoria, the future Queen of England, was born to her sister-in-law, the Duchess of Kent, she touchingly wrote: 'My children are dead, but your child lives, and she is mine too.'

VICTOIRE, DUCHESS OF KENT
1786 ~ 1861

Mother of a Legend

Victoire, daughter of the Duke of Saxe-Coburg-Saafeld, was 32 years old and a widow when Edward, Duke of Kent, proposed to her in 1818. She had previously been married to the Prince of Leiningen by whom she had two children, Charles, then 16 and Feodore, 11. Charles, as heir of the principality, had to finish his education in Hanover, but for Feodore her mother's marriage was to mean a new life in England. Victoire and Edward were married at Coburg in May, and there was a second double wedding ceremony, with William, Duke of Clarence, and his bride Adelaide at Kew in July. The royal race to produce an heir was on.

By the following year four duchesses were pregnant. Adelaide, Duchess of Clarence, miscarried her baby, but Augusta, Duchess of Cambridge, and Frederica, Duchess of Cumberland, both produced sons whom they called George.

But on May 24 Victoire, Duchess of Kent, had a pretty little daughter, 'as plump as a partridge', and the plump princess was first in line.

While he was eager for an heir, the Prince Regent did not want his brothers' offspring to be born in England and increase his financial burden. The Duke of Kent, anxious that his wife's confinement should be on home ground, argued his case. Eventually the Prince gave his consent, made a ship available for the sea-crossing and had apartments set aside at Kensington Palace.

The Duchess, already the mother of two, was well prepared for the event and brought with her Charlotte Siebold, who was not only a midwife of renown but a doctor as well. Her presence caused raised eyebrows and doubtless professional jealousy among the royal physicians, but Victoire was adamant. Charlotte Siebold, a

Victoire in old age.

woman doctor, was indeed a rarity, but she was highly thought of in Germany. Back in Coburg, three months later, she delivered another child, the son of Louise, Duchess of Saxe-Coburg-Saalfeld. He was called Albert, and destined to be the future Prince Consort.

Victoire had other firm ideas about motherhood. Her baby, born at Kensington Palace, while the Archbishop of Canterbury, the Duke of Wellington and other notable witnesses gathered in an adjoining room, was not to be handed over to a wet nurse. She dismissed the young lady from Islington who had been hired for the job and insisted on feeding the child herself.

The Prince Regent announced that the christening should be a low-key affair, for the royal family were not popular, least of all the Duke of Kent who, as a military leader, was known for his cruelty, and was also hugely in debt. The public were not in the mood for a show of lavish ceremonial, so the traditional gold font was taken from the Tower of London to

the Cupola Room at Kensington Palace. There Victoire's daughter was baptised by the Archbishop of Canterbury, and given the names Alexandrina Victoria: Alexandrina after the Czar of Russia, who was a godfather, and Victoria after her mother. The Prince Regent, also a godfather, vetoed other names which were suggested. Charlotte, he said, was definitely not allowed. No doubt because it would remind him too painfully of his own lost daughter.

Mounting debts prevented the Duke and his family staying at Kensington Palace, so that autumn they left London to live quietly at a cottage in Sidmouth, Devon. On the journey down to the West Country the Duke caught a chill from which he never fully recovered. After walking in the snow one January day he developed pneumonia and died within hours. Victoire, at the age of 34, was a widow for the second time; her little daughter was only eight months old. A few days later came the announcement that the old King George III had died at Windsor and his son, the Prince Regent, was now George IV. Baby Victoria (as Alexandrina was known) moved nearer to the throne.

Alone and penniless in a foreign country, ignored by most of her husband's relatives— even the new King was coolly indifferent towards her—Victoire might have taken her baby back to the comfort of her own home in Germany but for the advice of her brother Leopold. He had remained in England after the death of his wife, Princess Charlotte, and he urged the Duchess to stay and safeguard her daughter's claim to the throne. With his financial assistance she returned once more to the apartment at Kensington Palace which she made her home. Her elder daughter, Feodore, now in her teens, continued to be taught by her governess, the faithful Louise Lehzen, who had travelled with the family from Germany, but every spare moment Feodore spent in the nursery with her adorable half-sister—often affectionately called Drina by the family. The wide age gap between the two girls meant there was no jealousy, just mutual

*Feodore was not to spoil
Victoria's chances.*

a tiger, all of them gifts from kings and emperors of faraway places. And a magical moment for the little Princess was when she actually danced before the King at a children's ball at Carlton House.

Popular though Victoria was with the King, Feodore, 18 years old and very attractive and who already had had a secret romance with a son of the Duke of Sussex, had caught his eye for different reasons. It's likely that he was considering a second marriage—a move that would be disastrous for Victoria's future. So Victoire quickly foiled any chance of romance by marrying Feodore off as quickly as possible to Prince Ernest of Hohenlohe-Langenburg. And so, at five, Victoria lost her closest companion. At night she slept close to her mother, in the room in which she was born, and by day she played with her vast collection of dolls and dolls'

affection. It was hard not to be fond of the little princess with the blonde curls and the winning ways. Her grandmother, the old dowager Duchess Augusta who came to see her from Germany, gave her the nickname Mayflower.

William and Adelaide were the first to show kindness to the bereaved Duchess. Adelaide, who so longed for a child of her own, and the Duchess who was mourning her husband were able to commiserate with one another in their native German. Both Adelaide and William doted on their little niece. Gradually her uncles began to show interest in Princess Victoria and heaped gifts on her—the most precious of all being a much loved donkey which she learned to ride. Her earliest memory of her uncle, the King, was meeting him at Windsor when he said to her, 'Give me your little paw', and afterwards presented her with a miniature portrait of himself set in diamonds. She adored his wonderful menagerie at Windsor with the collection of llamas, zebras, kangaroos, monkeys, deer, even

*Baroness Lehzen,
drawn by the young Victoria.*

147

houses. She also began to have lessons with Lehzen who was firm but kind and devoted herself to her little charge. But it was a lonely childhood, watched over by governesses and nannies, and she rarely met children of her own age.

Life was to become even more cloistered as the Duchess isolated herself and her daughter from society. Early in her marriage the Duchess had found that she and her husband were not popular. The royal dukes, with their extravagant lifestyles, had provoked demonstrations against the royal family. By distancing herself from such excesses, Victoire no doubt hoped the public would be more sympathetic towards her precious daughter. She worried terribly that Victoria might be kidnapped, or that the Duke of Cumberland, cast in the role of wicked uncle, would claim the throne for his son George.

The brains behind the Duchess' strategy to get Victoria to the throne was an Irishman, Sir John Conroy. He had been a member of the Duke's staff and stayed on to become Comptroller of the Duchess' household after the Duke's death. He was ambitious and scheming and his intentions were obvious to everyone except the Duchess herself who appeared to be completely under his spell. Adelaide actually warned the Duchess against Conroy's influence, but the warning only had the affect of turning the Duchess against her friend. She consulted Conroy about everything, even about Victoria's education, which proved to be narrow and totally inadequate for a future monarch. Apart from Latin and religion, which were the responsibility of the Reverend George Davis, Victoria's lessons were given by Baroness Lehzen. Her reading was limited for she was allowed only improving books of a strictly moral tone. Fiction was banned until she married, when her husband introduced her to the delights of the novel. Poor Victoria was also ruled by the interfering Flora Hastings, her mother's lady of the bedchamber.

King George IV died in 1830 to be succeeded by his brother the Duke of Clarence who became William IV. Conroy, hungry for power, urged Duchess Victoire to apply to be Regent, hoping, ultimately, to rule through her. But overtures of friendship made to the new King and Queen were ignored. Victoire and Conroy felt hurt and insulted, and although Princess Victoria loved her uncle and aunt very much, she had to decline most of their invitations became of her mother and Conroy's attitude. So she rarely met them. She was forbidden to attend the coronation and was not allowed to attend the King's dances and drawing-rooms for fear she would come into contact with his Fitzclarence children. The profligate ways of her husband's family had made the Duchess determined to keep her daughter apart, unsullied by bad influences.

As Victoria moved to first in line to the throne, the Duchess set up what was in effect a rival court at Kensington Palace. In an effort to promote her daughter, she gave dinner parties, took Victoria round the country on meet-the-people tours and sometimes made use of the royal yacht. The pretty young future Queen was soon meeting more people, becoming more popular and endearing herself more to her future subjects than the King and Queen themselves.

Not surprisingly, King William's patience eventually snapped. It happened at his birthday dinner, when he announced in his speech that he hoped he would live until his niece was old enough to rule *unaided*. He had his wish, and on her 18th birthday he offered Victoria a household of her own and an independent income. Characteristically, she had to decline the household but accepted the allowance on condition her mother had control of the money.

Bitterly disappointed that Victoria had reached her 18th birthday while William was still on the throne, Conroy nevertheless still had one more card to play. He wanted Parliament to fix a period of Regency on the grounds that Victoria, though 18, was not mature or stable enough to rule. His request was refused. Still undaunted, he then tried to extract from the Princess a written promise that, on becoming Queen, she would appoint him secretary. Again he was refused.

On June 18, 1837 William IV died and the Duchess of Kent's daughter became Queen. Remarkably, the bonds that had bound mother and daughter for 18 years were broken. The bed Victoria had slept in since girlhood was removed from her bedroom and Conroy was barred from office in the new Queen's household. The pushy mother now had to bow to her daughter's wishes, and they did not include Conroy. Nor did they include the irritating Flora Hastings. Young as she was, Victoria had long ago recognised Conroy's influence and resented it, and she hated the way he and Lady Flora intruded in her own life. When mother and daughter moved to Buckingham Palace it was Victoria's trusted confidante, the loyal Lehzen, who was given a bedroom adjoining her own. Victoire had got her wish—her daughter was Queen. And that prob-

ably softened any sadness she may have felt at Victoria's rebellious behaviour. Meanwhile, Uncle Leopold, who had become King of the Belgians in 1831, was busy matchmaking. He had in mind a Consort for the new Queen. It was Victoria's marriage that brought about her real separation from Victoire, when the latter moved from Kensington Palace to Belgravia. Yet time was to heal the division between them and they became reconciled to the extent that the Duchess in old age once again had residences near her daughter, at Frogmore and Abergeldie. Her death in 1861 was a bitter blow to the Queen. For, despite their differences at various times, it was undoubtedly due to her mother's strength that the 'Grandmama of Europe' ultimately owed the grandeur of her position in the last half of the nineteenth century.

Victoria had a solitary childhood.
This portrait shows her working at her sketchbook.

149

The Saxe-Coburgs

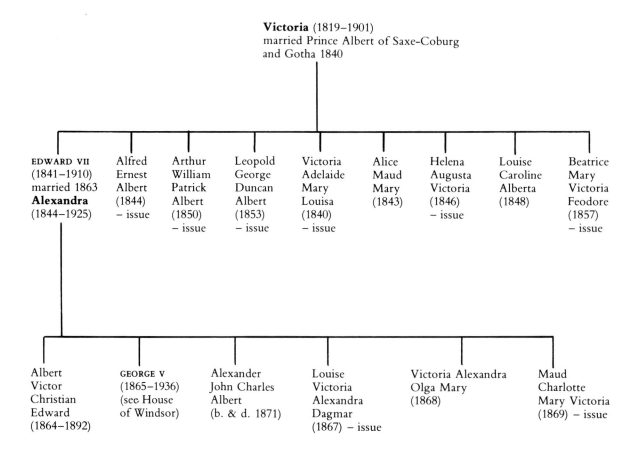

Victoria (1819–1901)
married Prince Albert of Saxe-Coburg
and Gotha 1840

EDWARD VII (1841–1910) married 1863 **Alexandra** (1844–1925)	Alfred Ernest Albert (1844) – issue	Arthur William Patrick Albert (1850) – issue	Leopold George Duncan Albert (1853) – issue	Victoria Adelaide Mary Louisa (1840) – issue	Alice Maud Mary (1843)	Helena Augusta Victoria (1846) – issue	Louise Caroline Alberta (1848)	Beatrice Mary Victoria Feodore (1857) – issue

Albert Victor Christian Edward (1864–1892)	**GEORGE V** (1865–1936) (see House of Windsor)	Alexander John Charles Albert (b. & d. 1871)	Louise Victoria Alexandra Dagmar (1867) – issue	Victoria Alexandra Olga Mary (1868)	Maud Charlotte Mary Victoria (1869) – issue

England enjoyed a long, settled period when Victoria came to the throne and she truly became grandmother of Europe. Her children, grandchildren and great-grandchildren were to marry into most of the ruling houses of the Continent. She was awe-inspiring and illustrious, not only to the world but to her family. It was a family dominated by strong women. It has been said that if Victoria and Albert's son had had half the character and intelligence of his sister Vicky, he would have made a superb king. That most of the Saxe-Coburg women married weak men didn't seem to matter —they had enough drive and enthusiasm, inherited no doubt from Mama, to shoulder any responsibilities.

Under Victoria's rule, Britain's economic growth was prolific. In 1851, when the Great Exhibition, organised by Prince Albert, was held at the Crystal Palace, over half the 14,000 exhibitors represented Great Britain and her colonies.

On the domestic front, nineteenth century parents still had large families as any form of birth control was considered socially unacceptable. Although the death rate was falling, an awful lot of babies and young children still died. Innoculation, immunisation and improved hygiene all helped, but there was still typhus, diphtheria and tuberculosis (consumption) to be avoided.

For royal mothers, many of the traditions surrounding birth had been forgotten or cast aside—but that didn't make having their numerous babies any easier or more pleasant. Victoria's medical advisers advocated plenty to eat and lots of wine to drink throughout pregnancy—which was probably why she was such a stout lady in later life. She hated pregnancy and birth and regretted bitterly that she went through seven deliveries before discovering the delights of chloroform to render her senseless.

The use of chloroform on the Queen caused great controversy at the time. It was administered by Dr Snow for the last hour of labour, dropped on to a handkerchief which was then held to Victoria's face. The medical profession considered it dangerous and totally unnecessary for a straightforward delivery. But the Queen didn't care.

Royal physicians were handsomely rewarded. The doctors in attendance at the Princess Royal's birth did especially well—£1000 for Dr Locock, £800 for Dr Ferguson, £500 for Mr Bagden, and £1,000 plus a £300 a year pension for the wet nurse—a doctor's wife from Cowes.

The Royal nursery typified Victorian upper-class ideas that children should be kept quite separate from adults until they were old enough to behave as adults. When in the drawing-room, dressed up and on display, children were supposed to be impeccably behaved.

Under the unsatisfactory head nurse, Mrs Roberts, Queen Victoria's children were declared 'overwatched, overdoctored and over-dressed'. At the age of two, little Vicky, the Princess Royal, was dressed in 'Garter blue velvet, Brussels lace, white shoes, pearls and diamonds'. Lady Sarah Lyttleton, who took over the nursery for eight successful years, soon changed the finery for simple straw hats and plain frocks, except for special occasions, and the little princes and princesses were often dressed in unisex kilts as an economy measure.

Toys came into their own during this period and children could choose from a bewildering display of playthings, from jigsaw puzzles and rocking horses to dolls' houses, magic lanterns, clockwork engines and toy theatres. Exciting mechanical toys reflected the changes that had taken place in adult life since the Industrial Revolution. There were plenty of outings, too, with family picnics and large gatherings at Christmas.

Despite the discipline and the sometimes harsh nursery routine, it was a good time to be a child—even a royal one.

*Queen Victoria surrounded
by her enormous family.*

Painted on the occasion
of her Diamond Jubilee.

153

VICTORIA
1819 ~ 1901

Grandmama of Europe

Victoria married her cousin Albert of Saxe-Coburg-Gotha in the Chapel Royal at St James's on February 10, 1840. She had first set eyes on him when they were both 17—a meeting arranged by her uncle Leopold—but the young prince made little impression on her. Their next meeting, more than three years later, was quite different. She proposed to him and he accepted. 'How I adore him,' she wrote. 'I feel the happiest of human beings.' Thus began one of the most famous partnerships of all time.

Victoria conceived her first child a month after the wedding, but childbearing frightened her. She described it as 'the only thing I dread', doubtless haunted by stories handed down to her of her cousin, the tragic Princess Charlotte who died in childbirth twenty years before. She also remembered the losses of her Aunt Adelaide, and she strongly disagreed with Uncle Leopold when he expressed a wish that she should have a large family.

On the night of November 21 Victoria awoke in some pain and found Albert so soundly asleep she had trouble waking him. Ten hours later, after a straightforward labour and delivery, a daughter was born. In attendance were Sir James Clark, her physician in ordinary, Dr Locock, her first physician *accoucheur* or obstetrician, with Dr Ferguson and Mr Bagden assisting, and Mrs Lilly, the midwife. The Queen made a special request that only her husband, Dr Locock and Mrs Lilly should be in the delivery room. The others—the Archbishop of Canterbury and privy councillors—who, by tradition should be present at a royal birth, were stationed in the next room, with the door ajar. There was slight disappointment that the first-born was not the son they had hoped for, but Victoria promised, 'The next will be a prince.'

They named the little princess Victoria, although it was often shortened to Vicky, and she was 'Pussy' to her family.

Unlike her mother, who firmly believed in the value of breastfeeding, Victoria followed the English royal tradition and refused to feed her daughter herself. As the reigning monarch she could hardly be criticised for the decision. Feeding times could well have interfered with state duties. But Vicky's wet nurse was not a wise choice. She had a taste for beer, which was blamed for her poor quality milk, and the baby grew pale and sickly, and suffered from colic. The royal nursery was not a happy place. Blame for mismanagement was placed on the unfortunate Mrs Southey who had fallen on hard times and been given the post of head nurse as an act of kindness. But she proved inadequate to the task and was dismissed. So too was Baroness Lehzen. After years of service to the Queen, she had outstayed her welcome. She fell into disfavour with Prince Albert who pensioned her off and sent her back to Germany.

Albert had more influence on life in the nursery than Victoria. He was a conscientious father as well as a devoted, caring husband. After the birth of Vicky, Victoria recalled 'his care was like that of a mother nor could [there] be a kinder, wiser, more judicious nurse.' Yet, like Victoria, whose childhood had been solitary, Albert knew little of family life and the needs of small children. His parents divorced when he was six and he spent a lot of his growing years with grandparents. But Albert was a modern man, something of a visionary, born before his time. At the University of Bonn he had read law, mathematics, and philosophy. But his interests were mainly scientific. And he faced fatherhood with the same scientific approach by setting out a daily schedule, an elaborate blueprint for raising children. However, he soon discovered that children cannot, will not, be brought up according to a book, and he was forced to relax his plans. Nevertheless, it was thanks to her Consort's modern ideas, that Victoria's children had a healthy start in life.

Soon after Albert's arrival in England he complained of a succession of colds, sore throats and swollen glands, all of which he put down to bad hygiene at the palace. With great foresight he ordered the modernisation of kitchens, bathrooms and lavatories in the royal house, so eradicating the risk of diseases such as typhoid and diphtheria which still carried off so many children at that time. All the children were vaccinated, the old treatments such as blistering and bleeding long forgotten. Castor oil and Grays powder were the modern cures for most complaints. Babies were no longer required to have their heads veiled when they went out; indeed, cold baths, fresh air, exercise and plain

'The Proud Parents.'

food was the spartan order of the day at the palace. And the children thrived. All of Victoria's nine children survived, and even Leopold, the invalid of the family who was a haemophiliac, lived to marry and father two children before he died at the age of 31. As parents, Victoria and Albert enthused and agonised, marvelled and grieved over the accomplishments and the shortcomings of their offspring.

Vicky, the Princess Royal, the enchanting baby who in her mother's eyes could do no wrong, was followed by the Prince of Wales and heir to the throne. He was a troublesome child even before he was born. Victoria passed the nine months of pregnancy in a cloud of depression with two false alarms of premature labour until, on November 9, 1841, in severe pain,

she gave birth to Albert Edward, the terrible Bertie, the future King Edward VII, large and bouncing with health. Afterwards Victoria complained miserably that she couldn't enjoy life at all if she was to be in a constant state of pregnancy, but once the gloom lifted she began to show some maternal pride. 'To think we have two children now ... it is like a dream,' she glowed. It was indeed a time to be happy. Victoria had produced the first Prince of Wales in almost 80 years.

Albert Edward was baptised in St George's Chapel, Windsor, in a grand ceremony befitting the heir to the throne. For the occasion he was dressed in a beautiful new satin and lace gown which is still worn at royal christenings today, and Frederick William III of Prussia was his

'The Royal Alphabet', a cartoon mocking Albert's concern to educate his children even in babyhood.

godfather. The ceremony was followed by a reception and banquet at which a huge cake, measuring eight feet in diameter, was cut.

When Bertie arrived, the nursery was ruled by Sarah Spencer, an ancestor of the present Princess Diana. She was the 50-year-old widow of Lord Lyttelton and had been lady-in-waiting to the Queen. But her best qualification was that she had brought up five children of her own, and she was a fitting replacement to the unsuitable Mrs Southey. She stayed with the royal children for eight years and they all loved her although she had wielded great power and believed in punishing them. Strict discipline became more and more necessary as the family grew in age and number. Every evening Sarah wrote a report on the children's progress to be handed to Victoria the following morning, so she was kept fully briefed on Bertie's latest temper tantrum or Vicky's aversion to milk puddings.

The problems caused by Vicky's beer-drinking wet nurse made Victoria much more careful about the choice of successive nurses. When Victoria's third child, Alice, was born, her nurse was made to follow a plain wholesome diet, and medicines were locked away. Victoria was overjoyed to have another daughter. Baby Bertie suffered so much from a runny nose and a bad temper, and was so hard to like that she had hoped for another bright lovable little girl like Vicky. But she was to be disappointed, for Alice turned out to be sensitive and complicated—a difficult personality for Victoria to cope with.

Alfred, Duke of Edinburgh, born in August 1844, was the easy one. Known as 'Affie' to the family, he was quick to learn, obedient and fearless. He had all the qualities lacking in the unfortunate Bertie. Helena, born two years later, was a blue baby at birth but she soon recovered. Nicknamed 'Lenchen', she grew up to be the tomboy of the family. She read little but adored sport and the outdoor life. She loved to sail and with her knowledge of mechanics could play at being ship's engineer on the royal motor yacht. She was also mad on horses and a keen rider. Like her father, she was born a century too soon.

Alive today she could well be the star of the Windsor horse show.

Victoria's third daughter, Louise, was born when civil unrest threatened the country. Louise was only three weeks old when Wellington advised the family to go to Osborne and stay there until peace was restored. They travelled by train, the new-born infant well wrapped against the cold March air, and stayed on the Isle of Wight for a month. On their return to Windsor they celebrated with a family christening at which the choir sang Gotha, a hymn the Prince Consort had composed himself. But Victoria's mind was not wholly on her new baby, for while there was unrest in England, there was revolution on the Continent, and royal refugees from France, Italy and Germany, many of them cousins of the family, were seeking safety within the walls of Buckingham Palace.

A third son was born to Victoria on Wellington's 81st birthday in 1850. He was christened Arthur after him and the old hero of Waterloo became his godfather. He was a good-looking child from babyhood and to Victoria, who preferred attractive children, he was to be her favourite son throughout her life. He followed in his godfather's footsteps and loved all things military. As a toddler he played with lead soldiers on the nursery floor and never grew tired of watching the Changing of the Guard; on holiday he loved to play with the fort Albert built for his sons at Osborne. Eventually he made the army his career. (He became a field-marshal and when he was in his nineties, during the Second World War, he still sometimes wore his uniform.)

Arthur's healthy happy babyhood contrasted with the life of inactivity which faced the next child, poor Leopold. He was the first of Victoria's children to be born with the aid of chloroform to relieve her labour pains. As usual, her physician Sir James Clark was in attendance but the chloroform was administered by an anaesthetist, Dr John Snow of Edinburgh. The effect was, said the Queen, 'soothing, quieting and delightful'. But although Leopold's arrival was easy, it was soon obvious that he was a sickly child. It was discovered that he had epilepsy, and then the symptoms of the dreaded disease of haemophilia became evident. The blood of a haemophiliac doesn't contain enough clotting agents and any wound can prove fatal. It's a strange disease which occurs only in males, but is carried only by females. And not every female in a family will be a carrier. When Leopold was found to be a haemophiliac, the Queen was distraught and bewildered. She protested that it certainly hadn't come from her side of the family—and in a way she was right. It seems that Victoria herself, by a quirk of genes, originated the haemophilia that was to spread, through her daughters Alice and Beatrice, into the royal houses of Europe.

Aware that sudden injury could mean death to Leopold, Victoria and Albert had to protect him from any dangerous activity. While he was pampered and cosseted because of his health, Victoria found it hard to identify with his needs as an otherwise intelligent, lively-minded child. It was Albert who read to him, played with him, and stimulated his young mind.

Victoria chose to have 'blessed chloroform' administered to her again when Beatrice was born in 1857. She was Victoria's ninth and last child. For 17 years there had been a baby in the palace nursery. Now Baby, as Beatrice was destined to be called for many years to come, was born to be the dutiful daughter, 'the comfort and blessing of my declining years'.

As a mother, Victoria seems to have been overwhelmed by having so many babies. Small babies, she considered, were mere little plants. She hated their bodies and limbs and their 'froglike' action and declared 'an ugly baby is a very nasty object—the prettiest is frightful when undressed.' Of her own offspring, she thought Leopold particularly ugly, a very common looking child with bad posture. Fortunately Victoria had in Albert what she called 'a capital nurse' who opened her eyes to the pleasures of watching children grow and develop. Certainly as parents, they spent more time with their children than was usual in those days, and they had high hopes and ideals for them. Maybe the

children were pushed too hard in the schoolroom, and pent-up energy just had to find release in the throwing of inkwells and books. They were certainly a noisy, lively, mischievous bunch and naughtiness had to be dealt with, rudeness, particularly to servants, was never tolerated. Disciplinary measures ranged from solitary confinement to smacking and loss of treats.

In the raising of their family, Victoria and Albert had an invaluable adviser in Baron Stockmar, who had been sent to England by King Leopold to assist the young couple. It was he who tactfully pointed out to Albert that his grand plan for educating his children was far too ambitious. He also advised that the children should be taught in England rather than abroad, so that they would not seem 'foreign' to the people. And so at the age of four or five the little princes and princesses had their first lessons from Lady Lyttleton. Later, with the help of specialist teachers, they all became fluent in German and French, and eventually each child had an individual tutor.

Bertie, who so exasperated his mother—he was slower to develop than Vicky and had a slight speech impediment—was first placed in the hands of a former Eton master, Henry Birch, but he made little headway with his difficult pupil and was replaced two years later by tutor and barrister Frederick Gibbs.

Despite these skilled tutors, Albert was still determined to play a big part in his children's education and in the evenings the older ones went in turn to his study to expand the day's work, revise essays, discuss literature.

Mama Victoria could not have hoped to devote so much time and patient dedication to school activities. As the reigning monarch she constantly had affairs of state on her mind. In the first years of her reign there had to be frequent meetings: with Lord Melbourne, her first Prime Minister who, at the age of 58, became her mentor, guide and father figure, later with Gladstone, Peel, Palmerston, Clarendon, and Disraeli. Every day she spent hours writing letters to her ministers, copious notes for her journal and memorandum. And she kept letters flowing constantly between her far-flung family of European relations.

Life for Victoria's children was not all hard work, though. It was the age of the toy, and the palace nursery was well stocked with the beautifully-made playthings which are today's museum pieces. Jigsaw puzzles were popular, there were ingenious clockwork toys from Germany, life-like dolls with beautiful waxen faces and dolls' houses crammed with Victoriana in miniature.

More and more books were being published for children; Albert enjoyed reading to his offspring and Victoria liked to be with them when they said their prayers. Sundays, after morning service, were devoted to the children. The royal parents joined in their activities, walking the dogs, riding, skating, flying kites; not for them the strict and sober English sabbath. With a father like Albert to show the way, Victoria's children had plenty of fun. He loved to romp with them, giving the youngest rides in a basket round the nursery floor. As they grew older they had jolly musical evenings together round the piano, and elaborate games of charades.

Christmas and birthdays were celebrated with special treats, children's dances at Buckingham Palace and parties—when Bertie was eight he had a group of Eton boys to tea. There were visits to the theatre, the zoo and the circus, which Victoria herself loved. One of the most exciting events in the lives of Victoria's elder children was the Great International Exhibition of 1851. It was Albert's brainchild and the sight of the Crystal Palace rising in Hyde Park must have been a wondrous experience to ten-year-old Bertie. Over six million visited the exhibition to admire the modern marvels, the latest in Man's achievements from around the world. And 11-year-old Vicky, present at the grand opening ceremony, was about to set eyes for the first time on her future husband, Prince Frederick William of Prussia.

Holidays were times when Victoria relaxed. Then the mother who could often be so critical at home, who could never understand that it was natural for a small child to have what she called 'tricks', and who reprimanded Vicky for standing on one leg, for 'violent laughing' and 'cramming in eating', learnt to laugh and have fun *with* the children. She began to take pleasure in some of the simple delights which were missing in her own childhood.

When Vicky was a baby there were seaside holidays at the Brighton Pavilion, but Victoria found the Pavilion lacking in privacy and by 1846 the family began spending summers by the sea at Osborne on the Isle of Wight. There, following her belief that 'children should be brought up in as domestic a way as possible', they had their Swiss Cottage. In the same way that Queen Charlotte's many children in their time had a model farm at Windsor, where they learned to sow and cultivate and harvest their own produce, Victoria's children learned the art of housekeeping and played at baking cakes, gardening and trying their hand at carpentry. Bathing in the sea, playing on the sands and scrambling over rocks were favourite pastimes during those idyllic childhood summers. Bertie, who as a tiny child had knock knees and wore splints in bed at night, grew stronger as the weeks went by. And there were wonderful days afloat, cruising in the royal yacht *Victoria and Albert* or the smaller steam yacht, *The Fairy*.

By 1855 the family had another holiday home, Balmoral, their beloved retreat and Albert's creation, to which they travelled overnight by the royal train. It was the place where Victoria was to find peace and seclusion in the long sad years to come. The children were to look back on their Scottish holidays in the late 1850s with sheer joy. Days spent pony trekking on the moors, hunting, sleigh rides in winter, deer stalking or just sketching and enjoying nature.

There were wonderful family picnics and evenings of music and dancing. And Victoria loved to dance, especially the boisterious Highland reels. But such happiness was soon to end.

In March 1861 Victoria's mother died, and she felt the loss so severely that she almost had a nervous breakdown. The old Duchess of Kent,

*Osborne House in the Isle of Wight
was especially loved by Victoria
for its seclusion.*

who had been the cause of so much friction before her accession, had been forgiven by Victoria and the two had become close again. Her death was a bitter blow to Victoria.

But nothing prepared her for the bitterest blow of all—the terrible loss, nine months later of Albert, the husband she so adored, who died of typhoid fever. His death on December 14, 1861, was due, too, to complete exhaustion. The Great Exhibition, the building of Osborne and Balmoral, concern over world events as well as Victoria's state affairs all took their toll and, finally, Albert succumbed to typhoid. Tired out, he lost the will to live.

It was Alice who helped nurse her father during his last days and afterwards cared for her grieving mother. Vicky was married and living in Berlin and Alfred, who had joined the Navy, was at sea when their father died, but Bertie and Helena were at the bedside, and Louise 13, Arthur 11 and Leopold 9 were called to the room to say goodbye to their father. Only Beatrice remained in the nursery. That night Victoria took the four-

year-old child in her arms, wrapped her in one of her father's nightshirts, and took her to her own bed. 'I live only for Beatrice now,' she exclaimed. And in a letter to Vicky four days after Albert's death she wrote: '*Sweet little Beatrice comes to lie in my bed every morning which is a comfort. I long so to cling to and clasp a loving being.*' Such was the pattern for the future. It was to little Beatrice, the perfect one, to whom the Queen turned in her grief, changing her from a bright and lively child to a shy, quiet, dutiful daughter. She had been Albert's last delight, his pet, and Victoria felt she must keep her close by. The Queen rarely went anywhere without her, and she was still called 'Baby' long after she was grown up. Victoria was determined Beatrice would never marry; she was never given the chance to mix with the opposite sex. Baby's place was with her widowed mother. It was her duty.

It was poor Bertie who was Victoria's greatest disappointment. Albert had carefully mapped out the future of his son and heir to ensure that he became a paragon of virtue, a perfect prince and a credit to both his family and his people. Bertie was kept apart from other boys and surrounded instead by serious, educated tutors, who kept him working for long hours.

But Bertie lived up to his early assessment and was slow, lazy and not very bright. He longed for friends of his own age, for laughter and fun—not stuffy lessons and tedium. As he grew older, the more Victoria and Albert despaired, and the Queen begged him to try to be like his father.

She wrote to Vicky that *'Bertie is my caricature. This is the misfortune and, in a man, this is much worse. You are quite your dear, beloved Papa's child.'* In Bertie, it seems, Victoria saw too much of what she might have become but for Albert's guiding hand.

When Albert had discovered that Bertie (well into his twenties) had slept with an actress, he was so appalled that he wrote to Bertie saying that he had inflicted him with *'The greatest pain I have yet felt in my life.'*

Bertie had apologised and Albert had forgiven him. But a few weeks later, after visiting his errant son at Cambridge, Albert had returned home exhausted and a few weeks later he was dead. The Queen became obsessed with the idea that wicked Bertie had been the cause of her beloved's demise and vowed to have nothing to do with him.

On the other hand, Bertie, Prince of Wales, by now a young prince-about-town, was enjoying heady freedom: triumphant tours of Europe, the near East and North America as well as a taste of academic life in Edinburgh, Oxford and Cambridge.

Bertie led an indulgent life because Victoria wouldn't allow him to do anything else. She spent her life writing him letters, complaining about his infidelities, his extravagances and idle ways. He was kept in complete ignorance of government business and never consulted or included in affairs of state.

Yet despite all this, Victoria had a fondness for Bertie, and although he lived in fear of her, Bertie felt affection for her. As the years dimmed Victoria's conviction that he had caused his father's death, she was moved to write to Vicky: 'Really dear Bertie is so full of good and amiable qualities that it makes one forget and overlook much that one would wish different.'

And how different they may both had been if they could have accepted each other's weaknesses and strengths from the beginning.

The four eldest children were the least affected by Albert's death. They were much involved with their own lives. Vicky, the future Empress of Germany, had problems of her own, and mother and daughter poured out their troubles in copious correspondence. Vicky's main problem was that although she lived in Prussia with her husband, Frederick, and they were poised to take the throne when Frederick's father King Wilhelm I died, she continued to be the very essence of an Englishwoman, extolling the vitues of everything at home above all else. Her mother even encouraged her to sign her name Victoria, Princess Royal and Princess Frederick Wilhelm of Prussia. It's not surprising that she was not well liked in her husband's country. *'I always feel like a fly struggling in a very tangled web,'* she wrote to Victoria, *'and a feeling of weariness and depression, often of disgust and hopelessness, takes possession of me . . .'*

Although on his father's death, Bertie had promised: 'I will become everything you wish', Victoria turned not to him but to Alice for care and consolation in the first weeks of mourning. Alice and Victoria's half-sister Feodora, also recently widowed, were her only companions. But even Alice was about to leave the royal nest. She was already engaged to Prince Louis of Hesse-Darmstadt and they were married the following summer, while still in semi-mourning at Osborne. Alice herself was destined to die at the early age of 35, on the anniversary of her father's death, after having caught diphtheria while nursing her children through an epidemic.

For Victoria's youngest children their father's death meant that normal family life was gone for ever. It seemed a curtain of darkness came down on the family; a curtain which they were never

*Victoria sits surrounded by her family
at Osborne House. On her right
is her grandson, the future George V
with the future George VI.*

*Seated to George V's right is
Queen Mary with her other children,
Princess Mary and the future
Duke of Windsor.*

allowed to lift. Gone were the dances, the parties, the fun. The youngest also missed their father's help with their education. His death left a gap which could never be filled. It is strange that Victoria, who herself experienced the loss and loneliness of life without a father, allowed this to happen to her own children, and that she did nothing to make life happier for them. But she was so immersed in her own sorrow that she found it impossible to take an interest in her family. No wonder some of them rebelled. The dark days of mourning and gloom seemed to stretch ahead for ever and, at 42, Victoria's widow's weeds became her habitual dress. Even little Beatrice commented on Mama's 'sad cap'.

Helena was the first to discover her social life was seriously affected. There was to be no coming-out ball for her; the Buckingham Palace ballroom was closed. She was on the verge of womanhood when she would normally begin to mix in society, but now there would be no celebrations, no balls, no state dinners. Helena, like her other brothers and sisters, escaped for a time to her elder sister Vicky in Germany. Vicky was always delighted to see them; she was their confidante, a shoulder to cry on. She understood their problems, and even the Queen heeded Vicky's advice. She was also a matchmaker.

In earlier times, Victoria would have been quite happy to see her children married off to suitable partners—Vicky had been engaged at 14 and married at 17. Now she tried to postpone the time they would leave her; and she dreaded that they might live abroad. Helena was 20 when Vicky introduced her to a Danish prince. Christian of Schleswig-Holstein was 42 years old and penniless, but he was kind and willing to make his home at Frogmore, which would mean Helena would in future be able to carry on a lot of public duties for her mother. She married him.

Louise was 19 when she broke new ground and became an art student. Encouraged by Vicky she went to the National Art Training School (which Prince Albert had founded), now the Royal College of Art, and even asked to be allowed to live in a studio, but this was refused.

Her work as a sculptor and painter gave Louise the outlet to express herself and she and Victoria found each other much easier to live with. Her best-known work must be the statue of her mother overlooking the Broad Walk in Kensington Gardens. At 22 she married Lord Lorne, an MP and son of the Duke of Argyll. Victoria was delighted that at last one daughter was marrying into British aristocracy and staying in England. Ironically, Louise was required to live overseas when her husband was appointed Governor General of Canada. But the marriage was not a success, and Louise left her husband in Canada, spent some time travelling round Europe, then made her home in England.

Even Beatrice, Victoria's last 'comfort and blessing', found love through Vicky. It happened at a family wedding in Darmstadt, when Vicky introduced her sister to Prince Henry of Battenberg. When Beatrice, then age 28, plucked up the courage to tell Victoria that she wanted to marry, her mother was so shocked at the thought of being left alone that she refused to speak to Beatrice for some months and, although they lived under the same roof, they communicated by letter. Victoria agreed to the marriage only on condition that Beatrice and Henry lived with her.

Like so many grandparents, Victoria seemed happier with her grandchildren and great-grandchildren who, in later years, arrived with their parents, servants and nannies to spend holidays at Windsor, Balmoral and Osborne. There were always some small children in Victoria's life, playing with dogs, riding in a little horse-drawn carriage or donkey chaise, playing games of make-believe in long castle corridors—though always trying to behave with the utmost decorum. They represented almost every royal house in Europe. Victoria's daughter, Alice, for example, whose fifth child Alix married Tsar Nicholas and was brutally murdered in the Russian Revolution, was grandmother to Alice (mother of Prince Philip), Queen Louise of Sweden, and Louis, Earl Mountbatten of Burma. Victoria's favourite grandson was the Kaiser: she died in his arms. Constant unrest in Europe, which was to culminate in the First World War, meant that brothers and sisters found themselves on opposing sides, as family ties clashed with national loyalties. Many of Victoria's family were to suffer hardship, deprivation and death as war and revolution swept the Continent.

Two of Victoria's children lived on until the Second World War—Arthur, Duke of Connaught, was 92 when he died in 1942—while Beatrice died in her late eighties in 1944.

Victoria reigned for nearly sixty-four years; in which she saw more change, both socially and politically, than any other monarch. As Queen, she had always taken more interest in foreign affairs than in events at home; it was a fitting tribute when, on Disraeli's suggestion, she was given the title Empress of India.

When the formidable old lady reached her Diamond Jubilee in 1897, Gladstone hoped she would abdicate and let Bertie take the Crown. But she was in control until her death in 1901.

Bertie, Prince of Wales and his wife Alexandra were, in fact, already grandparents themselves when the whole family assembled for the jubilee celebrations—the great procession through the streets of London, the rejoicing, the banquet. Victoria, frequently escorted now by her favourite son, Arthur, Duke of Connaught, was losing her strength. But she was still able to take on a royal tour of Ireland, rejoice at the relief of Mafeking, and knit blankets for troops engaged in the Boer War. The Grandmama of Europe was also Mother of an empire undreamt of by her ancestors.

But the young mother of 50 years ago, who had been so slow to flatter her children, so quick to criticise, and who had to learn to enjoy her offspring through the example of her husband, had always put her husband first. Her children came a very poor second. Although this was the custom of the age, Victoria carried it to its limits. Her jaundiced view of children is expressed in letters written to Vicky, then Crown Princess of Prussia, in 1876. *'You will find as the children grow up that as a rule children are a bitter disappointment—their greatest object being to do precisely what their parents do not wish and have anxiously tried to prevent ...*

'Most extraordinary it is to see that the more care has been taken in everyway the less they often succeed! And often when children have been less watched and less taken care of—the better they turn out!! This is inexplicable and very annoying.'

Feeling the way she did about babies, and coupled with her volatile, over-emotional nature and her absolute passion for Albert, perhaps Victoria should never have been a mother.

ALEXANDRA
1844 ~ 1925

Darling Motherdear

Edward, Prince of Wales, married the beautiful Princess Alexandra of Schleswig-Holstein-Sonderburg-Glucksburg in St George's Chapel, Windsor in March 1863. The match had been arranged before the death of the Prince Consort, for both Victoria and Albert had agreed that the Danish princess would make the perfect wife for their troublesome son. She had all the right qualities. Although her father was heir to the throne of Denmark, her lifestyle was not luxurious by royal standards. She was, therefore, unaffected, cheerful, dependable, and even sometimes made her own clothes. She was also stunningly beautiful. Beautiful enough, it was hoped, to hold Bertie's interest from all the other ladies who competed for the Prince's attention.

The wedding festivities were muted by mourning. Bertie's sisters wore dresses of white and lilac and Queen Victoria watched the ceremony screened from view in a gallery overlooking the altar. At the reception afterwards she ate with her youngest daughter, six-year-old Beatrice, apart from the wedding party.

After a honeymoon at Osborne, Bertie and Alix moved into Marlborough House and became leaders of fashionable London society. While Queen Victoria resumed her life of mourning, the 21-year-old Prince of Wales and his 19-year-old bride revitalised the social scene. They had boundless energy as they took in every event, Ascot, Cowes, garden parties and house parties, balls and banquets and nights at the theatre; the London season exhausted, they took holidays on the French Riviera or visited relatives in Germany and Denmark. Alexandra's social life kept her so busy that she barely thought about herself and the baby she was expecting in March 1864. January that year was exceptionally cold. Virginia Water was frozen over and Bertie led the royal party from Frogmore for a game of ice hockey. Alexandra, a spectator, was taking a sledge ride and listening to the band when she felt the first twinges of pain. Still, the baby was not due for another two months, she told herself, and ignored it.

That evening at Frogmore, Alexandra's lady of the bedchamber, Lady Macclesfield, herself the mother of 13, realised that Alexandra was in the last stages of labour. The nearest available doctor, Dr Brown, a Windsor GP, was called in and just before nine that evening Alexandra gave birth to a son. The second in line to the throne, weighing just three pounds three ounces, was then wrapped in cotton wool and swathed in a flannel petticoat belonging to Lady Macclesfield. As Alexandra had planned to have her confinement at Marlborough House, the event at Frogmore was completely unexpected, so next morning a servant was sent to a Windsor draper to buy baby clothes. And the only minister available to be present at the birth had been Lord Granville, Lord President of the Council. The Home Secretary was summoned, but everything happened so quickly that the baby was two hours old when he arrived. Later that evening Lady Macclesfield went to the Princess's room and found Bertie

with her, holding his wife in his arms. They were both weeping with joy.

Queen Victoria knighted Dr Brown for his royal services but she began to have doubts about Alexandra and disapproved of the irresponsible way she had continued to rush around with Bertie, keeping late nights and ignoring her pregnancy. A nurse, named Mrs Clark, was immediately found to take care of the baby, and the very next day, the Princess had no less than six doctors attending her. But Queen Victoria still found it necessary to travel from Osborne and spend several days at Windsor while Alexandra recovered. Writing to her daughter Vicky afterwards, she said she felt Alix had been 'utterly disgusted' by the experience of childbirth.

Queen Victoria began arranging her grandson's christening. She announced that she would hold the infant herself, and that he should be called Albert Victor, after her adored dead husband and herself. In fact, she declared that all their descendants should be given the name Albert or Victoria. Bertie and Alix had to agree. Their son was baptised Albert Victor, with the additional names Christian Edward after Alexandra's father and his other grandfather, the Duke of Kent.

Albert Victor cried throughout his christening and Victoria noted that her daughter-in-law looked thin, pale and sad, and quite 'gone off'. Alex was not only suffering fatigue after her delivery. Bertie, who had boundless energy, was able to turn night into day, consume enormous meals and generally live at a reckless pace without any ill-effects; but his wife was exhausted by the pressure. She was also very worried about affairs at home in Denmark and her parents' involvement in the war between Denmark and Prussia over the Duchies of Schleswig and Holstein. Alix longed to see her parents, and her brothers and sister again, and she and Bertie were off on their travels once more to visit far-off relations. But Alix could not bear the thought of being parted so soon from her young baby, so Albert Victor was taken along, too.

Queen Victoria was furious when she heard that the young heir had been taken out of the country without her consent, and demanded his return; but her request went unheeded.

Victoria continued to complain about the young couple's irresponsible attitude to parenthood, and her complaints increased when Alix gave birth to a second child a month before the expected date. She was upset because she had hoped to be present at the confinement; and it was later believed that the Princess had purposely announced the wrong date in order to avoid the presence of her mother-in-law. The baby, the future George V, was born at Marlborough House in June 1865, only a few hours after Alix returned from an evening concert, and once again the Queen wanted to name the baby. Bertie and Alix's choice of George did not meet with Victoria's approval at all. She did not think that the last of the Georges, George IV, had set a good standard of moral behaviour. But Bertie insisted. Eventually a compromise was reached and the baby was baptised George Frederick Ernest Albert. Following the royal tradition, little George was placed in the care of a wet nurse and soon Alix resumed her normal life.

The house parties, the racing, the fancy dress balls, the practical jokes, the fun continued for the Prince and Princess of Wales, but people began to notice that the Princess had lost her

The Prince and Princess of Wales with Albert Victor, George, Louise and Victoria.

sparkle, and looked pale and thin. It had taken her a long time to recover from Georgie's birth, and before long she was pregnant again. In November 1866 Bertie set off alone for Russia to attend the wedding of Alix's sister to the Tsarevitch at the Winter Palace in St Petersburg. His wife was not well enough to travel, so she stayed behind at Marlborough House and their two little sons went to stay with Queen Victoria at Windsor.

When Bertie returned to London six weeks later, he found his wife's condition had deteriorated. She was suffering acute pain in her hip and leg and could barely sleep at night without drugs, and because her throat was inflamed she was unable to eat. Yet Bertie and her doctors showed little concern. Eventually, acute rheumatic fever was diagnosed and because of her illness her doctors were afraid to give her chloroform when, on February 20, she gave birth prematurely to a daughter.

While the baby Princess thrived it was feared for a time that her mother might die. Alix's anxious parents travelled from Denmark to be with her and Queen Victoria spent days at her bedside. A month's rest in bed was still considered appropriate after a confinement, but the Princess of Wales took far longer to recover.

Bertie had his desk moved to her room so that he could deal with his correspondence while keeping Alix company. But he soon grew restless, the role of the attentive husband in the sickroom lost its attraction and he began looking for other interests. The Queen would not allow him to have any responsibility in affairs of State, no position was open to the energetic 25-year-old Prince of Wales, so Bertie began to return to the haunts and habits of his bachelor days. He stayed out late, so late that Alix, who refused to sleep until he returned home, often lay awake half the night waiting for him.

The new baby was three months old when Alix was well enough to be wheeled into the drawing room for the christening. 'The child ought to be called Victoria . . . But upon these subjects Bertie and Alix do not understand the right thing', wrote Queen Victoria, when her latest grand-child was named Louise Victoria Alexandra Dagmar. Shortly after the ceremony Bertie and his brother Alfred left for a holiday in Paris, and on his return tongues wagged as Bertie went to Ascot and other social events alone.

Later that summer Bertie took Alix to the fashionable spa resort of Wiesbaden. She was still terribly weak and when they set sail on the royal yacht *Osborne*, her wheelchair was taken aboard so that she could be transported around. With them went three-year-old Albert Victor (Eddy to the family), George and baby Louise. But despite the rest at the health spa Alix was slow to recover. By November that year the Queen noted that Alix was able to get about, even up and down stairs, but only with the aid of a stick, some-times two. In fact the Princess of Wales was to be handicapped not only by a limp but by deafness, too, for the rest of her life. She started to ride again and to indulge her love of dancing, though often in pain. And the following spring, still suffering, and again pregnant, she accompanied Bertie on an exhausting royal tour of Ireland.

Alix gave birth to her fourth child, a daughter, at Marlborough House in July 1868, only hours after attending a concert at Crystal Palace. This time there were no complications and to please the Queen the baby was christened Victoria Alexandra Olga Marie. Nevertheless, Victoria was not very impressed by the Wales' children:

'Such miserable puny little children (each weaker than the preceding one) . . . poor frail little fairies.' Four days after the arrival of the latest baby, the Queen wrote '. . . a mere little red lump was all I saw; and I fear the seventh grand-daughter and fourteenth grandchild becomes a very uninteresting thing—for it seems to me to go on like the rabbits in Windsor Park!'

While Victoria was unmoved by these happy events, Alix was a warm, affectionate, adoring mother who wanted her children with her all the time. She also wanted her husband. 'I would marry him if he were a cowboy,' she confided before her wedding, and in spite of his failings, his infidelities, his lack of concern, she still loved him. To get him away from distractions at home, she persuaded him that they should set out on an extensive tour, taking the children, of course, to see their relatives in Germany and Denmark, then to France, Austria, Greece, Turkey and Egypt. The Queen insisted that they should travel incognito, and take only the boys. Eventu-ally she was persuaded to allow Louise to go too; but the children could accompany their parents only as far as Denmark, then they would be sent home. The baby would stay with Grandma. It was while Alix was sailing up the Nile, her own little brood far away from her, that she adopted a 10-year-old Nubian orphan who she had taken back to Sandringham where he was christened. She was also moved by compassion for a little ram that was about to be slaughtered for food. He, too, was taken aboard the royal yacht to live out his days in the green pastures of Norfolk.

Nine months after her holiday in Egypt, Alix gave birth to her fifth child, a daughter who was christened Maud. It was her fifth pregnancy in as many years. Two years later there was a sixth child, a son born at Sandringham in the spring of 1871. He, like so many of Alix's babies, was born prematurely. She was quite unprepared and a local doctor had to be called to her aid. The infant was tiny and very frail; so frail that he was baptised that same evening and named Alexander John. To the grief of his parents he died next day and he was buried at Sandringham. Alix watched, weeping, from the window as the little coffin with its wreath of white flowers was carried from the house. Behind walked Bertie with Eddy and Georgie, wearing their dark grey kilts and black gloves.

Recovery came slowly once again. Alix made her annual trip home to her family in Denmark while Bertie toured the spas of Germany, and there were the usual shooting parties at Sand-ringham in the autumn, but that winter the Princess of Wales faced the worst crisis of her life; Bertie fell dangerously ill with typhoid fever. Queen Victoria travelled by the royal train to see him and, with Alix, sat for days at his bedside. Feverish and delirious his life hung in the balance and his family gathered at Sandringham, fearing the worst, hardly daring to leave the house. December 14, the terrible anniversary of his father's death came and went but still Bertie clung to life. By the end of the year the danger had passed. Gone and forgotten, too, were the differences between mother and son as Victoria was so thankful to have 'dear Bertie' well again. She had nothing but praise for Alix as, united in their anguish, they had come through the crisis together, while Bertie and Alix were closer than they had ever been since their marriage began. It was as a happy, united family that they rode through packed streets to St Paul's Cathedral on February 27, 1872, for a service of national thanksgiving. Bertie, still very weak, had to be helped into the carriage and Alix resented all the publicity surrounding what she considered an occasion for private prayer and thankfulness. It was, nevertheless, a wonderful chance for the people of London to display their affection for the Prince of Wales. 'I saw the tears in Bertie's eyes and took and pressed his hand! It was a most affecting day', wrote Victoria.

Alix, though still pale, fragile and terribly thin, and in spite of her deafness and her limp, re-tained her elegance and youthfulness. Her family now complete, she took her place at her husband's side as they attended the endless events of the royal year. Always dignified, she ignored, at least in public, Bertie's indiscre-tions; turned a blind eye to his amorous adven-tures. She went with him to the races at Ascot and Goodwood and yachting at Cowes; she was there beside him at the state banquets and recep-tions and the parties of the Marlborough House set. But Bertie, still the Prince of Pleasure, had his other interests. As he amused himself at the card tables, the theatres and clubs, he was always surrounded by the most glittering stars in the theatre and Society favourites—Lillie Lang-try, Sarah Bernhardt, the Countess of Warwick and Mrs Keppel. Alix, meanwhile, was more and more drawn to Sandringham, where her children were spending their babyhood.

In 1871, the year of Bertie's illness, Alexan-dra's eldest son Eddy (Duke of Clarence) was seven, Georgie six, and together they began their formal education. Their tutor was the Reverend John Dalton and it was his task to give his reluc-tant royal pupils a grounding in Latin and French, history, geography, mathematics and English. Georgie was an average pupil, some-times lazy, but he showed interest and at least he tried. Eddy, on the other hand, proved impos-sible to teach. He lacked concentration and was backward for his age. Their sisters were their mother's responsibility and Princess Alexandra worried little about their education. She appointed a governess for them, but the girls learnt little else but music. Otherwise they were allowed to run wild like their brothers. Queen Victoria was critical of them all. At seven Georgie shocked her when, having been sent from the meal table for naughtiness, he re-appeared with-out any clothes on. She said they were ill-bred and ill-trained and advised that they should not be allowed downstairs with their parents for too long, and never more than one at a time, and that they should keep regular hours. But Alexandra's devotion to her children amounted to an obses-sion, at least by royal standards. She insisted on bathing them herself whenever possible, reading bedtime stories to them and hearing them say their prayers. She was possessive and gave them the unstinting affection she would have given Bertie if only he had accepted it. Sons and daughters alike called Alix 'Motherdear' long after they were out of childhood; they were boisterous, fun-loving, affectionate in return. They had a happy childhood, free to run with their dogs, ride their horses and cycle round the Sandringham estate. But they had little discipline or education.

Eddy, as second in line to the throne, was his parents' chief concern. He was delicate, dreamy and dull. Alix wanted him to go to Wellington College, but he was not educationally suited, so, with Georgie for company, he became a naval cadet and was sent to the *Britannia*, an old wooden training ship at Dartmouth. Alix, always emotional, was deeply upset when it came to saying goodbye to her sons, but Bertie wanted them to have a more normal upbringing, mix with other boys of their own age, and so experience the kind of education he himself missed. While Georgie thrived at Dartmouth, poor Eddy was a disappointment. After training on the *Britannia* came long spells at sea, to the West Indies, Australia and the Far East. Each departure meant tears for Alix who wept whenever she had to be parted from her 'dear boys'.

Once again, while Georgie benefited from life at sea, the unfortunate Duke of Clarence was not a success. He was neither clever nor popular; nor was he attractive. Tall and thin, he had an exceptionally long neck and arms which led to his father giving him the nickname 'Collar and Cuffs'. After touring the world he had a period at Cambridge, where it was believed he became involved with homosexual circles, and in London his name even became linked with the mystery surrounding Jack the Ripper.

Alix, who strived to keep her offspring pure, simple and childlike, was blamed for his weaknesses. Having failed in the Navy he joined the Army and was given a commission in the Hussars. But, so far as anyone could see there was only one solution to the problem of Eddy and that was marriage to a suitable princess. Queen Victoria found the perfect bride: Princess May, daughter of the Duke and Duchess of Teck. The couple were not strangers; in fact they had known one another since childhood, having met

at children's parties and dances. Their marriage was arranged for February 1892.

In January, when Eddy should have been celebrating his 28th birthday he fell ill. It was thought he had caught a cold while shooting at Sandringham; the cold got worse and Eddie was found to be a victim of a flu epidemic. Then pneumonia developed. His condition rapidly worsened and, once again, the whole family gathered in a Sandringham sickroom fearing the worst. This time it came, on January 14. Albert Edward, Duke of Clarence, died in his mother's arms; his bride-to-be, Princess May, at his side. It was, May said afterwards, a 'dreadful night of agony and suspense.'

Princess Alexandra never really recovered from the shock of Eddy's death. Broken by sorrow she entered a long period of mourning from which she never fully emerged. And just as Victoria kept Albert's bedroom as it had been in his lifetime, so Alix preserved Eddy's room as he left it on that fateful day, with soap and toothpaste by the washbasin, a Union Jack draped over the bed, his uniforms hanging in the wardrobe. Often a fire was lit in the hearth and, on his birthday, flowers were placed on his pillow.

Bertie, who had so loved to tease Eddy, wept for the son he found so hard to understand: 'Gladly would I have given my life for his, as I put no value on my own.'

Alix now became even more possessive of her remaining children. Soon after Eddy's death, Georgie was created Duke of York. He also proposed to and was accepted by Princess May. Alix had mixed feelings about the match. 'It is sad to think we shall never be able to be together and travel in the same way—yet there is a bond of love between us, that of mother and child, which nothing can ever diminish ... nobody can, or ever shall, come between me and my darling Georgie boy.'

Princess Louise, the eldest of the Wales' daughters and the tomboy of the family with the nickname Harry, had been the first to leave the nest by marriage when in 1888 she married Lord

The three daughters of Bertie and Alix, painted by Hall in 1893.
From left to right, Louise, Victoria and Maud.

Fife, 18 years her senior. Now Alix clung to Victoria (whom she called Toria) and Maud. Alix, who had heard her children's prayers until they were in their teens, protected and fussed over them, dreaded the thought that they might leave her. Her daughters were so clinging and lacking in self-confidence that they became known as 'Their Royal Shynesses', and the 'Whispering Wales's'. 'Her whole life is wrapped up in her children', Bertie once said of his wife. But he, too, spoiled his daughters. Maud eventually married Prince Charles of Denmark and later became Queen of Norway. But Toria had to decline two offers of marriage. She was the daughter destined to care for her mother in her old age and became an embittered companion.

Queen Victoria died in 1901, and Bertie at last

succeeded to the throne as Edward VII. It was almost too late. He was 60 years of age and even then the coronation planned for June had to be postponed while he underwent an operation for appendicitis, a serious operation at that time.

Alix, without her own children to mother, now took on the role of grandmother. In 1905 when George, Duke of York, and Princess May went to India they left their own six children in her care. Alix was only too ready to spoil them. As Queen she took on many more commitments. Ever sympathetic, generous and kind, she became involved in the work of charitable insti-tutions and helped raise money for the poor. Nursing was another great interest. She involved herself with the army nursing staff sent to South Africa during the Boer War and the Queen Alexandra Imperial Nursing Service was named after her. She also worked for the hospital service at home and Alexandra Rose Day became a national institution.

In May 1910 Bertie died. For Alix, still gracious, elegant, dignified, 15 years of widowhood lay ahead. She took up new interests: photography, painting and embroidery. Her last days were spent at Sandringham with Toria her companion, and she died there.

MAY OF TECK
1867 ~ 1953

The Shy Queen

Princess May, the daughter of a German Duke, Prince Franz of Teck, and Princess Mary Adelaide of Cambridge was a great-grandchild of Queen Victoria. She was born at Kensington Palace in May 1867 in the same bedroom as Queen Victoria and spent most of her young life at the White Lodge, Richmond, where she was joined in the nursery by three brothers. When the family were hit by financial problems they moved to Florence, and stayed for two years until, at 18, May was ready to take part in court social life. Queen Victoria had picked her out as the ideal partner for the young Duke of Clarence, but when he died she married instead his younger brother George, Duke of York, the next heir to the throne.

They married in the Chapel Royal at St James's Palace in July 1893 when he was 28, she 26, and spent their honeymoon at Sandringham and Cowes, where May's sailor husband could enjoy the royal regatta. Then they settled down to married life at York Cottage, a stone-built villa on the Sandringham estate which had once been used as a hunting lodge and was their wedding present from the Prince of Wales. Their London home, York House at St James's, was still being refurbished when, the following summer, the Duchess was expecting her first baby. Princess Alexandra, who so loved babies, wanted her grandchild to be born at Buckingham Palace, but May decided to escape the oppressive heat of London in mid-summer and accepted her mother's invitation to have her first baby at home at Richmond. There, Princess Mary Adelaide was able to fuss over her daughter and Mr Asquith, the Home Secretary was present when, on June 23, 1894, May gave birth to a son.

Queen Victoria who travelled from Osborne looked with approval on her great-grandson and declared him a 'very fine strong boy, a pretty child'. She now had three living heirs and after the christening she posed for photographs of four royal generations. Once again, Victoria had wanted the new baby to be called Albert after her adored dead husband, but the Duke and Duchess wanted him to be named after Eddy, the Duke of Clarence. So the child was christened Edward Albert Christian George Andrew Patrick David. No leading member of the family, no patron saint had been forgotten. Later, he was known to his family simply as David—but in the

*May of Teck was born here
in Queen Victoria's bedroom.*

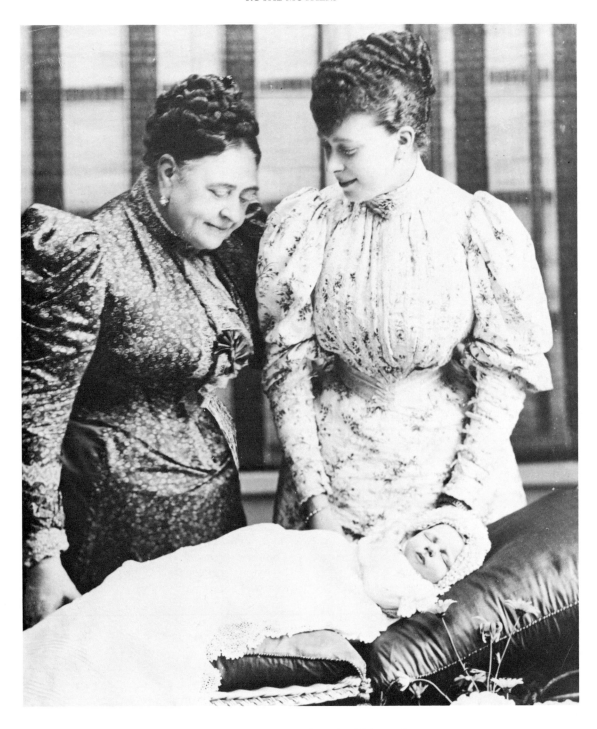

*Princess Mary (as she became known), with her mother
the Duchess of Teck, and her first child.*

years to come, he would be known as the Prince of Wales, King Edward VIII, and Duke of Windsor.

Right from the start, Princess May made it clear that she was not going to follow the example of her mother-in-law and make motherhood her career. She would never be 'Motherdear' to her children. When David was still a baby she left him in the care of a friend while she took a holiday in St Moritz and her husband went to Cowes. Princess Alexandra was strongly disapproving. Nevertheless, May continued to carry out her duty and fill the nursery at York Cottage with another generation of royal babies.

In 1895 she gave birth prematurely at Sandringham to a second son. He arrived on the exact anniversary of the death of the Prince Consort, and this time his great-grandmother's wish was granted. He was christened Albert, with the additions of Frederick Arthur George, and Queen Victoria was his godmother. But his family called him Bertie, and he was destined to become George VI. In the spring of 1897 the Duchess of Teck had a golden-haired daughter. 'My little diamond jubilee baby,' said Queen Victoria, who even wanted her called Diamond! But she was baptised Victoria Alexandra Alice Mary, and was known by her first name for the first few years before changing to Mary, and later taking the title Princess Royal.

Three years later May of Teck had her third son, Henry, the future Duke of Gloucester. Maybe, having spent her childhood surrounded by brothers, she preferred boys because she wrote afterwards, 'I confess I am just a little bit proud of myself for having produced another boy.' Then she went on to say, 'I think I have done my duty and may now stop, as having babies is highly distasteful to me tho' when once they are there they are very nice! The children are so pleased with the baby who they think flew in at my window and had to have his wings cut off.'

But Henry was not to be the last of the line. He was followed two years later by George, the future Duke of Kent and in 1905 by John. All of

May's babies, with the exception of David, were born at Sandringham and spent their early days in the comparatively cramped confines of York Cottage. But May spent little time with her children, preferring to leave them entirely to the care of nannies. The fact that she took little interest in the appointment of her children's nannies and seldom spent time in the nursery meant that her eldest children suffered disastrously. 'Before carrying me to see my parents at the end of the day, the nanny would pinch my arm and make me bawl,' recalled the Duke of Windsor. And the Duchess was so lacking in natural maternal warmth that instead of cuddling her baby to stop the tears she handed him back to Nanny. She liked her babies only when they were good and appealing. Nanny was ultra possessive and was only too happy to rush back to the nursery with her crying charge. The nanny was not only so neurotic about her responsibilities that she failed to take a holiday in her three years in royal service, she was also incapable of caring for the children. Bertie, in his turn, was so badly fed that he suffered digestive troubles that were to affect him for the rest of his life. Eventually the inadequate nanny had a nervous breakdown and swiftly departed to be replaced by the loving and capable Mrs Bill—Lala to the children. She was to rule the nursery for years to come and remained in touch with the children for the rest of her life.

Although May loved her children in her own way and she was kind and gentle, she was almost always overruled by her quick-tempered husband who was a stern disciplinarian, fanatical about punctuality and intolerant of the shortcomings of small children. May's extreme shyness prevented her from expressing her feelings and outwardly showing her affection. She normally saw her children for a short while after breakfast and again at tea-time, but frequent royal tours of the provinces as well as journeys overseas, sometimes for months at a time, meant that she missed much of their babyhood. In 1901 when David was seven, the others six, four and one, the Duke and Duchess went on a world tour

Princess Mary and Prince George.

wonder she sometimes puzzled over her relationship with her children, and once, referring to David, made the poignant remark: 'I really believe he begins to like me at last, he is most civil to me.'

While the Duke and Duchess were away their grandmother Alexandra, Princess of Wales, was able to indulge her love of children, allowing the York offspring to rampage through the big house at Sandringham, and be as noisy and as troublesome as they liked.

Deprived of so much maternal affection it is not surprising that the children were often troublesome. Bertie, who was sensitive by nature, seems to have suffered the most. Neglect made him timid and often tearful and his shyness caused the stammer that was to mar his adult life. It was later believed that his stammer was the result of being made to write with his right hand when he was naturally left-handed. His parents did little to help him overcome his difficulties and other children who jeered at his handicap went unchecked. All of the boys except David suffered, like their father, from knock-knees and to correct the deformity they were made to wear splints on their legs every night and often during the day as well.

When the two eldest sons, David and Bertie, were aged eight and seven, they were taken out of the care of Lala and put in the charge of a manservant, a nursery footman. He was Frederick Finch, a son of Wellington's footman, who became a devoted servant to the princes and later became Prince George's chauffeur. It was the faithful Finch who heard the boys' prayers night and morning, who looked after their clothes and made sure they wore those dreaded leg splints. At this time the princes began their education in the Sandringham schoolroom. They had specialist teachers for languages but their chief tutor was Henry Hansell, a scholarly academic who struggled to prepare his not very willing pupils for entry to the Royal Naval College at Osborne, and later Dartmouth. When Prince Henry was a pupil in Mr Hansell's

which kept them away from home for almost eight months. And in 1905, the year John was born, they were away for a further six months. They frequently sent their children messages by letter and postcard and sent them small gifts from the other side of the world, but the fast growing infants seemed like strangers to May when she returned. She found it so hard to understand them, for she had no insight into the workings of their minds. As a mother she was rigid in her outlook, distant, often critical. No

George and Mary, Duke and Duchess of York in 1906 with their children.
From the left, Mary, Henry, George, John, Edward and Albert.

Sandringham House seen from the lake.

schoolroom he was in such poor health that he had to be sent to Broadstairs to recover his strength. He was cared for by Sister Edith Ward who had nursed the Prince of Wales through his illness and between bracing walks by the sea he had his usual lessons. For Henry, the days in the Sandringham classroom were over. Mr Hansell had the imagination to persuade Henry's parents that boarding school, where he would mix with other boys, would be the best place for the young Prince. And so Henry, the future Duke of Gloucester, attended Saint Peter's Court Preparatory School at Broadstairs, where he was joined later by his younger brother George before both boys went to Eton.

Only Princess Mary escaped the harsh regime at Sandringham; she was her father's favourite who climbed trees with her brothers and was so disruptive in the schoolroom that her governess thought she should be separated from her brothers. Even Alexandra, her loving grandmother, suggested she should go to boarding school but the Duchess refused. May wanted her only daughter to be educated at home.

Life had changed dramatically for May and her husband in 1901 when that shadowy yet still formidable figure, the old Queen Victoria, died. She had been part of all their lives for longer than anyone could remember. When the new King Edward VII and Queen Alexandra moved into Buckingham Palace, May and George made Marlborough House their London home and, with increased royal duties to perform, they became yet more remote from their children. Nine years later, on the death of King Edward, George succeeded to the throne and May became Queen Mary.

The coronation in 1911 was a triumphant family occasion. David, the new Prince of Wales, wore his Garter robes, Bertie wore his naval cadet uniform and Henry and George, aged eleven and nine, were in Highland dress. Mary, their tomboyish sister, looked unusually dignified in a white gown of state. Only one member of the family was missing, the sad little Prince John who, from the age of five, lived apart from his brothers and sisters. It was believed that he suffered from epilepsy in such a severe form that he had to be nursed away from home. He had his own household where he was cared for by the capable Mrs Bill, a nursemaid and a manservant until his death, at the age of 14, in 1919.

Following soon after the coronation there was another display of glittering pageantry at Caernarvon when David, attired in knee breeches, purple cloak and gold coronet, and hating every embarrassing minute of it, was invested as Prince of Wales. It was a brilliant occasion, the inspiration of David Lloyd George, and it was to be the last event of celebration before the country plunged into the darkness of the First World War.

To his great disappointment, David, as next in line to the throne, was not permitted to take an active part in the war, but stayed on the sidelines on the staff of the Commander-in-Chief, first in France, then in Italy. But Bertie, as a sub lieutenant in the Royal Navy, joined in the fighting and was in the Battle of Jutland. Typically, as Queen, Mary supported the women's war effort. She spent time knitting for soldiers, and urged her family to follow her example. The war was a time of personal crisis for both Mary and the King, as so many of their family across Europe were now counted among the enemy. When peace came on a changed world King George decided that his family should have a new name. The house of Saxe-Coburg-Gotha took the name of Windsor.

Princess Mary was the first of the Queen's children to marry, when, in February 1922, she married Viscount Lascelles (later the Earl of Harewood) at Westminster Abbey. It was the wedding of the year and Queen Mary, as mother of the bride, arranged the event with great enthusiasm. But the event was eclipsed a year later by the marriage of the Duke of York to the 'so pretty and engaging and natural' Elizabeth Bowes-Lyon. The family had to wait another eleven years for the next wedding, when in 1934, George, Duke of Kent, married Princess Marina of Greece and, the following year, Henry, Duke of Gloucester, was wedded to Lady Alice Montagu-Douglas-Scott.

Mary, who found it so hard to know her own children, took a natural delight in her grandchildren. When the King was convalescing at Bognor after a serious illness in 1929, the company of the toddling Princess Elizabeth, the daughter of the Duke and Duchess of York, was an important part of his recovery. Suddenly the ageing Queen appeared to enjoy the chatter of small children. In 1935, the Silver Jubilee Year of the King and Queen when they celebrated not only 25 years on the throne but a further thanksgiving for the King's recovery, Princess Elizabeth and her little sister Margaret Rose drove through cheering crowds to be with their grandparents for their service of thanksgiving in St Paul's Cathedral.

King George V, the one person who always came first in Queen Mary's life, lived for only eight months after the jubilee. He died in January 1936 a few weeks after delivering his Christmas Day message to the nation. Bravely, his widow concealed her grief. During the King's illness, Bertie, Duke of York, had commented to the Prince of Wales, 'She is really far too reserved; she keeps too much locked up inside her. I fear a breakdown if anything awful happens. She has been wonderful.'

The 'awful' thing happened, and Queen Mary was left to face alone the biggest crisis of her life. Her son's abdication. Having lost her husband, Queen Mary now had to summon all her courage, all her inner strength, to survive yet another terrible blow. David's announcement that he would marry Mrs Simpson and renounce his throne meant that she was now to lose her son, the as yet uncrowned King Edward VIII. As usual, she kept her feelings to herself; throughout the crisis she was restrained and dignified, every inch a Queen. What it cost her, emotionally, we shall never know.

Queen Mary, always stately, quiet, reserved, who never succumbed to changes in fashion because her husband liked her the way she was, became an ever more devoted grandmama. As well as Elizabeth and Margaret Rose there were the Lascelles children, George and Gerald, then came Edward, Alexandra and Michael of Kent, and William and Richard of Gloucester. In old age she somehow found the love she could not show her own children; she was generous with extra pocket money and Christmas and birthday treats. But there was still more sorrow to come in her old age. In 1942 her son George, Duke of Kent, was killed in a air crash in Scotland while he was on active service, and ten years later Bertie, her second son who became King George VI, died in his sleep.

Queen Mary died in 1953 at the age of 86 only two months before the coronation of her granddaughter Elizabeth. She had survived two world wars, seen six monarchs on the throne, and lived to see her great-grandchildren, Prince Charles and Princess Anne.

A royal nursery in miniature? One of the rooms in Queen Mary's elaborate doll's house.

The Windsors

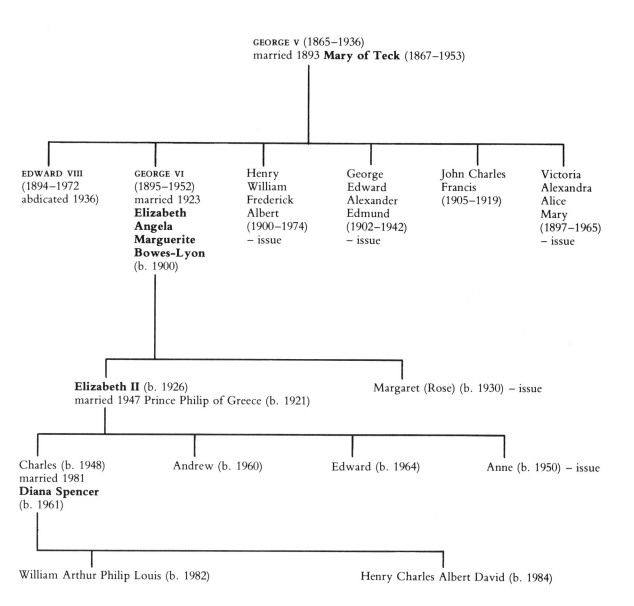

GEORGE V (1865–1936)
married 1893 **Mary of Teck** (1867–1953)

EDWARD VIII
(1894–1972
abdicated 1936)

GEORGE VI
(1895–1952)
married 1923
**Elizabeth
Angela
Marguerite
Bowes-Lyon**
(b. 1900)

Henry
William
Frederick
Albert
(1900–1974)
– issue

George
Edward
Alexander
Edmund
(1902–1942)
– issue

John Charles
Francis
(1905–1919)

Victoria
Alexandra
Alice
Mary
(1897–1965)
– issue

Elizabeth II (b. 1926)
married 1947 Prince Philip of Greece (b. 1921)

Margaret (Rose) (b. 1930) – issue

Charles (b. 1948)
married 1981
Diana Spencer
(b. 1961)

Andrew (b. 1960)

Edward (b. 1964)

Anne (b. 1950) – issue

William Arthur Philip Louis (b. 1982)

Henry Charles Albert David (b. 1984)

Today's princes and princesses marry for love. No one can deny that they marry 'well', but they are still allowed a relatively free hand in their choice of marriage partner. Their lives are almost unclouded by the violence and dangers that royal families faced for centuries. Nowadays, such incidents are isolated: the attempted kidnapping of Princess Anne from her car in The Mall in London; the Trooping of the Colour ceremony during which blank shots were fired at the Queen, and the potentially hazardous tours that are undertaken to sensitive countries.

The mothers of the House of Windsor have strength and resolve, combined with great self-control and restraint. They rarely display emotion in public and their private lives have been kept just that, although the Prince and Princess of Wales have allowed a glimpse of their thoughts and lifestyle through the media.

Queen Elizabeth the Queen Mother was perhaps the most courageous of them all. She had enjoyed a private life with her husband and daughters until the day Edward VIII abdicated and thrust the family into the spotlight. Even if Elizabeth had speculated on the outcome of the affair between Edward and Mrs Simpson, and wondered what might happen if . . . could she ever have foreseen that her husband would so suddenly become King? Unprepared though she was, she rose well to her new role. Seeing her daughter take the responsibilities of State after her beloved Bertie's early death must have been a double blow. She would surely have wished Elizabeth a few more precious years in peace with her family.

But young Elizabeth had learned her lessons well. A woman ahead of her time she balanced both the affairs of state and the needs of her young children to become a true working mother. She kept the children with her, and the youngest two were even allowed to play at her feet in her study as she worked. Her children—and grandchildren—are devoted to her in a way that has rarely been seen in royal relationships.

Now that tradition has all but lost its grip on royal mothers, the lying-in and witnessed births have been replaced by short stays in hospitals and the most up-to-date equipment for safe, almost pain-free birth.

Princess Anne was one of the first of the modern royals to have a baby in hospital. She has proved to be a brisk, no-nonsense mum who cheerfully declares herself not particularly maternal. Although she enjoys the company of her children when she is with them, royal duties and her work for the Save the Children Fund keep them apart for many weeks of the year. She has admitted, 'There are times when I don't see very much of my children. But when I'm around they're with me and we do things together.' In fact, she is merely repeating the pattern of her own childhood, when she and Prince Charles were often separated from their parents. 'I don't remember ever feeling deprived,' says the Princess of those childhood partings, 'because nobody told me I was deprived. I accepted my parents' absences because they'd always done it. When they came back, they made a lot of time for us and spent holidays with us.'

She is bringing up her children as plain Master and Miss Phillips with no titles and no fuss. That she is allowed to do so is an indication of how un-royal the family has become in its thinking.

It's true to say that being royal today has become a job of work as much as a way of life, and motherhood is a far more pleasurable occupation for these royal wives than it ever was in history. Husbands take an active interest in their children as children, and not as potential pawns in a game of power and politics. Contraception and modern health and birth practices have removed the necessity for royal women to produce a child every year. And those that are born can expect long and happy lives.

Like Princess Anne, Princess Diana had her children delivered in hospital, staying just 24 hours after Harry's birth. She has never made a secret of her love and commitment to her children, and has gone to great lengths to avoid long separations. However, having proved her point by taking baby William on tour, she has since decided that the children really are better off in the nursery than being taken half way

*The Duchess of York
with her baby Elizabeth.*

round the world. But through her actions, she made the statement that she is a mother first and the Princess of Wales second.

Today, royals are allowed to be mothers to their children to the degree that they wish. If they choose to breastfeed them, they can—and both Anne and Diana did. If they want to leave them to a fleet of nannies and rarely see them, they can. That they choose to spend time with their children—our monarchs of tomorrow—and enjoy it, says a lot for the evolution of the monarchy, and a lot more for motherhood today.

ELIZABETH BOWES-LYON
1900 ~

The Calm After the Storm

Lady Elizabeth Bowes-Lyon, the youngest daughter of ten children of the Earl and Countess of Strathmore, married Bertie, Duke of York, in Westminster Abbey in April 1923, and afterwards moved into the White Lodge in Richmond Park. It was a 'grace and favour' house, the former home of the late parents of Queen Mary, but the newly-weds were not happy at Richmond. It was too far from London and the house too big and draughty. They needed a town residence, and this they found at number 145 Piccadilly.

So much work had to be done on the four-storey house that when the Duchess's baby was due in 1926 she went to her parent's home, 17 Bruton Street, for the confinement. Three doctors were present to deliver the first of a new generation of royal children, and it proved to be a complicated birth. Afterwards came the delicate announcement that 'a certain line of treatment' had been successfully undertaken, which meant that the child had been born, feet first, by Caesarian section. The information was couched in discreet terms because the Duchess disliked having such intimate details made public.

The Home Secretary, Sir William Joynson-Hicks, followed the old tradition and was one of the first to inspect the baby who had arrived shortly after 3 a.m. on April 21. Later that day the King and Queen, George V and Queen Mary, arrived for their first glimpse of their pretty fair-haired granddaughter who was described as having large dark-lashed blue eyes, tiny ears and a lovely complexion. 'We always wanted a child to make our happiness complete and now that it has at last happened it seems so wonderful and strange,' wrote the proud father to Queen Mary. 'I am so proud of Elizabeth at this moment, after all that she has gone through during the last few days.'

The Duke and Duchess chose the names Elizabeth Alexandra Mary, and the Duke asked the King for his approval, adding that he did not think it would be confusing to have two Elizabeths in the family—and Elizabeth of York sounded so nice. Approval was duly given and the infant baptised by the Archbishop of York in the private chapel at Buckingham Palace with water from the River Jordan. She wore the lace and satin robe handed down by Victoria's family and the silver gilt font designed for Victoria's daughter was used for the ceremony.

The Duchess breastfed her baby for the first month, then she handed little Elizabeth into the care of an old family retainer, Nurse Clara Knight ('Alla' to her charges), who had looked after the Duchess in her own childhood. She knew Alla was motherly, reliable and kind, and that life for the baby would fall into a cosy routine.

Elizabeth of Glamis began motherhood with the experience of a golden childhood behind her. She, in turn, had an instinctive love for children. And, as 50 years on, her grandson Prince Charles was to say: She has always been one of those extraordinarily rare people whose touch can turn everything to gold—bringing happiness and comfort—making any home she lives in a unique haven of cosiness and character.

The Duchess was never allowed to forget that her baby was special, for the public claimed her as their own. Press photographers and public followed in pursuit of the royal pram so that outings in Green Park had to be abandoned and, instead, Elizabeth had her airings in the gardens at Buckingham Palace. Suddenly the new royal infant became a trendsetter and Princess Elizabeth clothes, look-alike frilly dresses, bonnets and coats, as well as dolls and picture books filled the shops. The Duchess of York had to share her baby with the nation.

She also had to travel with her husband on extensive overseas tours. Little Elizabeth was only eight months old when the Duchess had to face the heartbreak of the first long separation.

After spending Christmas at Sandringham, the Duke and Duchess took their little daughter to St Paul's Walden Bury, the Strathmore family home in Hertfordshire, where she was to stay with her grandparents for the first month of her parent's absence. She would be looked after by the faithful Alla in the familar surroundings of the Duchess's old nursery. From Hertfordshire, Elizabeth would be taken back to London to be near the King and Queen who were also taking a close interest in their little grandchild.

The parting, said the Duchess, 'quite broke me up'. She knew that it would be more than six months before she would see her baby again. On January 7 the Duke and Duchess sailed from Portsmouth on a voyage to New Zealand, then on to Australia for the opening of the first session of Parliament in May 1927.

Elaborate plans were made for the Duchess to receive a weekly cable in code giving news of her daughter's progress. Photographs were taken every month so that she always had the latest picture of her baby, and letters were waiting in every port. The Duchess had planned to be reunited with her child at the new family home, 145 Piccadilly, but on her return to England six months and 30,000 miles later she learned that Elizabeth was waiting for her at Buckingham Palace. King George V and Queen Mary, who had been so stern, so cool and distant with their own children, had developed a warm loving relationship with their granddaughter. In fact they were so indulgent towards her that the Duchess feared she might already be very spoilt. 'There's Mummy,' said the Queen, when the Duchess arrived, and Elizabeth grinned happily and held out her arms to her mother who had been away so long that she had even missed her first birthday.

Years later, when Elizabeth married, her father, then George VI, promised that there would be no overseas tours for her until her children were well out of babyhood. The long parting had affected not only the Duchess, but the Duke, too.

As soon as Elizabeth learned to talk she called herself 'Lilibet'; her parents thought it endearing and the name was adopted by the family. In 1930 Lilibet was joined in the nursery by her sister, Margaret Rose, born during a thunderstorm at Glamis Castle, the Strathmore ancestral home, on the evening of August 21. She, too, was born by Caesarian section, but she was late arriving. Mr Clynes, the Home Secretary of the day, stayed at the nearby home of the Earl of Airlie for more than a fortnight waiting for the event. Bonfires were lit on hilltops and bagpipes played to welcome the baby. Of course, there was popular expectation that the second York baby would be a son, but the Scots were delighted. Boy or girl, this was the first royal child so close to the throne to be born in Scotland since 1600, and a team of Scottish doctors had been chosen for the delivery. The Duke and Duchess wanted to call her Ann Margaret but the King disapproved of Ann. Even as a married man and a parent, Bertie dared not disobey his father in such matters; his daughter, therefore, was called Margaret. But they added Rose, after the Duchess's sister Lady Leveson-Gower, who was the baby's godmother.

Lilibet must have welcomed the newcomer with mixed feelings. A four-year age gap is hard to bridge. But she was quick to call her little sister

'Bud' explaining: 'You see, she isn't a real rose yet, only a bud.'

Alla, ruling her nursery at the top of the house, was joined by Margaret 'Bobo' Macdonald and her sister Ruby, who were appointed as under-nurse and nurserymaid. The next few years were to be the happiest for the close, loving family. Life for the royal sisters was sheltered, ordered, secure. Lilibet and Margaret Rose enjoyed comparative peace and seclusion as the Duchess tried to keep her daughters out of the limelight.

Lilibet could sometimes be glimpsed through the garden railings as she played with her Lascelles cousins, the sons of Princess Mary. And at four she had her first seaside holiday when she went with her nanny to visit King George V, recovering from his illness at Bognor. A sandpit was provided for her in the garden at Bognor and the merry laughter of 'our sweet little granddaughter' was a tonic to the convalescing King. A special bond had grown up between them. At Christmas the words 'Glad tidings of great joy I bring to you and all mankind' prompted little Lilibet to say 'I know who is that old man, kind. He is you, Grand Papa, and I does love you.'

In 1931 the Duke and Duchess took over the Royal Lodge in Windsor Great Park as a country retreat for their expanding family. It had last been used by the Prince Regent, then abandoned, and had fallen into a tumbledown state of disrepair. The Duke and Duchess restored, rebuilt and lovingly revitalised the place making it into a comfortable modern family home. Close by, Lilibet had her own little thatched home—*Y Bwthyn Bach*, a miniature house presented to the Princess as a wonderful sixth birthday gift from the people of Wales. There the two sisters spent countless hours of childhood pretending to be ordinary grown-up housewives. Another birthday present was a Welsh corgi—the first of a long line of companions.

Life in the York household was altogether happy, informal, relaxed, with none of the old barriers that existed between the nursery and the grown-up world downstairs. There were morning cuddles when the children were taken to their parents before breakfast, and squeals of delight at bathtime. As they grew older meals were taken together whenever it was convenient so the girls did not suffer the terrible shyness endured by their father.

With the arrival of Margaret Rose, Alla was kept busy looking after the newborn baby's needs and Lilibet turned to Bobo for attention. The little girl depended increasingly on the under-nurse for companionship until Bobo became indispensable. She was later appointed dresser to the Princess, travelling everywhere with her. Today Bobo Macdonald is still in the Queen's service, and one of her closest friends.

It was soon obvious to the Duchess that her two daughters had totally contrasting personalities. Lilibet, as a tiny child, seemed aware of her position in life. She had a maturity beyond her years; she was serious and dignified. Her little sister was fun-loving, often naughty, fond of mimicry and practical jokes, and was quick to show her emotions. While Lilibet displayed the gravity which was the hallmark of the stiff and starchy Queen Mary, Margaret Rose was extrovert and demonstrative in her affections. She would jump on her father's knee for kisses and cuddles, just when he was about to scold her for some highspirited prank. Her behaviour convinced Queen Mary that she was terribly spoiled. Sometimes sisterly disputes were settled by a battle royal in the nursery.

The Duchess often worried that her little girls were being given too much publicity. They were featured in magazines and newspapers worldwide, and although she was flattered to think that others found her daughters so attractive, she worried enough about Elizabeth's popularity to write to Queen Mary: 'It almost frightens me that the people love her so much. I suppose it is a good thing, and I only hope she will be worthy of it, poor little darling.'

The Duchess's fears were not altogether unfounded, because Princess Margaret, at the tender age of five, was not unaware of her charms and said to her father: 'I'm pretty, you know', to which he tactfully replied: 'Of course you're pretty, but then you've got a pretty mother.'

*Princess Elizabeth and Margaret were much more
in the public eye than their parents had been.*

It was agreed that the two princesses should be educated at home in the old tradition and Lilibet had her first lessons at her mother's knee. The Duchess taught her to read and gave her daughter her first lessons in French. Where other royal mothers may have failed to understand their children, hard as they tried, the Duchess was in her element. She even turned teaching her daughters how to address dignitaries into a game by acting out the part of a prime minister or a bishop, so the girls had fun choosing the right responses.

Marion Crawford, a young, energetic, highly qualified Scot, was appointed governess in 1932. She had been recommended for the job by the Duchess' sister, for she had been with the family for some time. Now she was destined to educate a future Queen, and she stayed with the royal family for 17 years. Formal lessons, divided into half-hour periods, were given in the mornings; afternoons were devoted to dancing, music and art. And Queen Mary, who kept an interested and often critical eye on her granddaughters' progress, gave extra history lessons. These entailed outings to museums and art galleries and lectures on family history—of which she herself had so much personal knowledge. When she was older, Lilibet had religious instruction from Canon Crawley, who was a member of St George's Chapel Chapter, and for the important subject of history she went to Eton for tutorials from the Vice Provost, Sir Henry Marten. But Margaret, to her great disappointment, had to continue learning history from Queen Mary.

Outside the schoolroom, the royal year was punctuated by weekends at Windsor, visits to St Paul's Walden Bury, summer at Glamis and Balmoral, Christmas at Sandringham. But the gentle routine of family life ended abruptly when, only a year after the death of George V, the new, as yet uncrowned King Edward VIII renounced the throne. In 1937 Bertie, Duke of York, Edward's younger brother became King George VI. Princess Elizabeth, ten years old and now next in line to the throne exclaimed sadly, 'Nothing could ever be the same again.' And she

wished, at least, someone could build a tunnel from Buckingham Palace back to 145 Piccadilly so that she could sleep in her old nursery. To comfort her, it was decided that Bobo Macdonald would share her bedroom.

The weeks leading up to the coronation were filled with activity. The whole family were involved in fittings for robes; the two princesses were to wear matching dresses of ivory lace over satin, with purple velvet robes trimmed with ermine and gold tassels, and little light-weight gold coronets. When the great day came they drove to the Abbey with their grandmother. There amid the pageantry and spendour of age-old tradition, Lilibet aged 11 and Margaret Rose, 6, saw their father crowned King. Afterwards the two little princesses stood with their parents on the balcony of Buckingham Palace and waved to the sea of cheering faces below.

The day of public exultation marked the end of their carefree childhood, lessons with Mother, dancing classes with Madame Vacani, afternoon drives with Alla through Battersea Park or Hyde Park. From then on the sisters were to appear more often with their parents in public, they were to travel more, and Princess Elizabeth, as heir presumptive, had to be prepared for her possible future role. Gone were any thoughts that the princesses might be sent to school. The Queen had voiced ideas that the experience of school could be good for her daughters but these were vetoed by the King and other traditionalists who regarded palace lessons from governesses and tutors the only way to educate children so close to the crown. But the world was about to change. Lilibet and Margaret Rose were to be the last of the generation educated at home.

The family were on holiday at Balmoral when war broke out late in the summer of 1939. The King and Queen hurriedly left for London leaving their daughters in Scotland. For the two Princesses, the outbreak of the Second World War meant an extended holiday. When their mother returned it was to explain to them the dreadful truth. It would be dangerous for them to return south, at least for the time being, so the

*Summer 1946
in the gardens of the
Royal Lodge, Windsor.*

girls, then aged 13 and 9, stayed on at Balmoral.

Windsor Castle, the ancient stronghold, with its great stone walls and fortifications was considered the safest place for the royal children. There was at one time a fear that German paratroopers might attempt to storm the castle to take the Princesses hostage. Their safety was a constant worry and it was suggested that they might be evacuated overseas, but the Queen refused to be parted from them. 'The children won't go without me,' she said. 'I won't leave the King. And the King will never leave.' And so while Lilibet and Margaret spent the war years at Windsor, the King and Queen continued to use Buckingham Palace as their daytime headquarters, returning to Windsor to sleep at night and staying there at weekends. They also spent a lot of time away from home, visiting areas which had suffered the worst devastation and travelling thousands of miles by royal train, sleeping on

189

board whenever necessary. It was miraculous that the royal couple themselves escaped injury, for Buckingham Palace was hit nine times. On one occasion, the Queen stood at the window as she watched an enemy bomber approaching—and seconds later, six bombs fell on the building. The private chapel, the scene of so many christenings, was destroyed that day, and most of the windows were blown out. The Queen's response was typically courageous. 'I'm glad we have been bombed,' she said. 'It makes me feel we can look the East End in the face.'

Eventually an air raid shelter was constructed for the family's safety at Windsor and for the Princesses, siren suits, gas masks and air-raid warnings became part of life. Even the royal dolls were catered for—small pink and blue suitcases containing dolls' clothes were often carried down to the shelter as well. But dolls were not favourite playthings. For Lilibet at least, animals always came first. It was a love she inherited from her mother. From toy horses on the landing at 145 Piccadilly, she soon graduated to her first Shetland pony, and her Pembrokeshire corgis, Dookie and Jane, became constant companions.

While the Queen in London ran a twice-weekly sewing circle making things for the troops, toured hospitals and tried to comfort families made homeless by the bombing, her children at Windsor carried on with their lessons, went to Girl Guide meetings and met evac-uee children. Separated from her daughters, the Queen worried constantly and wrote them letters, to be opened should she die in the raids.

On the lighter side—in spite of the rationing, the blackout, and austerity, the family, gathered together at weekends, brought ever closer by the shared hardship of war, contrived like families everywhere to find simple pleasure in home-spun entertainment. There were elaborate games of charades and evenings round the piano when Princess Margaret played and sang and entertained her parents with her gift of mimicry so that for a while at least, problems were forgotten. And there was the annual Christmas panto, written, produced and acted by the Princesses and their friends.

At last in the spring of 1945, Victory Day came. The King and Queen and the Princesses, now teenagers, joined in the nation's rejoicing. With Winston Churchill they stood on the Palace balcony to wave again and again to the crowds, and that evening Lilibet and Margaret Rose were allowed to join the excited throng.

Soon the Queen's eldest daughter had something else to celebrate. Love was in the air. The King, reluctant to lose a dear daughter, said she was too young; she must wait. She waited until the summer of 1947 when, on the family's return from a royal tour of South Africa, her engagement was announced to the world. Princess Elizabeth was to marry Lieutenant Philip Mountbatten RN.

ELIZABETH
1926 ~

A Working Mother

'I have watched you grow up all these years with pride under the skilful direction of Mummy who, as you know, is the most marvellous person in the world in my eyes . . .' Thus wrote King George VI in a moving letter to his daughter, Princess Elizabeth, at the time of her marriage in 1947 to Lieutenant Mountbatten, formerly Prince Philip of Greece. On the eve of the wedding the groom-to-be was invested as a Knight of the Garter and created Duke of Edinburgh, Earl of Merioneth and Baron Greenwich of Greenwich. And on November 20 King George and Queen Elizabeth looked on with pride as the couple were married in a blaze of post-war pageantry in Westminster Abbey.

Elizabeth and Philip, Duke and Duchess of Edinburgh, were to have Clarence House as their London home. But in the autumn of 1947 it was still being restored after wartime bombing so, for the time being, the newlyweds were given apart-ments at Buckingham Palace. And there, just a year later, Princess Elizabeth became a mother.

At 9.14 in the evening of Sunday, November 14, 1948 Princess Elizabeth gave birth to a son—Prince Charles—in the Buhl Room at Buck-

Elizabeth with Prince Charles as a baby,
photographed by Cecil Beaton.

ingham Palace. But although crowds outside the palace gates sang and cheered with delight, and the Trafalgar Square fountains flowed with 'blue for a boy' water, the birth was tinged with sadness. For Elizabeth's little prince arrived at a time of family crisis. King George, age 52, and about to depart on a tour of Australia and New Zealand, was found to be seriously ill with a grave circulatory problem and it was feared he might lose his right leg. He was determined that the gravity of his illness should be kept secret from his daughter, at least until after her baby was born. And the child, due at the end of October, was about a fortnight late. Meanwhile Queen Elizabeth, calm and reassuring as wife and mother, continued to fulfil her public duties during those difficult weeks. Not until November 16, the baby safely delivered, was it publicly announced that the overseas tour was to be postponed and the truth about the King's health was made known.

The arrival of Prince Charles signalled, once and for all, the end of the custom of the Home Secretary being present at a royal birth. The King had decided, after the long wait for Princess Margaret Rose, that this archaic practice, which had begun with the great warming-pan scandal in the reign of James II, no longer had a place in the modern world. The King informed the Home Secretary of his grandson's arrival by telephone.

On that Sunday evening in 1948, Prince Philip filled the waiting hours swimming and playing squash with his private secretary Mike Parker, while Princess Elizabeth, in labour, was attended by gynaecologist Sir William Gilliatt, the King's physician Sir John Weir, midwife Sister Helen Rowe and an anaesthetist from King's College Hospital. Afterwards Prince Philip congratulated his wife with roses and carnations; the baby was toasted in champagne.

In 1948, although the war was over, its aftermath effects were still felt. Newly-registered infants were presented with identity cards, ration books, orange juice and cod liver oil. It was fitting, therefore, that there should be economies in the royal nursery, too, so little Prince Charles slept, for the first month of his life, in the dressing room adjoining his mother's bedroom, in the Moses basket which 22 years before had been Lilibet's. He also inherited his mother's cot and big black pram, which were brought out of storage, as well as her childhood treasures such as the rattle with an ivory handle which had been a gift from Queen Mary. Prince Charles had two nannies, Helen Lightbody and Mabel Anderson, but Princess Elizabeth, the first of a new generation of royal mothers, spent more time with her baby than most other royal parents in the past. For the first weeks she breastfed her son until she caught measles and, reluctantly, had to stop; and she and Prince Philip spent many happy hours playing with him in the nursery that had once been hers.

When he was a month old, he was baptised Charles Philip Arthur George in the Music Room at Buckingham Palace. Like so many royal babies before him, he wore the family christening robe, and holy water from the River Jordan was used for the ceremony.

Elizabeth and Philip were at last able to move into their own home, Clarence House, in July 1949, and eight-month-old Charles installed in freshly painted blue-and-white nursery quarters. The Princess—a great believer in fresh air—insisted that her son should be taken regularly for airings in St James's Park.

When Prince Charles celebrated his first birthday in November, his father was at sea, and soon afterwards Elizabeth flew out to join her husband in Malta to celebrate their second wedding anniversary together. It was to be the first of many partings from her baby son, for Philip had returned to his career in the Royal Navy and the Princess had many official duties. But on August 15, 1950 they gave him a playmate, whom they called Anne Elizabeth Alice Louise, and who weighed in at six pounds.

The Princess, who only eighteen months before had gazed in wonderment and pride at every expression, every change in mood of her baby son, and wrote, adoringly, 'I still can't believe he is really mine', was now a mother of two. Princess Anne, born at Clarence House, was welcomed by gun salutes and flying flags. Her father, home on leave, was there when she was born, and so was her grandmother, the Queen.

Life for the royal children fell into a secure, happy routine which began at seven each morning. After breakfast they joined their mother for half an hour before their morning outing in the park. Then came lunch, and afternoons were

Elizabeth, the young Queen, finds time to play with Charles and Anne.

spent again in the park, or playing on a rug on the lawn at Clarence House, or visiting. Teatime with banana sandwiches and sponge cake was at 4.30, followed by playtime with Mother before she helped bath her children and put them to bed. Although Princess Elizabeth tried to spend as much time as she could with her babies, her father's fragile health meant she had to take on more and more public duties. Then in December 1950, in the face of public criticism, Elizabeth left her children with her parents and flew to Malta to spend Christmas with her husband.

But the happy days when, as a naval officer's wife, Princess Elizabeth could travel freely with her husband, were soon to end. In the early months of 1951 the Princess joined Philip whenever duties allowed, in Italy, Greece and Malta. But her father's health was deteriorating rapidly; more rapidly than anyone realised. Celebrations for his younger daughter Princess Margaret's twenty-first birthday went ahead as planned, but it soon became apparent that he was desperately ill. Eighteen months earlier he had had an operation to relieve arteriosclerosis and save his leg, now he had a stubborn cough and he was losing weight. In fact the King had lung cancer, and on September 23 he had his left lung removed. A fortnight later, when Princess Elizabeth felt that her father was recovering, she flew with Prince Philip in place of her parents to begin a royal tour of Canada and the USA. Nevertheless, the Princess took with her a sealed envelope containing a declaration of Accession, to be opened in the event of the King's death while she was overseas.

Christmas, however, was a happy occasion with the whole family reunited at Sandringham. Elizabeth found her three-year-old son and his baby sister being spoiled and fussed over, and endearing themselves to their grandparents just as she herself had done twenty years before. Her father valiantly made his Christmas message in spite of his failing voice and on January 31 he sadly waved his daughter and son-in-law goodbye as they flew off on the first leg of an Australasian journey planned to keep them away from home for five months. The King then wearily returned to Sandringham to resume his winter holiday, but on the morning of February 6, 1952, his valet found that he had died in his sleep. The 25-year-old Elizabeth was now Queen; her son, still a toddler, next in line to the throne.

Four generations mourned the King's passing; his grandchildren, too young to understand, his daughters, his wife and his mother, the still dignified, but frail, 85-year-old Queen Mary, who died only two months before the coronation in 1953.

Prince Charles, aged four and a half, wearing a cream silk shirt and trousers and his hair brushed smooth, was present in the Abbey at the coronation. He sat in a special box between his grandmother, the Queen Mother, and aunt, Princess Margaret, with a full view of the moving pageant before him, and afterwards he appeared on the palace balcony with his diminutive blonde-haired sister, and waved to the crowds below. For Elizabeth it would be no longer possible to even pretend she was an ordinary mother. From then on the pattern of life for her and her family would be set in one direction. Bound by duties of state, she would have to put her job first. And Prince Charles, in his turn, would be prepared for kingship.

Shortly after her accession, the Queen and her family moved back into Buckingham Palace, while in May of the coronation year the Queen Mother and Princess Margaret settled into Clarence House. In fact, they simply exchanged houses. And as Prince Charles' fifth birthday drew near, the Queen and Prince Philip prepared for a six-month Commonwealth tour. In their absence, Charles would have to start his education in the Palace schoolroom where Lilibet and Margaret Rose also had their lessons. But for Charles it was going to be different. For a prince destined to be a king of the twenty-first century, life would not be so rigid or remote; there would be less formality. Elizabeth broke with tradition and decided that her children would never bow or curtsey to her, and that they should be addressed simply by their Christian names by the staff at the palace. Neither did she make her little son swear an oath of allegiance to her at the coronation.

Katherine Peebles, who had been governess to Charles' cousins, the children of the Duchess of Kent, became his governess. Under 'Mispy's' guidance he took his first lessons in history, which were often given deeper meaning with sightseeing trips to monuments such as the Tower, and to museums. He learned to swim in the Palace pool, he was taken to dancing classes, and to a gymnasium to exercise his young limbs and, in the spring of 1955, his geography lessons took on real meaning. With his sister Anne, he sailed on the new royal yacht *Britannia* to Malta, where they were greeted by great uncle Lord Louis Mountbatten, then on to Tobruk, for a joyful reunion with their parents.

Both children grew up loving animals, a love passed on to them by their mother. Both took to the saddle as soon as they could walk and their mother gave them their first riding lessons in the Royal Mews. Dogs, too, filled their young lives from the moment they were given their first Corgi puppies—Whisky and Sherry. The Queen also passed on to them the tenancy of the little Welsh cottage which she and her sister had enjoyed at Windsor. But Anne, short of temper and impatient for action, was not keen on dolls and domesticity. She prefered to play with Charles' go-carts, trains and tricycles.

When Anne was five, she was joined in Mispy's classroom by two little girls of her own age: Susan Babington-Smith and Caroline Hamilton, while Charles broke royal tradition and went to the pre-preparatory school, Hill House in Chelsea, where he was enrolled as a day boy for two terms. He did well in most subjects except maths, but he was dogged by recurring tonsillitis which ended in his having his tonsils removed in an operation carried out at Buckingham Palace.

From Hill House Charles, still a quiet, shy and reluctant schoolboy, graduated to his father's old prep school, Cheam in Surrey, and while he was there his mother created him Prince of Wales, an event which caused her nine-year-old son acute embarrassment. The Queen chose to announce her decision at the close of the Empire and Commonwealth Games in Cardiff. Because she was suffering from sinusitis, her speech was taped, but Prince Philip made the introduction. With his headmaster and some friends Charles watched the end of the Games on school television and heard his mother's voice say: '. . . I intend to create my son Prince of Wales today. When he is grown-up I will present him to you at Caernarvon.'

Charles became ill during his last term at Cheam with appendicitis. This time he went into hospital—Great Ormond Street—for the operation. After his convalescence, it was time to move on to the spartan regime of his father's other old school, Gordonstoun, in the rugged north of Scotland. There, too, he became ill. He caught pneumonia and the Queen flew to his bedside in a local nursing home.

Away from their respective classrooms, Charles and Anne discovered a wide range of interests. Their father introduced both of them to sailing, but both suffered terribly from sea sickness. Riding proved much more popular, especially with Princess Anne. When her mother presented her with her first pony, 'High Jinks,' she at once demonstrated signs of her future

Princess Margaret with her children,
David and Sarah.

195

prowess in the show ring. Both brother and sister went to riding school at Windsor, ice skating at Richmond, learnt to dance and play the piano. And to give Anne some opportunity of mixing more with little girls of her own age, she became a Brownie, and later the First Buckingham Palace Company of Girl Guides was formed. They met once a week in the summer house in the grounds, and when the Queen was home Anne would invite one or two of the girls back for tea.

The Queen, whose royal duties—her long overseas tours, official visits at home and affairs of state—kept her busy for long periods at the beginning of her reign, saw little of her son and daughter in their childhood years. It was frequently their aunt, Princess Margaret, or their ever-devoted granny, the Queen Mother, who gave Charles and Anne their holiday treats, their trips to the Regent's Park Zoo, the theatre or cinema, and who took charge of them at Windsor, Sandringham or Balmoral.

Years before, when she was still a young girl, the Queen expressed a wish to have two sons and two daughters; that, she said, would be the ideal family. In February 1960, when Charles was eleven and Anne nine, and when it was popularly assumed that the Queen had completed her family, it became obvious that she had other ideas. Elizabeth II became the first reigning monarch to become a mother for 103 years when she gave birth to Prince Andrew in the Belgian Suite on the ground floor of Buckingham Palace. The prince was born at 3.30 p.m. on February 19 and weighed 7 lb 3 oz. Later he was christened Andrew Albert Christian Edward. So after nine years, Nanny Mabel Anderson had a baby to care for in the Palace nursery again. In the following days the Queen received four thousand letters, telegrams and messages of congratulation, but she could not bask for long in her personal happiness. Within hours of the birth she sat, propped up by pillows, dealing with papers from her despatch box.

The birth of the Queen's 1960 baby boded well for the new decade. A week later there was more cause for royal celebration—the engagement of

Princess Margaret to Mr Antony Armstrong-Jones. Five years after ending an affair with Group Captain Peter Townsend she was in love again. Antony Armstrong-Jones may not have been a good match by the old standards. He was a commoner; his father thrice married; he didn't even have a title. But he was eligible and acceptable; the marriage would not shake the monarchy. The Queen was happy to give her consent.

At the Abbey wedding in May, Princess Anne was a bridesmaid. Bouncy, extrovert, tomboyish, she was bursting to break out of the confines of the Palace classroom, but she had to wait until 1963 when she was 13. Then the Queen and Prince Philip decided she could become a boarder at Benenden in Kent where she was to be treated like any other pupil.

On November 3, 1961, it was the turn of the Queen's sister, Princess Margaret at the age of thirty-one, to become a mother. Her husband Tony, who three days before had been created First Earl of Snowdon, drove his wife from their Kensington Palace home to her mother at Clarence House for the confinement. The Queen Mother's fourth grandchild, a son weighing six pounds four ounces, who was later christened in the Music Room at Buckingham Palace and named David Albert Charles, would be known as Viscount Linley. With his nanny, Miss Verona Sumner, he was soon out and about with the younger generation of royals and later joined Prince Andrew for lessons at the Palace with Miss Peebles.

A big year for royal birth days was 1964. Princess Alexandra led the way with her leap year son, James Robert Bruce Ogilvy, born on February 29. Ten days later at the age of 38, the Queen gave birth to her fourth child. Not the daughter she may have hoped for, but to Prince Edward Antony Richard Louis, the baby of her family. The following month the Duchess of Kent had her second child, Lady Helen Windsor, and on May Day Princess Margaret gave birth to Lady Sarah Frances Elizabeth Armstrong-Jones.

With both Charles and Anne away at boarding

school, the Queen now had a second family in the nursery. This was to be her very private family; so private in fact that when Andrew was born his name was not announced until his birth was registered a month later, and no photographs were allowed of the christening. For the first 16 months of his life Andrew wasn't even seen in public, leading not surprisingly to rumour that all was not well with him. But when the Queen had shared Charles and Anne with the nation, they had been plagued by press and public attention. So this time Andrew and Edward were to have more privacy.

Both younger sons enjoyed a freedom with their mother that Charles and Anne had never known. She was much more relaxed and confident with them. Right from the start she enjoyed the peak of health with her last two pregnancies. Both boys were delivered by Sir John Peel, a brilliant obstetrician, assisted by the Queen's Physician-in-Ordinary, Sir John Weir (a sprightly 84-year-old by the time Edward arrived). As both doctors believed in the use of anaesthesia for childbirth, they were joined by an anaesthetist, Vernon Hall. Sister Helen Rowe, who was at the births of all the Queen's children, completed the team.

By 1964 the Queen had time to adjust to the pressure of her royal duties, now she was able to spend much more time with her children, to mother them and enjoy them. Whenever possible she pushed the youngest in his new shiny pram, bought just before the arrival of Andrew, on a morning airing in the grounds of Buckingham Palace. The little princes often played at her feet as she worked instead of being banished to the nursery, while on Nanny Anderson's night-off the Queen was glad of the opportunity to bath her sons and put them to bed. And mindful, perhaps, of the criticism about the secrecy surrounding Prince Andrew, she held three-month-old Prince Edward in her arms for all to see when she appeared on the Palace balcony after Trooping the Colour.

The ever-growing number of junior royals meant that there was no longer room for all the

Prince Charles in 1969 playing a game of bagatelle at Sandringham, with Edward (aged 5) and Andrew (aged 9).

family to be at Sandringham for Christmas, so instead the festival was kept at Windsor, where the young Snowdons and Kents, Ogilvys and Gloucesters could romp together at one huge gathering. And more and more, as time went by, and Princess Margaret and her husband drifted apart, Lord Linley and Lady Sarah were seen with the Queen and her youngest children.

In 1969 the Queen for once relaxed her dislike of publicity for her children. First there was the long promised investiture of Prince Charles as Prince of Wales at Caernarvon, a ceremony stage-managed by Lord Snowdon, the Constable of the Castle. And then the royal family was seen as never before, on a full length feature film shown worldwide. The film, *The Royal Family*, directed by Richard Cawston, showed the Queen not only as a monarch occupied with the affairs of state but as a parent, a mother who also happened to be Queen. And into every home were flashed intimate family images of barbecues and snowball fights, shared hobbies and fireside evenings.

Both Andrew, who was described as tough and independent, and his quieter brother, Edward, went first to Heatherdown Preparatory School near Ascot before following in Charles' footsteps to Gordonstoun.

In 1973 Princess Anne became Mrs Mark Phillips, but for the time being, Anne's equestrian career was to come before thoughts of motherhood. When she married Captain Mark Phillips in November she made it known that one of her wishes was to have a private life. And she turned down her mother's offer of a peerage for her husband primarily because she wanted her children to be free of any restraints a title could have on their future lives. Never afraid to show her feelings, and often curt and surly in public, Anne's relationship with her mother was often stormy. Her rejection of a title for her husband and children clearly disappointed the Queen, but Anne was adamant.

Children were not uppermost in her mind in 1973. There was even a nagging doubt that, following a string of gynaecological problems and an operation for an ovarian cyst in 1971, she might have difficulty conceiving. In the meantime, horses filled the lives of both Anne and Mark and the Princess already had a string of major successes to her credit.

Triumphs at Wembley, Burghley and Badminton won her the title of Sportswoman of the Year in 1971. Later came the European Championships in Kiev. Her ambition was to be picked for the British Equestrian team in the Olympic Games in 1976. 'Right now,' said the Princess, 'I've got this ambition to achieve the Olympics. It seems to me that having a family can wait a bit longer.' And when she was selected for the team she was determined that nothing would get in her way. Yet by the spring of 1977 she was able to tell her mother that her first grandchild would be born in her Silver Jubilee year. But Anne still firmly refused a title for her offspring.

Under the care of the eminent gynaecologist Mr George Pinker, Princess Anne was one of the first mothers to be given the Alpha-Feto Protein Test, a blood test used to detect spina bifida. And it was also due to his advice that she decided to break with tradition and have her baby in hospital; mainly, it was rumoured, because she is of the rhesus negative blood group and could, therefore, have had a 'blue baby'. Anne, always practical, said: 'It's like the dentist. You want to go where the equipment is.'

The place chosen for the birth of the Queen's first grandchild was the Lindo Wing of St Mary's Hospital, Paddington, and the Princess was driven there by her husband at 4 a.m. on November 15. That morning the Queen was ten minutes late for an investiture at Buckingham Palace. The Queen, who had previously joked about her future grandchild saying: 'We might well expect it to have four feet', was beaming when she appeared in the Throne Room. She said, simply, 'I apologise for being late but I have just had a message from the hospital. My daughter has given birth to a son and I am now a grandmother.'

A cry of delight went up from the 800 people in the audience who applauded enthusiastically. The baby, weighing six and a half pounds, was born at 10.46 a.m. after a normal labour and delivery. An epidural injection enabled the Princess to remain fully conscious, yet comfortable, throughout the birth, and Captain Phillips was there at her side—albeit reluctantly—to encourage her. Anne herself was less than ecstatic: 'Three-day eventing at Burghley is a doddle compared to this,' was her comment.

'This is one of the happiest days of my life,' said a radiant Queen Mother, as the nation echoed her joy on becoming a great-grandmother. Anne may not have been a favourite with the people, but the birth of her son was welcomed. She chose to breastfeed her son and stayed in hospital for three days before returning to Buckingham Palace to recuperate. And while she was there the baby was given a traditional royal christening in the Music Room, just before Christmas, and named Peter Mark Andrew. It took Anne and Mark three weeks to announce their son's names—simply because they could not decide.

The Royal Family at Windsor on the
occasion of the Silver Wedding in 1972.
Photographed by Lord Litchfield.

A few weeks later the Princess took her baby to the Phillips' new home, Gatcombe Park, in Gloucestershire, and there Master Phillips was installed in his new nursery, in the care of Nanny Mabel Anderson. It was Mabel Anderson who, years before, had charge of Anne at Buckingham Palace; a no-nonsense nanny of the old school, strong on discipline and no time for spoiling but utterly dependable. And Anne, a no-nonsense mother, knew that she was just the person for her child.

Master Peter Phillips, at the time of his birth fifth in line to the throne, thus began a childhood which, though undoubtedly cushioned by wealth, was stripped of the pomp and panoply which restricted Anne in her young life.

When Peter was four, Princess Anne gave him a sister, Zara Anne Elizabeth. She weighed a healthy 8 lb 1 oz. when she was born on May 15,

1981. This time Anne had been keen to have the baby at home, but Mr Pinker advised otherwise, so once again the Lindo Wing at St Mary's became the royal birthplace.

The labour and delivery of Zara were swift—just six hours after Anne arrived at the hospital—and perfectly straightforward. She was a very noisy baby, her father revealed. Anne, who again left hospital three days after the birth, described her second pregnancy as 'boring', adding 'I am not particularly maternal. It is an occupational hazard of being a wife.'

Before long both Peter and Zara were sitting in the saddle, riding Smokey, their pony, as Princess Anne believes in children starting young. And Peter and Zara, casually dressed in tee shirts and dungarees, were often seen with their mother at local equestrian events, learning to take an early interest in the sport.

The Princess may not be a demonstrative mother in the style of her sister-in-law the Princess of Wales, she may not have the same easy line of small talk with a five-year-old, but she treats her offspring with down-to-earth commonsense. Her approach is refreshingly natural—as was demonstrated when she delivered a sharp smack when they misbehaved in public, then took them home in disgrace.

The independent daughter of the Queen may not fit into the mould of her predecessors, but her children will be well prepared for life in the twenty-first century.

DIANA
1961 ~

A Thoroughly Modern Mother

When on July 29, 1981, 20-year-old Lady Diana Spencer married the Prince of Wales there was no doubt in anyone's mind that she would one day be well suited for motherhood. Her love of children was already well known to the great British public who lapped up every detail about the girl who was to become their new princess. She had worked as a nanny and as an assistant at the Young England kindergarten school in Pimlico. Whereas most young people in her set posed with their horses, she was photographed with children, and they obviously loved her.

Some people felt she should have waited a little longer after her wedding to allow herself time to adjust to her superstar status without the added emotional changes of pregnancy. But Diana, Princess of Wales, cut short her extended honeymoon at Balmoral to fly to London for a consultation with the royal gynaecologist Mr George Pinker. It was still too early to confirm that she was pregnant: that announcement came from Buckingham Palace in November. At one time such a statement would have been couched rather coyly to the effect that the princess would not be undertaking any public engagements after a certain date. Today there is no room for any doubt or speculation. The world is informed her Royal Highness is indeed pregnant and told the estimated time of the baby's arrival.

For a time the Princess suffered miserably from morning sickness—one of the side-effects of pregnancy that she admitted she did not expect. But once that wore off she looked radiant for most of the time. Her delight at the prospect of motherhood was obvious, and shortly before the birth she was spotted shopping in Harrods for last minute items for the nursery.

Prince Charles, too, was overjoyed at the thought of parenthood and set out to be the ideal father from the start. He read every available book on pregnancy and ante-natal care and child rearing, and he consulted his mother about early education. One thing was certain, neither he nor Diana wanted their child to have the lonely upbringing they both suffered. Affairs of State had kept Charles and his mother apart for weeks at a time, although he developed a close relationship with his grandmother who once said 'the nice thing about having grandchildren is that you don't feel guilty about spoiling them'.

The Princess missed her own mother for a different reason. Her parents separated when she was six and she and her sisters and brother remained with their father at Park House on the Sandringham estate. Although she was outwardly a happy child, much loved by her father, her mother's absence must have saddened her.

In line with the modern approach to childcare, Diana chose not to have a uniformed nanny of the starched and college-trained old school. Instead she appointed 39-year-old Barbara

Princess Diana with Prince William
on her first wedding anniversary in July 1982.

Barnes, who had been recommended by friends, Colin and Anne Tennant. Barbara, as she likes to be called, wears no uniform and she has had no formal training. Her qualifications are long experience and sound commonsense.

Barbara Barnes, a great believer in fresh air, said: 'I like to approach things with a sense of humour. And I don't see any different problems in bringing up a royal baby—I treat all children as individuals.' She added that she hoped the Princess would be strongly involved in bringing up her own children. 'I think it will be a great help—they are not my children after all.'

Mr Pinker described Diana as 'a particularly healthy young woman'. In fact the only alarm the Princess had during her pregnancy was when she fell down a flight of stairs at Sandringham four months before her baby was due. Prince Charles advised her to lie down, and sent for the local doctor, who confirmed that the Princess had suffered no injury and everything was fine.

The Queen is said to have wanted her grandchild to be born at Buckingham Palace but Mr Pinker stressed the importance of a hospital delivery, especially for Diana's first baby.

At dawn on June 21, 1982, ten days before her 21st birthday, Prince Charles drove his wife from Kensington Palace to the Lindo Wing of St Mary's Hospital, Paddington. She was then in the early stages of labour. Her small, simply furnished hospital room was a far cry from the velvet draped, silk cushioned splendour of the medieval lying-in chambers of past princesses.

Charles may not have been over-enthusiastic about being present at his child's birth, but he obviously wanted to please his wife and he was no doubt persuaded, too, by social pressures. He stayed with Diana throughout the day and watched his son arrive into the world at 9.03 p.m. 'A very grown-up thing', as he said afterwards. The baby, the second in line to the throne, had fair hair and blue eyes, weighed 7 lb 1½ oz. and was described by his father as 'beautiful'. His wife, he said, was 'in marvellous form'—as, indeed, she was, for she stunned

everyone by leaving hospital just 21 hours later; a testament to her youth and fitness. Relaxed and unselfconscious, she was ready to smile for the cameras as she took her baby home.

It is thought that the Princess followed the example of her sister-in-law, Princess Anne, and had an epidural injection to help her in labour, for Prince Charles described the birth as 'natural—well, very nearly'.

Diana breastfed her baby, which helped her back to her super-slim self so quickly after the birth, and she worked hard at exercising and disco-dancing to recover. Her son, meanwhile, was installed in a brightly decorated nursery, with furniture hand-painted with bunny motifs. And among the many toys was the same familiar ivory-handled rattle, given to his grandmother when she was born.

The christening was held in August, when he was baptised by the Archbishop of Canterbury in the Music Room at Buckingham Palace and given the names William Arthur Philip Louis. He shared his big day with the Queen Mother, who was celebrating her 82nd birthday. But it was the infant prince who won most of the attention. He cried so loudly that the Princess had to put her little finger in his mouth to calm him. Unlike royal mothers of the past, Queen Mary among them, Diana does not approve of dummies. William, she said, had to make do with his thumb.

But the Princess does believe in love. 'Babies need a lot of loving', she declared, and there were plainly to be plenty of kisses and cuddles for the little son with the chubby cheeks and serious expression. Both his parents adored him. Diana had, from the earliest stages of her pregnancy, expressed her determination to be with her baby as much as possible. Talking afterwards to young mothers during her 'walkabouts' she said she wished she could spend more time with her children.

Rumours of a battle royal over taking William on tour began as much as three months before his birth. Tours of Canada, New Zealand and Australia had been cancelled because of the

Princess's pregnancy, and she knew they would be rescheduled after the baby's arrival. Diana was adamant that she either took her baby with her or she would not go at all.

As we have seen throughout history, royal mothers and their babies have always endured lengthy separations and those mothers have always accepted them, believing that duty came first. But the Princess of Wales is of a new breed. She believes that her duties as a mother come first and she will never allow her children to suffer emotionally because of royal traditions. She firmly believes that separating a mother and baby in the first precious months is deeply upsetting for both of them.

And this is one fight that Diana won. Early in 1983, when William was seven months old, he broke with tradition and accompanied his parents on a six-week tour of Australia and New Zealand. He also broke the old rule whereby the heir to the throne does not travel by the same flight as his father. As he was carried down the plane steps into the bright Australian sunshine he looked a little dazzled, a little sleepy, but he had stood up to the journey well. Down under, he was the star of the royal show. There were photocalls and crawlabouts for the world's press and television, and he took his first swim in a pool in New South Wales.

But there was a stressful parting later that summer when Diana agreed to leave William behind during a two-week tour of Canada in June, although it meant missing his first birthday. When Charles and Diana phoned 'Wills', as they call him, they were rewarded with a few squeaks down the line.

William had just turned two when his brother Harry was born, on September 15, 1984. Again Charles stayed with Diana during her nine-hour labour at St Mary's Hospital, then he went home for William, and television viewers everywhere watched as father and son walked hand in hand up the hospital steps to meet the new arrival.

Harry, baptised Henry Charles Albert David, was described by his father as someone for Wills to fight with. But from the moment Harry was taken home, William showed nothing but affection for his little brother, as he tried to climb into his cot to kiss and cuddle him. Maybe Charles was recalling his own childhood, when his aggressive younger sister Anne often bullied him. Even his own angelic-looking mother Lilibet and her sister Margaret Rose solved their conflicts with kicking and biting. It is well known that the second child of any family can suffer sibling jealousy aroused by a natural rivalry, but how much more likely when the eldest child is also heir to the throne.

'It is almost impossible to bring them up as ordinary children, however hard you try,' Prince Philip once said, speaking about his own family. Charles and Diana are trying very hard. In private life, within the confines of Kensington Palace and Highgrove House, their home in the Cotswolds, the Wales family can be as relaxed and loving, as natural and as normal as they like. They can play with their children not only at bathtime but at breakfast, too, if they wish. They can even take them on some overseas tours. In spring 1985 Diana endeared herself to the baby-worshipping Italians by introducing William and eight-month-old Harry to cheering crowds, as they sailed on the *Britannia* after a tour of Venice.

In some ways William and Harry have less freedom than their father enjoyed. Charles, for example, was regularly pushed in his pram round St James's Park. Today the risk of terrorist attacks and kidnapping, not to mention crowds of sightseers, make such a simple outing impossible. Any day-to-day activities of the young Princes make news. William's curiosity in excavating wastepaper baskets, and the mischievous way he tossed his shoes down the loo were reported in the press. Diana knows that her children are not, indeed cannot ever be regarded as 'ordinary'.

Diana is fashion conscious, a trend-setter, her style is admired around the world. From the time her engagement first hit the headlines, 'Lady Di' look-alikes blossomed everywhere. Small wonder, therefore, that the clothes she chose for her children also made fashion news. The

Charles and Diana with their two children on the Royal yacht Britannia.

smocked and embroidered romper suit William wore for his first photocall was reminiscent of the garments his father once had and was criticised by some fashion pundits—but similar models in the shops were a sell-out. And the navy snowsuit with the appliqué motif worn for another photo session when William was 18 months old also became a best-seller.

Diana Princess of Wales knows that her children, especially William, will always be in the public eye. The other wives of the royal house of Windsor, the Kents, and the Gloucesters, know on the other hand that their children, on the outer periphery of the royal circle, will have more freedom, more choice. The children of the Queen's sister, Lord Linley and Lady Sarah Armstrong-Jones, are planning their own lives, making future careers for themselves in carpentry and theatre design. Even the Queen's own daughter, Princess Anne, as Mrs Mark Phillips, has already chosen 'normality' for her children. They will always be royal cousins, close to the crown; they will receive invitations to grand occasions, welcomed to exclusive events, share in those marvellous royal Christmasses. But they will be expected to make their own way in the world.

William and Harry, like it or not, will be groomed for royal service; their education directed towards the responsibilities of State duties. It *has* to be different. William's introduction to school life at the age of three seemed ordinary enough. Instead of the traditional but now outdated lessons with a governess in a palace schoolroom, he went to a nursery school at Notting Hill Gate. His loving parents naturally accompanied him on his first day, but with barely a second glance he strode in to meet his new companions. When Charles was a little boy his parents took pains to treat him like an 'ordinary' child. Even birthday presents were kept purposely modest so as not to arouse envy among other pupils. William, in his turn, dressed in red shorts and check shirt and clutching a 'Postman Pat' flask containing his mid-morning orange juice, certainly did not appear any more princely than the rest. But the police with sniffer dogs who made sure the area was safe, and the photographers and television crew who lay in wait for the new pupil to arrive marked this little boy as very special indeed.

Later, speaking on television during an interview with Sir Alistair Burnet, while viewers watched Wills and Harry pounding the piano, Princess Diana recalled her feelings on her son's first day at school. Yes, she admitted, she had felt sad 'because it's opening another chapter in my life, and certainly William's. But he's ready for it. He's a very independent child.' Speaking of her role as Princess of Wales, she said 'I feel my role is supporting my husband whenever I can and always being behind him, encouraging him. And also, most important, being a wife and mother. And that's what I try to achieve. Whether I do is another thing, but I do try.'

In all her efforts the Princess of Wales knows she has the full and loving support of the Queen, who became Diana's best friend in the early days when she was a new recruit to the family circle. It was obvious to all those surrounding the Queen that she was delighted with her new daughter-in-law. Diana in her turn can grow more confident, can enjoy the warmth of a large and loving family with the Queen as its head. It was the Queen who helped bring her nephew, Lord Linley and, most especially her niece, Lady Sarah, through the terrible trauma of the break-up of their parent's marriage. In fact whenever storm clouds hover over the marriage of any of the Queen's extended family she is quick to close ranks and defend. That Princess Diana feels at ease with the Queen there is no doubt. 'I have the best mother-in-law in the world,' she said.

Children are an utter joy to the Princess and her husband. They are sensible, caring, modern parents, in love with each other and happy with their life together. Thanks to Diana, royal motherhood has swung sharply away from the formality of the traditional image. The Princess of Wales, who will one day be Queen, is bringing the next generation of royal children in touch with the modern world.

Index